For Fred —
In friendship +
for the many years of
mentorship + guidance,

Farah

COSMOPOLITAN POLITICAL THOUGHT

Cosmopolitan Political Thought

METHOD, PRACTICE, DISCIPLINE

Farah Godrej

UNIVERSITY PRESS

OXFORD
UNIVERSITY PRESS

Oxford University Press, Inc., publishes works that further
Oxford University's objective of excellence
in research, scholarship, and education.

Oxford   New York
Auckland   Cape Town   Dar es Salaam   Hong Kong   Karachi
Kuala Lumpur   Madrid   Melbourne   Mexico City   Nairobi
New Delhi   Shanghai   Taipei   Toronto

With offices in
Argentina   Austria   Brazil   Chile   Czech Republic   France   Greece
Guatemala   Hungary   Italy   Japan Poland   Portugal   Singapore
South Korea   Switzerland   Thailand   Turkey   Ukraine   Vietnam

Copyright © 2011 by Oxford University Press, Inc.

Published by Oxford University Press, Inc.
198 Madison Avenue, New York, NY 10016

www.oup.com

Oxford is a registered trademark of Oxford University Press

Library of Congress Cataloging-in-Publication Data
Godrej, Farah.
Cosmopolitan political thought: method, practice, discipline / Farah Godrej.
p.   cm.
Includes bibliographical references and index.
ISBN 978-0-19-978206-2 — ISBN 978-0-19-978207-9 (pbk.)
1. Political science—Philosophy. 2. Cosmopolitanism. I. Title.
JA71.G615   2011
320.01—dc22   2011002584

9 8 7 6 5 4 3 2 1

Printed in the United States of America
on acid-free paper

For my parents, with whom this journey began;
and
for Greg, with whom I share the joy of returning home.

Contents

Acknowledgments

THIS BOOK, LIKE most, is not entirely my own. It is the combined result of years of intellectual support, good conversation, and emotional sustenance offered by many colleagues and friends. To all of them, I am deeply grateful. For planting and cultivating the seeds of this inquiry, I thank Fred Dallmayr and Anthony Parel. For their intellectual friendship and spirited scholarly engagement, I am indebted to Richard Avramenko, Andrew March, Piya Chatterjee, Bronwyn Leebaw, and Leigh Jenco. Many other friends and colleagues took the time to read and comment on parts of the manuscript, others engaged me in important conversations, and still others offered recommendations, thoughts, and words of encouragement. Among these, I thank Joseph Prabhu, Susan McWilliams Barndt, Michaelle Browers, Russell Fox, Lisa Ellis, Daniel Bell, Tamara Ho, Setsu Shigematsu, Keith Harris, Leona Helmsley, Dvora Yanow, Peregrine Schwartz-Shea, Hans-Herbert Koegler, Corey Brettschneider, Keally McBride, Margaret Kohn, Sharon Snowiss, Andrew Norris, Ronald Terchek, Kirstie McClure, Tracy Strong, Mark Bevir, Joshua Foa Dienstag, Brian Walker, Rajeev Bhargava, Michael Frazer, Andrew Murphy, Stuart Gray, Jakob de Roover, Tony Spanakos, Dustin Howes, Brooke Ackerly, Vinay Lal, and Roger Ames.

I am extremely fortunate to have studied with the finest of teachers. Bruce Douglass, along with Mark Warren and Gerry Mara, provided extraordinary mentorship through years of graduate training at Georgetown. Cynthia Enloe, my undergraduate mentor at Clark University, awakened my critical thinking skills. At the University of Chicago, Martha Nussbaum, Lloyd Rudolph and Susanne Hoeber Rudolph all pointed me toward the possibility of theorizing beyond traditional boundaries.

I have participated in many workshops and conferences that allowed me to develop my arguments. These include the southern California Political Theory Colloquium, the Comparative Political Thought Workshop at Princeton University, the political theory colloquia at the University of Wisconsin–Madison, the University of California–Los Angeles, University of California–Santa Barbara, the Gandhi Society of Calgary, and the annual conferences of the American Political Science Association, the Society for Comparative and Asian Philosophy, the Western Political Science Association, and the Association for Asian Studies. The Center for Ideas and Society at the University of California–Riverside funded a research leave from teaching duties, during which these arguments were sharpened. A prior version of chapter 3 was published as "Towards a Cosmopolitan Political Thought: The Hermeneutics of Interpreting the Other," *Polity* 41 (2), and is reproduced with permission of Palgrave Macmillan. Excerpts from chapter 4 have been published in "Nonviolence and Gandhi's Truth: A Method for Moral and Political Arbitration," *The Review of Politics* 68 (2) and in "Gandhi's Civic Ahimsa: A Standard for Public Justification in Multicultural Democracies," *International Journal of Gandhi Studies* 1, 2011.

The University of California–Riverside provided me with an academic home where I grew as a scholar; it has been a privilege to share this home with colleagues who have generously supported me. For this, I express my gratitude to Karthick Ramakrishnan and Bronwyn Leebaw, whose friendship, advice and encouragement have proven invaluable. Piya Chatterjee deserves special mention for her efforts to provide a nurturing space for junior faculty. I also wish to thank John Christian Laursen, John Medearis, Martin Johnson, Shaun Bowler, and Steve Clark. For long hours spent in the joint pursuit of meaning, I must thank Veronica Benet-Martinez, Jennifer K. Walter, Ala Khazendar, and Sindhu Venkatanarayanan. Each of these friends has uniquely inspired me in ways that defy description: Jill Davis Doughtie, Brinda Sarathy, Sara Anjargolian, and Katie Goldberg. At Oxford University Press, this book has flourished under the stewardship of Angela Chnapko and Joellyn Ausanka and has been immeasurably improved by the insights of its anonymous reviewers.

Above all, I owe the most to my family. My parents, Perveen and Byram Godrej, instilled in me an instinctive appreciation for exploring the unknown, and taught me how to grapple with a complex world. My sister Delara is the most steadfast friend I could have asked for; she has stood by me and listened carefully when it mattered the most. And finally, to my partner and closest companion in all of life's adventures, Greg: his love, compassion and patience underlie my efforts and ultimately make possible this endeavor.

COSMOPOLITAN POLITICAL THOUGHT

1

COSMOPOLITANISM, COMPARATIVE POLITICAL THEORY

AND CIVILIZATIONAL ALTERITY

IN RECENT YEARS, two movements of thought have emerged that should be of interest to political theorists. First, the idea of "cosmopolitanism" has become the focus of much normative interest within political theory.[1] Driven initially by a recovery of ancient Stoic and Greek claims about the *kosmou polites* or "world citizen," many political theorists and political philosophers have begun investigating the postures, practices and structures that could be characterized as "cosmopolitan." These are characterized by the turn away from the local affiliations and attachments of one's birth (such as nation, ethnicity or community identification), toward an understanding of the self as bound through its capacity for rationality to all human beings worldwide and a "fundamental devotion to the interests of humanity as a whole."[2] Simultaneously, political theory has begun to exhibit awareness that it cannot go on defining itself as a mainly Westcentric mode of inquiry, and that its relationship to intellectual resources from "non-Western" civilizations bears some reflection. The subfield of comparative political theory takes for granted the notion that encounters with the otherness of non-Western resources should be considered a legitimate and necessary part of political theory.

Motivated by the emergence of these discourses, I take cosmopolitanism as my central problematic. I ask the question, what might it mean for the practices of political theorizing—especially in the encounter with non-Western texts, ideas, practices and modes of inquiry—to be cosmopolitan? In what follows, I suggest that each of the above movements, while generally welcome, remains incomplete and is characterized by important gaps that deserve sustained attention: in one case, the lack of reflection on what the recent development of cosmopolitan discourse means for the activity of political theorizing, and in the other case, the relative scarcity of methodological reflection within the emerging field calling itself comparative political theory. Moreover, I argue that these *aporiae* are not unrelated. As yet, with few exceptions, these two discourses tend to make little reference to one another, but the assumptions underlying them suggest a need for each to engage with the other. I suggest here that methodological questions about the practice of comparative political theory are linked to the reenvisioning of political theory as a more cosmopolitan endeavor. The advance of comparative political theorizing requires urgent reflection on what modes of inquiry and approaches to otherness might be characterized as cosmopolitan. Meanwhile, the discourse on cosmopolitanism similarly requires reflection on its relationship to practices and modes of theorizing in the study of non-Western intellectual resources. Taken together, this calls for reflection on what constitutes a cosmopolitan political thought, or a more genuinely cosmopolitan mode of political theorizing. My project seeks therefore to articulate not only the question of what exactly is meant by a cosmopolitan political theory, but the relationship between "comparative" political theory and a more cosmopolitan field of political theory as a whole. It argues that political theory itself can evolve toward cosmopolitanism only when explorations of comparative political thought occur at the center, rather than at the margins of, the discipline. Although my intervention is targeted at political theory and its practices, I also suggest that such reflection would be valuable for scholars of cosmopolitanism and could serve as an added voice to pluralistic discourse on the topic.

In calling for a cosmopolitan practice of political theory, this book addresses a third (and not unrelated) *aporia* that underlies the preceding two *aporiae* and relates more generally to the self-understanding of political theory. Political theory has long been committed to problematizing and examining our relationship with alterity; indeed, the very dichotomies of "self" and "other" are said to have originated within and been elaborated through political theory. Recent attempts by political theorists to defend the central place of political theory in the broader discipline have rested on the idea that political theorists were the first to raise and focus attention on the discipline's "ethnocentrism"; that they have posed questions of gender and race when these were ignored by others; and that they have served, as such, as the "moral voice" of political science.[3] Concerns about alterity are thus seemingly central to the self-definition of political theory. However, these concerns are dramatically undermined by the exclusively Westcentric nature of political theory. Political theory's preoccupation with alterity stands in profound and ironic contrast with its failure, until relatively recently, to look beyond Western intellectual resources—and beyond their premises and foundational questions—in any meaningful way. Given its preoccupation with the general question of alterity, political theory's relative silence on this question seems deafening. How a cosmopolitan political thought might engage this aporia and what implications this might have for the practice of political theorizing constitute the subject of this book.

COMPARATIVE POLITICAL THEORY AND COSMOPOLITANISM: THE APORIAE

I turn first to the emergence of the subfield calling itself comparative political theory. Disciplines such as literary theory, history, anthropology, cultural studies, and postcolonial theory had long established that texts, ideas and practices beyond the West constituted an important, legitimate field of inquiry. Philosophers and classicists had been exploring the ideas of their non-Western counterparts as early as the nineteenth century.[4] Yet strangely, such discourse has remained relatively rare in political theory, the one field in which the implications of the West's relationship to its non-Western other seems the most urgent. Few avenues of intellectual exchange dealt with the question of what methodological questions would be raised by such a project. Even in the immediate aftermath of 9/11, the main vehicles of intellectual exchange in political theory remained relatively silent on the implications that such a newly found— and deeply tension laden—proximity to otherness may have for the field.

Comparative political theory (CPT) saw itself as a corrective to this obvious gap, It commenced as an imperative to study political thought from all corners of the globe, and particularly civilizations outside the West.[5] One of its earliest proponents Fred Dallmayr called for a "move toward a more genuine universalism, and beyond the spurious 'universality' traditionally claimed by the Western canon and by some recent intellectual movements."[6] Long seen as the founding father of comparative political theory, and deeply influenced by Continental thinkers like Heidegger, Gadamer, Bakhtin and Derrida, Dallmayr traced CPT's intellectual lineage to "comparative philosophy." Dallmayr's *Beyond Orientalism*—one of the earliest and most urgent articulations of the comparative imperative—called upon the work of the philosopher Raimundo Panikkar, revealing the impact of Gadamerian hermeneutics on early comparative political theory literature.[7] Panikkar considered the predominant mode of cross-cultural encounter

> a philosophical stance that opens itself to other philosophies . . . This enterprise is only possible through entering into dialogue with other philosophical

views. It should further cultivate the attitude of learning from them. In medieval Latin this process was called *imparare* . . . an open philosophical attitude ready to learn from whatever philosophical corner of world, but without claiming to compare philosophies from an objective, neutral and transcendent vantage point.[8]

The learning involved in such a dialogical and hermeneutic process, Panikkar claims, is reflective and critical, aware of the contingency of its own assumptions, and ready to question its most basic foundations.[9] Panikkar emphasizes that this continuously open and learning-oriented process is the core of "comparative philosophy": the forging of a common language, mutual comprehension and "fecundation" through the crossing of boundaries, the immersion in another universe of discourse, "[overcoming] our parameters and plunge into a participatory process," while "think[ing] and speak[ing] directly in that other linguistic universe."[10] It is this hermeneutic, process-oriented vision that Dallmayr draws upon as the intellectual— and methodological—antecedent of comparative political theorizing.[11]

Another methodological commitment of some CPT involves repudiating a Huntingtonian "clash of civilizations" model emphasizing the radical incommensurability of cultures. Roxanne Euben has argued that comparative political theory aims to make the strange familiar and the familiar strange, contributing to "conversations about the nature and value of politics among . . . a variety of traditions" and raising the possibility that "non-Western perspectives may provide new (that is, new to the West) answers to our old questions."[12] For Euben, CPT must emphasize synthetic and hybrid interactions rather than dichotomies and binaries, and demonstrate the extent to which apparently incommensurable traditions have interpenetrated one another over the years. Euben's exploration of Sayyid Qutb thus reveals that many Western critiques of modernity by thinkers such as Arendt, MacIntyre, and Charles Taylor are mirrored by and clearly recognizable within twentieth-century Islamist thought. Dallmayr casts this as a "dialogue of civilizations" in direct contrast to Huntington's "clash."[13] Much work within CPT (following Dallmayr and Euben) and related fields relies on the language of intercivilizational dialogue, similarity and mutual implication.[14] Related to this repudiation of Huntington is the rejection of the triumphalism that suggests that the Western "discovery" and perfection of liberal democracy represents the apex of moral and political order.[15] Other traditions offer compelling alternatives to the reigning Westcentric consensus, or are less hostile to this consensus than they are often made out to be.[16]

While thinkers like Dallmayr, Euben, and Parel self-identify as comparative political theorists, the literature often loosely subsumed under the label comparative political theory is hardly monolithic or static. It is characterized, above all, by a fluidity and rich diversity of motivating assumptions, methodologies and even disciplinary commitments. The task of gauging what thinkers and works might come under this label is, as often happens, fractious and rarely prone to consensus. Philosophers like Stephen Angle or Roger Ames, for instance, may identify as philosophers rather than political theorists, yet many of their works are inspirational to current generations of comparative political theorists.[17] In other cases, scholars from area studies, comparative history or religious studies are often leaned on for insights within comparative political theory.[18] The very attempt, therefore, to define comparative political theory as one thing rather than another, is itself fraught with dissent.

Equally diverse are the kinds of arguments that have arisen for the purpose and significance of this turn beyond the West:[19] the critical or normative value of encountering and reflecting upon alienness,[20] the postcolonial imperative to resuscitate modes of knowledge dismissed by Orientalist modes of domination,[21] the purely explanatory power of understanding other societies for social science and policy relevance,[22] or the importance of taking seriously the increasing contact between cultures as a result of globalization.[23] The "comparative" label, many have argued, is not to be understood narrowly to imply comparison between specific units or entities only. Rather, it implies the broader sense in which the term "comparative" is used in political science, namely the study of units other than ones traditionally studied (in the case of political science, American politics; in the case of political theory, Euro-American or Western thought). As a result, some debate has ensued about whether "comparative" is the best designation for a subfield that includes almost any mode of studying non-Western thought. But in general, the name has stuck, and comparative political theory continues to be associated with a general inclusivity, openness toward and a deep curiosity about otherness.

The methodological and disciplinary stances that inform the diversity of CPT's proponents are no less wide-ranging. One genre is what we might call conceptual comparison, such as Anthony Parel's drawing of parallels between "the Aristotelian *politikos* and the Confucian *junzi*, Indian *dharma* and the pre-modern Western notion of 'natural justice,' the Islamic prophet-legislator and the Platonic philosopher-king."[24] Many CPT scholars undertake a history of ideas or a history of political thought *within* non-Western traditions. For some, the purpose of such exegetical operations is simply greater clarity and shedding of light on the tradition itself,[25] for others, it is to answer a specific question about a tradition, a thinker or an idea, and its possible relationship to ideas in other traditions.[26] Other scholars compare the history of particular ideas across two (or more) civilizations,[27] and, in some cases, cite the relevance of such a comparison for global-historical and pragmatic political purposes.[28] Some theorists focus on contemporary interpretive and commentarial debates in scholarly communities of non-Western traditions, assessing the implications of these debates for political problems within and across traditions. In her work on Koranic interpretation, for example, Michaelle Browers examines how contemporary Muslim intellectuals across the Arab world are employing various interpretive strategies toward Islam's main texts such as the Koran, the *hadith* and the *sunna*.[29]

Browers and others also engage in conceptual analysis, asking how ideas like the state or civil society have been conceptualized in other traditions, what the histories of these concepts are, and whether they are equivalent in any sense to our Western understanding of the concept.[30] Rochana Bajpai and Rajeev Bhargava's work on Indian secularism and minority rights discourse is a particularly intriguing example of such analysis. This is especially so given their placement outside the American academy, as well as their use of nontraditional sources like the Indian Constitution, legal battles, and other nonacademic discourses.[31] Occasionally, some works of CPT focus on the cross-cultural normative implications of non-Western thinkers or texts for political problems within the West. They ask the question of whether concepts, norms or ideas can be adopted across cultural-geographic boundaries, and interrogate the implications of these transcultural movements.[32] Added to these are the variety of self-reflective methodological commentaries that rigorously debate ways to define and sharpen the very point and purpose of the comparative political theory agenda.[33]

Yet, despite the decentralized plurality of motivations and approaches, the language of cosmopolitanism has intervened only briefly in this discourse on comparative political theory. Fred Dallmayr hints at the possible emergence of cosmopolitanism in political theorizing: he characterizes this as an attitude that seeks no uncritical attachment to the superiority of its own ways of life and modes of theorizing, and speaks of it as "letting be" or a "hermeneutics of difference."[34] The *cosmopolis* Dallmayr envisions would constitute a hermeneutically informed "civilizing process for our global age,"[35] and is characterized by "mutuality and reciprocal recognition,"[36] in a multicultural world that would be democratic and nonhegemonic. More recently, Roxanne Euben has traced the possible beginnings of a premodern Islamic cosmopolitanism.[37] She has produced a countergenealogy of cosmopolitanism as something not emerging in the West alone, but available to be excavated from the doctrinal sources and political practices of Islam.

But despite these provocations, comparative political theory remains relatively silent on the question of whether these initiatives alone constitute a more cosmopolitan evolution in political theory's self-understanding, and how, if at all, the tasks and purposes of a more cosmopolitan political thought might be reconceived. The assumption is that a series of assorted encounters with otherness and a general incorporation of otherness into our existing practices, conventions and discourses over time occasions a more cosmopolitan mode of theorizing.[38] The implication is that the intent to include otherness by broadening the frontiers of the field and of its objects of inquiry, by studying, say, Gandhi, Confucius or Sayyid Qutb, in addition to Kant, Hegel, Locke or Marx, will produce the evolution of a cosmopolitan political thought. Cosmopolitan theorizing is implicitly equated to a broadening of boundaries beyond the West, or an inclusivity characterized by openness and sympathetic treatments of otherness. But this focus on substantive broadening of parameters still leaves unanswered a host of questions about practice and method: namely whether certain kinds of practices and modes of inquiry might be preferable to others, and what the implications are for political theorists for choosing this or that method or practice of inquiry in the course of their engagement with foreign ideas and thinkers.[39]

I turn now to a simultaneous movement, the emergence of a discourse on the idea of cosmopolitanism. Contemporary cosmopolitanisms within political theory[40] cohere around a normative position that is identified with certain basic assumptions: individualism (humans as the ultimate unit of moral worth), egalitarianism (humans as having equal worth), and universalism (the scope to which this moral theory should be applied). Martha Nussbaum asserts that the ancient Greek and Roman traditions of Stoicism first address the notion of the *kosmou polites* or the "world citizen." For the Stoics, every human being "in virtue of being rational and moral . . . has boundless worth."[41] Stoic cosmopolitanism calls for us to recognize the community of rational beings worldwide as the source of our most fundamental moral and social obligations, and of a universal political community. Kant, meanwhile, is said to have been the modern reinventer of this tradition, using it as the basis for his regulative ideal of a cosmopolitan law and political community in *Perpetual Peace*.[42] Although this narrative tends to dominate, different cosmopolitanisms have different emphases. Some cosmopolitanisms display a strong commitment to global justice,[43] others to cosmopolitan law,[44] others to universal human rights,[45] global democracy[46] or the idea of a cosmopolitan culture and citizenship.[47] Cosmopolitanisms are distinguished also by their varying moral or institutional emphases as well as their claims about justice versus culture and identity.[48]

What unites most of this scholarship is that it is rooted firmly in the works of Western thinkers and implies that the West's intellectual heritage contains the resources for a cosmopolitan theorizing. The discourse on cosmopolitanism has remained for the most part an internal Western discussion that privileges the Western experience, as though it were self-evident that other sources need not be consulted.[49] At no point does this cosmopolitanism turn the lens on the disciplinary practices of political theory itself, scrutinizing either the substantive or methodological premises of the field.[50]

Indeed, innovative interventions have been put forth by the counterparts of political theorists in other disciplines, and humanists of various stripes—anthropologists, literary theorists, philosophers, geographers—have been engaged in creating a flourishing space of interdisciplinary discourse on cosmopolitanism. This discourse often recognizes the parochial nature of dominant older versions of cosmopolitanism and acknowledges its rootedness in Western categories, while seeking to pluralize these understandings. Bruce Robbins asserts that in contrast to the old cosmopolitanism of Nussbaum and her Stoic interlocutors, a newer and more refined notion of cosmopolitanism is emerging in the contemporary era. Cosmopolitanisms are now "plural and particular, both European and non-European, weak and underdeveloped as well as stronger and more privileged."[51] Cosmopolitanism can now refer not only to moral codes, obligations, political structures and institutions, but to styles of residence, historical excavations of literary patterns of production, individualized experiences and patterns of migration and transmigration, communication, mass media, and biblical analysis. Newer and richer understandings of cosmopolitanism are emerging, as its core principles become more diffuse and correspondingly "less clear . . . what its value is supposed to be."[52] This plurality of definitions often seeks to remedy the unlocated, abstract nature of cosmopolitanism, acknowledging instead the multiplicity of its situated and embodied formulations. Robbins and others call this "actually existing cosmopolitanism," suggesting that its normative power must often recognize the actual historical and geographic contexts from which it emerges.[53] Paul Rabinow asserts that the term "cosmopolitan" should be extended to transnational experiences that "are particular rather than universal and that are unprivileged and often coerced."[54] Moreover, these interdisciplinary interventions display a strong—and troubling—recognition of cosmopolitanism's often un-self-conscious attachment to a Western genealogy and of the categories of experience and analysis that often accompany this genealogical story. Arjun Appadurai calls for anthropology to "study the cosmopolitan cultural forms of the contemporary world without logically or chronologically presupposing either the authority of the Western experience or the models derived from that experience."[55]

In a perfect illustration, the South Asian area studies scholar Sheldon Pollock provides an alternative to the reifying story that cosmopolitanism originated in Greece and Rome, by focusing on the practices of culture and power in imperial Rome, rather than on theory or moral commitment alone. Focusing on such practices gives us a rather different vision of Roman cosmopolitanism from what we might infer from the writings of, say, the Stoics. In other areas of life such as religious practices, there seems to be evidence of a general indifference in the Roman *cosmopolis* to the cultural diversity of conquered peoples, perhaps even an imperial policy of toleration. But in the domains of both the literary and the political, Pollock argues,

Romanization represented what has been called a "decapitation of the conquered culture"—an obliteration of local literary cultures, and an imposition of Roman cultural and political behavior.[56] The Stoics and Cynics may have thought themselves to be *kosmou politeis*, citizens of the world, but this seems at least in part owing to the fact that "they had been able to transform the *kosmos* into their *polis*, or, rather ... to transform the *orbis* into their *urbs*, the world into their own city."[57] In contrast to the Roman imperial *cosmopolis*, Pollock points to what he calls the Sanskrit *cosmopolis*, the literary and political world produced by the spread of the Sanskrit language, which was created not by conquest, but by traders, literati, religious professionals, and the like. It was voluntaristic, in that those who participated did so through free will (within limits). There was no classification, enumeration and standardization across this cosmopolis (unlike the Roman one), nor was there a need to transform it into a metropolitan center, along with attendant concepts of a center and periphery. Rather, every center was "infinitely reproducible across cosmopolitan space."[58] And, even if these cosmopolitanisms were similar in transcending the local and stimulating feelings of living in a large world, their modalities, Pollock points out, were radically different: the one coercive, the other voluntaristic. Moreover, these cosmopolitanisms involved "two profoundly different visions of the 'cosmos' [as] meaningful for human life: in the one case, the 'circle of the lands' (*orbis terrarum*) that have fallen under Roman power, in the other, 'all that moves with life' (*jagat*)."[59] In one case it involved a strategic/political vision of the cosmos as located in territorial power, and in the other, an all-inclusive metaphysical vision of the cosmos as embracing the underlying unity of all life-forms. Cosmopolitan practice and doctrine, Pollock thus demonstrates, are neither products of the modern age, nor are they restricted to the EuroAmerican West.

Other scholars shed light on the often "presentist" preoccupation in associating cosmopolitanism only with its contemporary expressions, or the "statist" understandings of cosmopolitanism, which organize it in terms of the nation-state and its concerns, subjects, affiliations and conceptual categories. Pheng Cheah points out the anachronism involved in opposing cosmopolitanism to nationalism, precisely because it precedes both the nation-state in history and nationalism in the history of ideas.[60] Newer treatments of cosmopolitanism seek to remedy what Pollock calls an "astonishing ahistoricism" which "retreats into the present"[61] and reconstructs past cosmopolitanism in terms of present categories, often summarily ignoring the existence of vastly cosmopolitan practices in ancient or premodern times.[62]

But political theorists in particular have given little consideration to what these multiple understandings of cosmopolitanism—whether fragmented or cohesive, whether situated and embodied or abstract and ideal, whether historical or presentist—might have on their modes of inquiry. This is not to say that scholars writing in political theory have not produced interventions that critically and robustly interrogate existing formulations of cosmpolitanism.[63] Rather, such interrogations generally continue to remain detached from any reflection on their implications for the very practices of political-theoretic inquiry. Most strikingly, they remain detached from conversations among comparative political theorists and from larger questions about the point and purpose of the comparative political theory project.

This book takes its cue from the intuition that the relationship between comparative political theory and cosmopolitanism requires conceptual elaboration. My intention is not to argue for one singular conception of cosmopolitanism over all others. Nor is it to provide a manifesto for the practice of comparative political theorizing as restricted to one set of activities rather than another. It is to suggest, however, that each of these emerging areas of interest lie in a necessarily complicated relationship to one another. Political theory more generally requires critical self-reflection on the question of what it would mean for the discipline to be genuinely cosmopolitan. Moreover, such reflection is intertwined with methodological questions facing comparative political theorists and others concerned with the turn beyond Westcentric modes of inquiry. The question of cosmopolitanism has thus far remained removed from its implications for the practices of political theorizing, and I will argue that the turn toward a more genuine cosmopolitanism in the practice of political theorizing is long overdue. Moreover, the manner in which scholars approach the study of otherness has implications for the self-understanding of political theory as a whole. The evolution of political theory's self-understanding toward a genuine cosmopolitanism is unavoidably implicated with certain crucial methodological challenges. It also involves a corresponding rearticulation of the political theorist's methodological mandates, especially as they move beyond the parameters of their traditional objects and methods of study.

In the following chapters of this book, I wish to make a distinction between cosmopolitanism and a cosmopolitan political thought. The former is a body of literature with a particular set of normative claims about structuring our moral commitments as well as our political, legal or institutional structures. The latter would be a way of thinking about the practice of our political theorizing itself. I wish to offer an understanding of cosmopolitan political theory that distinguishes it from the cosmopolitanism that has recently been the focus of normative interest in political theory, and turns the lens onto the practice of political theory itself. I will call this a cosmopolitan political thought and argue that its development is linked to the methodological questions about the practice of comparative political theorizing. In so doing, I argue that a clearer understanding of the scope and methods of comparative political theory is crucial to the development of a cosmopolitan political theory. This book is therefore an argument for both challenging existing understandings of cosmopolitanism and for applying the idea of cosmopolitanism—understood in a particular way—to the discipline of political theory itself.

Binaries, Dichotomies and Oppositional Framings

Such an inquiry could not proceed without problematizing the usage of certain categories. To what extent does the language of "Western" and "non-Western" result in precisely the sort of reification we wish to avoid? Have we not recognized the dangers of regarding "West" and "non-West" as stable categories, of ignoring the fluidity, internal multiplicity and interpenetration that characterizes them? As Roxanne Euben reminds us, surely we need to recall that the West, as well as the non-West, are not "civilization(s) with homogeneous roots and clearly delineated historical and contemporary boundaries."[64] Even so, I insist that the history of domination and exclusion in global politics and in knowledge-production makes it important for us to rely on the West/non-West distinction, for the purpose of this project.

In elaborating the necessary usage of the West/non-West dichotomy, a prior task is to address what precisely is meant by "Eurocentrism" or "Westcentrism" to which I will make repeated reference. Broadly speaking, we may use Eurocentrism to refer to the cognitive hegemony of epistemic categories emerging from the Western European and American experience. In much scholarly literature, Eurocentrism is seen as a projection of "the West" and its disciplinary categories as a universal standard of knowledge against which all others are measured.[65] As I will argue in chapter 5, Eurocentrism refers to those modes of understanding that see knowledge as emerging from the EuroAmerican West, and frame all other ways of knowing and being according to its presumptions. They locate subjectivity and agency *to* know in the West, while treating other ways of life and other standards of knowing as objects to be studied, rather than sources of knowledge. As such, Eurocentrism is not only a set of institutional structures but also a posture toward knowledge. It is an attitude that almost anyone trained within certain boundaries cannot avoid imbibing, and is often implicit rather than explicit. It includes the intellectual habit of privileging Western experiences as constitutive of human experience, while relegating all others to the realm of the anomalous or the irregular. Many scholars remind us that this habit permeates practices of inquiry and knowledge production. Not only what counts as valuable knowledge, but also valuable ways of framing knowledge and conducting inquiry, are all subject to the dominance of EuroAmerican modes of thought.[66] Moreover, such Eurocentrism is often insidious in its effects, for it not only ignores non-Western material, it often causes scholars to fail to take seriously alternatives to Europeanized theory as necessary resources for critical analysis. They treat foreign sources as case studies, rather than as sources of alternative *general* theorizing for the EuroAmerican world and its problematics.[67] Rarely are non-Western intellectual resources seen as sources of theoretical inquiry, rather than its objects.

The distinction between West and non-West—and the usage of such terminology—does not necessarily refer to "traditions" clearly bounded by geography or culture. Rather, it refers to patterns of historical privilege and exclusion within modes of knowledge production, both substantive and methodological. This is nowhere more true than in political theory. While there is by now much recognition of the need for an examination of the content of intellectual resources, scarcely have the frames or modes of knowledge production emerging from the West been subject to scrutiny.[68] And, few scholars have considered what impact such scrutiny might have on the practices and methods of inquiry pertaining to the study of otherness. Rarely do we reflect on whether such methodological choices have the ability to *reinscribe* rather than *dislocate* the un-self-conscious Eurocentrism inherent in them.[69] Choosing to study something in a particular way is laden with background assumptions about what constitutes an appropriate mode of knowledge gathering, and a cosmopolitan political theory cannot but engage in a series of critical interventions into these assumptions. The critical interventions I propose here are all too keenly aware of the plurality and elasticity of categories such as "West" and "non-West." Yet, my usage of them suggests that these categories remain pertinent because they reveal how knowledge production and transmission have continued to reflect and be inflected by disparities in power.

In addition to West and non-West, this project will often rely on another binary formulation that may seem troubling: that of self and other. Throughout this book, I will make reference to the idea of civilizational "otherness" as a motivating imagery for the turn beyond Westcentric resources. The language of otherness has been given urgency by the works of Edward Said and subsequent postcolonial or subaltern treatments. No doubt such language is problematic if it seeks uncritically to contrast an undifferentiated other with respect to an equally undifferentiated West. But as I will soon show, the category of otherness can serve as a useful heuristic to distinguish between those modes of inquiry that predominate and those that are relatively ignored; between those understandings of the political world that are seen as self-evident, normalized and routine, and those that are seen as alien, irregular or atypical. This project concerns itself with a specific mode of otherness that has long been neglected by political theorists—namely, that of civilizational alterity. Binary framings require acknowledgment and engagement when there is no alternative language for expressing the ways in which knowledge production is dichotomized. This oppositional framing is eventually what we wish to move past, creating a field of understanding in which *all* things can be at play—the binary and beyond the binary. A cosmopolitan political thought aims to move through *and* beyond the simple binaries of "self" versus "other," and "Eurocentric Western thought" versus "Indian thought," as though these were discretely and impermeably bounded. In turn, it seeks to move toward webs of coeval engagement among Western, Indian, Chinese, African, Japanese or Islamic political resources, in all their multiple genealogies, and with full recognition of the debts that these owe to one another at their porous boundaries. Western philosophy is, for instance, deeply indebted to the Islamic, constructing its own notion of secularism in contrast to the Islamic constitution of the *umma* as a politico-religious community. Indeed "Western political thought" is itself an essentialism that elides its debt to the very traditions it has constructed itself as superior to. A cosmopolitan political thought necessitates an increasing awareness of such permeabilities so the "Eurocentric" center no longer remains the center. But such a web of coeval engagements that seeks to break through oppositional framings cannot avoid making reference to the dichotomies that have thus far constructed and constrained the world of knowledge production.

Methodological Claims and Reflections on the Promise of Cosmopolitanism

What about the cosmopolitan aspiration might be valuable to political theorists—in particular to comparative political theorists—and why might they rely on the promise of this trope? The cosmopolitan aspiration has, to some extent, already been pinpointed as valuable. Yet, little has been done to sharpen its relevance specifically for the project of engaging with civilizational alterity. The promise of cosmopolitanism, I believe, rests on refining our conception of cosmopolitanism, its approach to specifically civilizational alterity, and the contributions of its methodological interventions into the existing practices of political theorizing.

Notice that cosmopolitanism need not be implicated in a mandatory rejection of all EuroAmerican thought as necessarily hegemonic and thus unsuitable for inquiries pertaining to other contexts. It may be true that reading certain kinds of Western texts and accepting the presumptions of certain Western modes of inquiry can be emancipatory for non-Western peoples. It may also be true that a scholarly and rigorous political theory must be concerned with more than simply the dislocation of Eurocentric views.[70] But cosmopolitanism seeks to show that standards of rigorous scholarship can often be located in sites of discourse and practices of theorizing beyond the West, and that an un-self-conscious replication of one set of standards is not always the path to such rigorous scholarship. Rather, such rigor often requires an unsettling of the idea that disciplinary training within a single context—namely the

EuroAmerican one—is methodologically sufficient to study political inquiry within a radically different context.

But the promise of a cosmopolitan political thought inheres in more than the turn away from the insularity of Westcentric analysis. Rather, its promise lies in a series of claims about method. I conduct my intervention through a series of provocations grounded in intuitions about the practices of political theorizing and debates about method. Sheldon Pollack urges a shift in thinking about cosmopolitanism from a focus on ideas to one on action, from philosophical propositions to practices.[71] A shift toward cosmopolitanism requires not large-scale reflection about grand methodological questions, but a series of moderated interventions having to do with particular *practices* of political theorizing—what sorts of subjects we choose to focus on, what kinds of questions we ask, how we seek to frame these questions, and how we locate ourselves with respect to the resources we seek to study.

I suggest then that cosmopolitanism is not an ideal to be contemplated in the abstract and then applied in concrete cases, but rather that its very definition will only emerge as a result of specific, localized interventions into practices of political theorizing. I seek not to posit an a priori definition of cosmopolitanism as attached to this or that value or to a particular set of moral commitments. Rather, we may give shape to the notion of cosmopolitanism through certain practices of engaging with non-Western intellectual resources. The situated interventions I propose will depart from illustrations of particular texts, ideas or traditions; most often, I will rely on examples within Indian political thought, particularly on Gandhi's political thought as it emerges from, yet reinterprets, the Vedic tradition. The promise of the cosmopolitan vision I offer will thus be implicated in a series of methodological claims, clarified and deepened by reflection on the very questions about method that motivate my interventions.

What methodological claims and reflections might motivate these interventions? First, I indicate continually that a cosmopolitan political theory must be both transgressive in its hybridizing thrust, yet cognizant of the connections between civilizations and their cultural products. It will be transgressive in the sense that it will be drawn to engage in fusions and theorizing across cultural boundaries. In so doing, it will take ideas, texts and methods out of their original context, calling upon them and interpreting them in new ways and new contexts. It will take as self-evident that hybridity and synthesis rather than purity are the condition of humankind. "Hybridity" should not be misunderstood to mean the mongrelization of once-existing pure and unalloyed forms,[72] or of idealized cultural monads, whole and untouched by any other. Rather, an encounter with otherness is the very prerequisite for any tradition's resources to become the target of scholarship. Such encounters are "always already" transformative once they have brought such resources to the attention of the external "gaze."

But the cosmopolitanism I describe simultaneously recognizes that such fragmentary and hybridizing modes of theorizing cannot occur in an unchecked riotous fashion as texts, ideas, practices and methods of inquiry float free of connection to any tradition. In fact, the very prerequisite for the transgressive, synthetic moments described here will be a firm grounding within the heuristic value of intellectual lineages. It will require a nuanced and fully informed respect for the shaping power of traditions over their own intellectual products. Fractured, hybridized understandings first place such fragments within larger wholes, no matter how artificially constructed or easily deconstructed these may be. The promise of a cosmopolitan political thought will emerge from an ability to see family resemblances linking certain resources to one another and thus preserve the unique historicity of a lineage; while simultaneously engaging in transgressive syntheses that bring about unforeseen excavations of existing resources. It neither negates the placement of such resources within traditional lineages, nor reifies it.

In other words, to place both Gandhi and Tagore's metaphysical views and their subsequent understandings of pluralism within the context of Vedic cosmology is not to accede to essentialist constructions of Vedic texts as foundational to Indian political thought. It is compatible with a recognition of the synthetic capacities inherent within these thinkers, each of whom incorporated elements of Vedic thought, Enlightenment thought, as well as nonclassical folk knowledge into their ideas. And, it does not preclude excavating their writings for normative insights that travel across cultural boundaries, beyond their own spatiotemporal contexts.

Second, such nuanced ability to move between the poles of fragmentary hybridizing and holism requires attention to the multiple subjectivities and ever-shifting positionalities of the scholar undertaking the study. Cosmopolitanism requires an intervention into the subjectivity and vantage point of the scholar investigating alterity. Certain self-conscious positionalities and self-reflexive engagements with one's own location are crucial modalities of a cosmopolitan theorizing. It involves two primary positionalities on the part of the scholar. The first, which I call self-dislocation, requires her to leave her disciplinary home, immersing herself in the practices, modes of inquiry, scholarly conventions, and intellectual resources of another tradition. Chapters 2 and 3 describe in detail the activities involved in this self-dislocation. A cosmopolitan political theory is one in which theorists actively seek out this kind of dislocation both literally and imaginatively. They immerse themselves intellectually *and* existentially within the alien worlds they are trying to understand. This positionality will often require a self-conscious exit from the disciplinary home located within the parameters of Westcentric practice, and a resituation within another, while grappling with the discomfort of encountering alterity.

But this self-dislocation must be followed by the second positionality, which I call self-relocation. Cosmopolitanism's promise, I will argue, lays in a necessary movement or return home, a movement that calls into question the very settled presumptions learned from that home. Here, the scholar resituates herself within the debates and frames of inquiry of her disciplinary home with a reconstituted vision that creates the possibilities for intervention into Eurocentric categories of inquiry. It requires that she struggle with introducing these dislocating insights into familiar theoretical conversations, precisely so that they challenge the very self-understandings that define these discourses. In chapters 4 and 5, I address the components of this self-relocating movement, which pertains to dislodging of Westcentric normative commitments, as well as dominant preoccupations and modes of framing and motivating inquiry.

Consider the scholar who is singularly positioned in the West and simply seeks un-self-consciously to bring its methodological, substantive and practical prejudices to bear on a foreign tradition. In contrast, a scholar situated in multiple contexts and immersed in the practices of inquiry of another tradition *in addition* to his or her own is far better equipped to conduct inquiry into the resources of that tradition. Moreover, such multiple positionalities also heighten the capacity for the unsettling of the West's attachment to its own substantive and methodological commitments.

Bringing the insights of another tradition to bear on Westcentric inquiry is a crucial component of a cosmopolitanism understood in this way. It illustrates the possibility that Westcentric normative commitments and modes of inquiry may eventually become targets of intellectual intervention from the vantage point of immersion in otherness. It is this dual movement, fostered by the alternate moments of self-dislocation and self-relocation that I argue is crucial to a cosmopolitan political thought.[73] These multiple subjectivities and shifting positionalities may also eventually decenter the Eurocentric notion of "self." The construction of the "self"—so central to Enlightenment thought—is not shared in the same ways in other political philosophies. A cosmopolitan political thought, in acknowledging the fluid locations of this "self" and placing it in a multiplicity of relationships to various traditions, opens the door to a destabilizing of the Enlightenment's own predominant ways of constructing self-hood.

Third, cosmopolitanism requires an elaboration of the centrality of the metaphor of travel to the practice of political theorizing. The theme of travel, of course, has a long history as a prominent trope within Western political thought. The very name "theory" comes from the Greek *theoria*, a term used initially by Herodotus, defined alternately as to "see the world," to be a spectator, or to observe.[74] Its etymology, Roxanne Euben reminds us, connects the practice of theorizing to travel, direct experience and vision. It suggests that the systematic investigation and attainment of knowledge involves exposures to other lands, along with the comparisons they make possible, thus fostering the "epistemological journey from habit to knowledge."[75] But once we look deeper, it becomes clear that the use of travel in political theory has not always coincided with actual, physical dislocative experience. When it has done so, it has tended to suggest that the value of travel lies simply in witnessing or observation, with little reference to what comes after. And, rarely have the dislocative experiences of political theorists investigated the resources of civilizational alterity with anything other than imperial interest.

Theory has thus long been associated with the idea of travel and visiting, but until recently has rarely demonstrated a prolonged engagement—either literal or imaginative—with ideas and cultural worlds outside the West. Kant, who associates the idea of cosmopolitanism with travel and hospitality, most notably never left Konigsberg. Drawing on Kant, Arendt proposes a concept of impartiality based on "going visiting" but specifies that this visiting must rely on the imagination.[76] Political theorists who traveled outside the EuroAmerican world often did so in order to point to the novelty and exotic nature of the practices they encountered (think here of Montesquieu and de Tocqueville), placing the value of the encounter in the observing or witnessing of these practices. This notion of observation treats such practices as objects of analysis to be gazed and wondered at, but rarely articulates the importance of the moments beyond the witnessing and chronicling. Moreover, such travel was almost never undertaken to investigate a non-Western civilization's political-theoretic resources, seen as legitimate sources of intellectual authority on par with the West's own. Most often, travel by Europeans occurred within the context of the imperial experience, designed to "constitute and silence a diverse array of cultural Others,"[77] by cosmopolitans seeking either "to study the world or to control it."[78] For instance, both the German and Anglo-Orientalist projects from the eighteenth century recognized the sophistication of Vedic thought but had to prove, nonetheless, that it was not quite up to par with Enlightenment thinking. Thus, the very Eurocentrism of political theory emerged because of mobility, imperial travel, and indeed, a certain kind of dislocation. It is in these very encounters with otherness that Eurocentrism established its own sense of exceptionalism.

How does self-dislocation in a cosmopolitan political thought move beyond the West's earlier interweaving of self-dislocation with travel, imperial power and theorizing? To begin, cosmopolitanism's self-dislocation requires actual physical dislocation from the comforts of home. The study of civilizational alterity cannot rely solely on theorizing as an exercise of imagination, for the very purpose of encountering alterity is to disturb the knowledge arising from home and hearth. Such provocations are qualitatively different when experienced in embodied actuality, and are often unavailable to the armchair traveler. Chapters 2 and 3 will elaborate on what makes such physical dislocation so crucial.

A cosmopolitan political thought must also move beyond wondering and gazing at otherness. The dislocations of cosmopolitanism must amount to more than the simple equation of knowledge expansion with the wonders of observation. When travel is equated with witness, it suggests an impermanence, a wandering-about and surveying novelty without the deeper understandings that come with long-term familiarity. Accounts of travel that rely on moments of witness suggest that alterity can be experienced visually as a spectator from an external vantage point. Self-dislocation deepens and moves beyond the trope of travel understood simply as the experience of observation. Instead, it turns to the metaphors of dwelling in, residing in, and existence within otherness, to immersion and participation in ways of life by inhabiting a perspective internal to the tradition and to its members. Rather than gazing at an object and transcribing the results of this observation, self-dislocation in cosmopolitanism suggests that viscerally experiencing the provocations of alterity requires replicating the perspectives of the adherents of an intellectual tradition. Other tradition's sources of intellectual value are to be understood from the perspectives internal to that world. In turn, this requires detachment from the presumption of the superiority of Westcentric training for the investigation of other traditions.

Finally, self-dislocation in a cosmopolitan political thought occurs in a complex dialectical relationship to self-relocation. Self-relocation need not be a matter of strictly spatial or geographical return to the West, but rather of a broader targeting of intellectual interventions toward the Westcentric disciplinary home. It constitutes an acknowledgment that the center too can be the target of an intervention that originates from its non-Western periphery. The distinction between these two positionalities need not assume that these moments of self-dislocation and self-relocation are easily separated, or that they imply perfect ideal-type polarities between "insider" and "outsider," between internal immersion *within* otherness and external gaze *at* otherness. Nor should either of these modalities imply a disavowal or rejection of the practices and modes of theorizing gleaned from the other. Rather, they point to the ultimate possibility of the scholar's self-reflexive positionality at the intersection of boundaries between intellectual traditions, the simultaneous capacity for inhabiting what I call "multiple insider perspectives." It requires neither complete disavowal of the disciplinary home, nor a complete transformation into a member of another tradition. Rather than focusing on outcomes of achieving insider or outsider status, I use the trope of inhabiting perspectives. I suggest therefore, that the hallmark of cosmopolitan theorizing is the ability to move between multiple perspectives as insiders *and* outsiders at crucial moments. Indeed, this suggests that the Enlightenment's narrowly Westcentric understanding of the entity of "self," as well as its dichotomous understandings of inside and outside, can be challenged. Seen in this way, the metaphors of location in a cosmopolitan political thought are used as means to subvert the very processes that enabled Eurocentric thinking to establish itself in the ways it did.

Cosmopolitanism, Universalism, Liberalism

In its emphasis on localized and situated interventions, the cosmopolitan political thought I envision differs not only from universalisms that have often dominated political theory, but also from certain anti-universalist critiques. One motivation for broadening the parameters of political theorizing suggests that Western political thought has achieved its presumption of universal validity through a kind of tribalism masquerading as universalism. Its worldview is founded on philosophical and theological claims emanating from a specific historical context, yet, it claims that the reach of this worldview is universal. The tendency of key Western thinkers has repeatedly been to suggest that their presuppositions about models of humanness and political order, although derived largely from Greek and Christian sources, were universally applicable. Some argue that such a universalism is morally and politically objectionable, as well as intellectually flawed, in that it entails "jumping to conclusions." If the purpose of political theory is to investigate the best available models of political order, then it seems odd to arbitrarily privilege ideas drawn from the Western experience, and then claim that they apply elsewhere, with no examination of what other traditions have to offer. In the absence of any serious investigation of alternatives, the universalism of Western political thought seems unempirical. Such anti-universalist arguments often suggest that a more genuinely global mode of theorizing should seek a set of varied answers to questions that are perennial.

But the idea of collecting a more complete set of answers provokes one to ask, what questions are we trying to answer? Many of these critiques fail to register that such queries are motivated by the preoccupations of Westcentric theorizing. Collecting varieties of theories in response to so-called "perennial" questions only reinscribes the particularity of the West's own presumptions about what constitutes political inquiry. Rather than simply "adding value" to existing conceptions of political theory by making the treatment of non-Western texts fit the categories of Western inquiry, the cosmopolitanism I describe entails a willingness to question the very premises that motivate our own inquiries. It requires a refusal to systematize *both* questions as well as responses, and a change in the sorts of questions we ask and the problems we focus on. Of course, this may be obvious to most political theorists who recognize that adding value requires problematizing existing concepts and categories. But many attempts by theorists to add such value through the exploration of non-Western thought seem unaware of how their very efforts to do so could remain bounded by specifically Western frames of theorizing. Much of this book (particularly chapters 2, 3 and 5) is dedicated to demonstrating how CPT may be vulnerable to reinscribing much of the Eurocentrism it wishes to avoid, unless it engages the radically different motivating queries of non-Western traditions.

Of course, Western political theory is a category subject to much contestation and fragmentation. How it is defined often depends on who its practitioners are, and how they go about their practices of theorizing. Recent reflections on the state of the subfield have aptly pointed to the variety and diversity of activities loosely coalesced under the wide umbrella known as "political theory," many of them often unrecognizable to one another. Andrew March has pointed out the "fruitful, fortunate and productive absence of a settled consensus on the meaning and purpose of 'political theory,'"[79] echoing John Gunnell's characterization of the field as "fractured into a number of parochial professionally and intellectually inspired discursive enclaves."[80] Timothy Kaufman-Osborn reminds us that the methodological commitments of political theorists range from psychoanalytic inquiry to deconstruction, hermeneutics, history of political thought, analytic philosophy and postcolonial theory, while their substantive leanings vary from Rawlsian liberalism to Straussianism to Marxism to neo-Aristotelianism or republicanism.[81] But we do not require a monolithic concept of political theory in order to acknowledge that specific histories and experiences, no matter how loosely connected, give rise to particular preoccupations and modes of inquiry. Kaufman-Osborn points out that despite its apparent heterogeneity, political theory continues to be narrowly preoccupied by liberalism's central concerns and has rarely been able to break free of the confines of its basic presumptions.[82] It may be, then, that a cosmopolitan political thought adopts the posture of deliberate challenge toward liberalism's presumptive centrality to the project of political theory. Anticipating my arguments in the concluding chapter, the outcome of a cosmopolitan political thought may indeed be to target specifically liberal presumptions for controversion, rather than simply exploring non-Western alternatives and calling for their inclusion in existing debates. Its focus on topics that genuinely problematize liberalism's most settled presumptions will, at times, explore non-liberal models as sources of theorizing, and identify which elements of liberalism could productively be displaced by such interventions.

I turn now to a description of the chapters in this book. Chapter 2 points to the complexity of even the most preliminary question: what resources within a tradition might be of interest to a political theorist? It asks whether we can we turn to different intellectual traditions without reproducing the categories of Westcentric theorizing. A cosmopolitan political thought requires a method of investigation allowing each tradition and its members to identify and assign value to its own intellectual resources, according to standards internal to that tradition. But even this can be problematic if it reifies essentialist understandings of the civilization and its resources. The challenge, then, is a dual one: avoiding ethnocentric reference to our specific practices, without acquiescing to canonical constructions that paint traditions in sweeping essentialist terms.

I argue for an alternative possibility that involves three critical interventions: genealogical investigation, internal investigations of power and dissent, and finally, immersion within the practices of knowledge production. Such an approach should reveal the narrow specificity of the West's modes of political inquiry, emphasizing the precise aspects of those resources that displace Westcentric presumptions, and the ways in which they do so. In so doing, cosmopolitan scholarship not only avoids reproducing highly specific notions of what constitutes political theory, but also self-consciously seeks out modes of intellectual production that displace and even replace those very settled preconceptions.

In chapter 3, I argue that the next task will be to undertake the interpretation of particular texts and the analysis of particular ideas. Given the unique challenges this poses, the existence of Western interpretive techniques is often insufficient in allowing us to understand well the ideas contained in these texts. Using the Vedic Hindu concept of *dharma* (variously translated as duty, moral law, or force of moral order) and Gandhi's appropriation of Vedic hermeneutic techniques to illuminate interpretive dilemmas related to *dharma*, chapter 3 will argue for a particular approach to the interpretation of non-Western texts and ideas. I call this approach "existential immersion" and argue that such interpretive study must involve immersion in the practices and life-worlds of members and adherents within a tradition. But a good cosmopolitan scholar will have to alternate between an internal immersion in the lived experience of texts or ideas and an external stance of commentary and exegesis. Struggling with the conflicting imperatives of these moments is precisely the task of a more nuanced approach to a cosmopolitan political theory. The scholar must be able to read texts and thinkers as both deeply situated and highly nomadic, both based in adherence yet focused on criticality, both historically grounded yet ready to travel beyond context. This in turn requires a commitment to struggling with two conflicting moments: the first, of immersion in specific contexts, and the second, a commentative task requiring a return to external vantage points. Chapter 3 argues that this radical "self-dislocation" involved in existential immersion is a necessary— if paradoxical—task of the cosmopolitan political theorist, a prelude to a cosmopolitan mode of engagement that eventually unsettles the disciplinary home.

But how is such unsettling engagement meant to occur, and what precisely is to be done with the new modes of knowledge gained through this process of self-dislocation? Chapter 4 turns to the question of "self-relocation" and argues that the vision of cosmopolitanism I outline rests crucially on a particular understanding of self-relocation. Yet this too is a theoretical minefield that raises crucial methodological issues. In chapter 4, I present two possible models or modes of transcultural learning, showing that each is implicated with a set of complex concerns that make it difficult either to pry them apart from one another, or to resolve them unproblematically. The first one suggests that texts can speak polyvocally, and that creative interpretation across time and space is a necessary outcome of transcultural borrowing. In so doing, texts and ideas will often mutate in a piecemeal manner, leading to the transcultural application of ideas in a fractured and disaggregated manner. The second suggests that the appropriate method of importing texts or ideas across cultural boundaries is one that faithfully preserves the holistic nature of the idea or text. This model maintains the connection of the text or idea to all contextual factors, allowing it to travel only by replicating the webs of meaning within which it is placed. Using Gandhi's theory of nonviolence as an illuminating lens, I argue that the pitfalls of transcultural borrowing and creative learning underscore the crucial importance of prior existential engagement with traditions and their cultural products.

Chapter 5 turns to the question of Eurocentrism, asking whether and how the posture of self-relocation may challenge the Eurocentric presumptions of political theory. Is not making Western audiences, disciplines and concerns the target of one's interventions itself an indication of Eurocentric preoccupation? Some critiques imply that the very project of self-relocation underscores the entrapment of a cosmopolitan political thought in the web of Eurocentrism, for it suggests a return to the institutional infrastructures and demands of an academy that reproduces the dominance of Western categories, by speaking within the forms of discourse supported by those categories. The central dilemma animating our study of otherness may be the choice between viewing traditions as only meaningful to their own members in their own languages, or acknowledging that any attempt to speak about ideas across traditions will be Eurocentric in the sense of relying on standards of scholarship learned in one tradition.

In chapter 5, I argue that the choice provided by this view is all too narrowly construed. It asks the wrong questions, and misconceives both the imperative to deconstruct Eurocentrism, as well as the resources and opportunities available to the theorist. Deconstructing Eurocentrism is not simply the flight away from modes of inquiry infiltrated by Eurocentric assumptions, and the recovery of those that have resisted them. The cosmopolitan project requires asking what resources are available in a tradition *despite* the pervasiveness of Eurocentrism, and how these resources may challenge Eurocentric modes of knowing. The approach to such resources is one that may require an imaginative vision, an ability to excavate both from a tradition's past as well as from beneath the façade of its Eurocentric structures.

In the concluding chapter, I ask how this analysis may clarify, deepen, or reconfigure the concept of cosmopolitanism we began with. Cosmopolitanism in political thought, I argue, is an ongoing displacement by scholars who are located, at different times, in different relations of insidership and outsidership to different traditions. It is continuing destabilization; it is continuing confrontations with the hegemony of liberalism's normative *and* structural hegemony. Cosmopolitanism becomes an ongoing set of practices by scholars themselves, a disciplined carrying out of dislocative and relocative practices which leads to a shift in disciplinary self-understanding. According to the current *status quo* in political theory, new, competing counter-formations that challenge liberalism's hegemony are easily integrated into a constellation of minoritarian satellite discourses, while liberal norms remain both substantively and structurally unthreatened. A cosmopolitan political thought moves toward a disciplinary practice in which liberalism and other Westcentric modes of thought take their place in a series of plural and coeval engagements of thinkers and texts from all traditions, moving through and past the dichotomies that ground these encounters. It is from this possibility that we can begin to envision a political theory *beyond* Eurocentrism, that is, after the presumptions of Eurocentrism's primacy have been challenged and disestablished, and post-Eurocentric possibilities of engagement can occur.

2

CANONS, TRADITIONS AND COSMOPOLITANISM

Choosing the "Units" of Analysis

IN ORDER TO turn the endeavor of political theory in a more genuinely cosmopolitan direction, a preliminary task is to ask the following question: what are relevant resources for the task of political inquiry in traditions outside the West? This issue needs to be confronted rather more directly than the current scholarship has tended to do. One could respond, for instance, that every tradition has its well-recognized texts or ideas. A cursory glance at existing works of comparative political theory reveals that thinkers and texts such as Gandhi, the *Bhagavad Gita*, Confucius, Mencius, Sayyid Qutb, Ibn Khaldun and Frantz Fanon are often the least contentious choices of many theorists.[1] This relies on the assumption that if a thinker or a text is relatively well-known in the West, this must constitute sufficient reason for them to be taken as serious objects of inquiry in political theory. But what of less well-known thinkers and their writings such as, say, B. R. Ambedkar or Ashis Nandy in India, Mbembe or Senghor in Africa? They are highly influential within their own traditions, but relatively unheard of in the West. Surely their obscurity in the West alone cannot be grounds for excluding them, and surely Western recognition alone is suspect ground from which to assign intellectual merit to some resources and not to others. Even among those who readily agree on the need to engage non-Western resources, there is little reflection about *which* texts, ideas or modes of scholarship bear investigation in traditions that are relatively unfamiliar to us, and what criteria we might use to identify them.[2]

Can we turn to new intellectual resources without reproducing—intentionally or otherwise—the categories and modes of inquiry pertaining to a Westcentric understanding of political theory? The failure to make explicit how non-Western frameworks, categories and motivating inquiries are often radically different from Westcentric ones makes much of comparative political theory vulnerable to a lack of awareness. It leaves open the often unexamined suggestion that political inquiry everywhere must have the same shape as our own, or must conform to our expectations about appropriate forms of inquiry. A cosmopolitan evolution in political theory's self-understanding requires a critical interrogation of how its self-identification is replicated beyond subject matter produced in the West, and the articulation of an alternative possibility.

I argue that a cosmopolitan political thought requires a method of investigation that allows each tradition and its members to identify and assign value to its own intellectual resources according to standards internal to that tradition. Such an approach requires commencing the study of foreign intellectual resources from a self-conscious immersion in the concepts, categories and modalities of inquiry that structure the larger traditions from within which these resources emerge. In so doing, the approach should seek out those insights that either displace the centrality of Western preoccupations with particular kinds of questions or explore seemingly familiar questions in ways that reveal the narrow specificity of the West's modes of political inquiry. Moreover, such an approach should emphasize the precise *aspects* of the resources that displace Westcentric presumptions and preoccupations and the *ways* in which they do so. As a result, the encounter with radically different modes of political inquiry not only avoids reproducing highly specific notions of what constitutes political theory, it also focuses on modes of intellectual production that challenge, displace or even replace those settled self-definitions. It does so precisely because it takes as a point of departure the immersion in the study of the standards and methods of a tradition, rather than the external stance of gazing at the tradition from afar, while implicitly seeking confirmation of one's own standards and expectations.

Ultimately, such an approach remains indispensable for a cosmopolitan political thought that can grapple intelligently with the paradox of alterity and familiarity. It must recognize that the otherness of the other is rarely either fully alien or fully comprehensible to us, and that the connection between intellectual resources and traditions from which these resources emerge are neither definitive and primordial, nor utterly irrelevant. It is such an approach, I will argue, that allows us to both recognize and move beyond the binary polarities that often underlie and subtly interpose themselves into the study of political inquiry produced by civilizational alterity.

POLITICAL INQUIRY WITHIN AND ACROSS BORDERS

Many approaches by comparative scholars sometimes presume that other traditions must replicate the West's understanding of what counts as a valuable resource for political inquiry, because political inquiry everywhere has the same shape. Therefore the turn toward radically other intellectual resources must be a matter of finding the same kinds of methods, resources and questions that animate our own inquiries. Here, I shall outline the basic ways in which such presumptions lie implicit within the works of some scholars.

The most stringent version of such a presumption manifests in an outright evaluative or prescriptive claim. That is, some scholars argue for *excluding* the study of certain non-Western resources because they do not display what seem to be appropriate political inquiries and categories. Bhikhu Parekh argues, for instance, that there is nothing recognizably like political thinking in ancient India; despite a long tradition of systematic *philosophical* exploration, premodern Hinduism developed no systematic tradition of *political* philosophy.[3] Ancient Indian philosophy, he claims, was deeply metaphysical in nature, dealing only tangentially and sporadically with matters pertaining to political life, producing incidental and fragmentary discussions of political life scattered throughout various texts, which, in the absence of a well-established tradition, seem fragile, tentative and nonargumentative. Implicit in a claim like Parekh's, is the idea that we need to assess texts from all traditions on the basis of whether they meet "our" criteria of merit, whatever those might be.

A Straussian might similarly argue that in order for something to be recognized as political philosophy, it must aspire to ahistorical foundational wisdom or objective knowledge of the good. Any texts or ideas that do not provide such knowledge can only be considered historical or cultural relics.[4] Of course, one does not need to be a Straussian to hold to this view. Surely not just anything can be considered political theory, some suggest, and turning to foreign resources runs the risk of making us uncritical apologists for radical otherness at the cost of rigor in our enterprise. In the worst case, we may become free-for-all relativists who blindly accept that something is valuable and appropriate as a resource purely because of its otherness. The philosopher John Passmore claims that what is commonly called "Chinese philosophy . . . consists almost entirely of the pronouncements of sages,"[5] without clearly explaining the distinction between philosophy and poetry or sagehood, both of which he regards as the same "woolly-minded" thing.[6] Of course, in arguments such as these, what counts as appropriately political is rarely a question that is investigated; rather, the implication is often that the content of the "political" is clearly uncontested, and that the animating inquiries of these other traditions are not recognizably political *to us*. This suggests in turn that Western answers to the question of what constitutes political theory (or the content of "the political") *should* serve as the only guiding framework for considering resources beyond the West.

But most scholarship on non-Western resources rarely takes such a radically pre-scriptive—and exclusive—position on the necessity of replicating the West's own approaches. Instead, much of the time, presumptions about replicating the shape of Western political inquiry, rather than being explicitly stated, are often embedded in the very texts, thinkers and ideas that many scholars choose to focus on. Sometimes, such presumptions manifest in the tendency to gravitate un-self-consciously toward a "great books" or "history of political thought" version of political inquiry, in which emphasis is placed on the thinkers and texts that seem equivalent to canonical works in the Western tradition. Confucius' writings are often uncontroversially accepted as legitimate sources of political inquiry, as are those of the Vedic texts, Gandhi, Say-yid Qutb, al-Farabi, or Ibn Rushd. But little reflection occurs on *why* precisely these resources might be worthy of investigation or *what* about them might be valuable for the purpose of cross-cultural theorizing. Often, it is implied (rather than inves-tigated or proven) that what is theoretically worthwhile is precisely the fact these resources address questions that are recognizable to Western-centered political the-orists. Sometimes, it is also suggested that they present a form of argumentation that is recognizably like political theorizing; namely, addressing the questions of what constitutes the good life or the best form of political organization.[7]

From its earliest inception, the subfield of CPT had already identified as its raison d'etre the uncovering of necessary equivalences among different traditions of politi-cal thinking.[8] In one of the earliest articulations of CPT, Anthony Parel and Ronald Keith identified the project explicitly with the "study of substantive equivalence or *parallelism*" in the development of different traditions. It is the presence of such "equivalences," Parel claimed, that "makes the comparative study of political phi-losophy possible."[9] Roxanne Euben's study of the mid-twentieth-century Egyptian Islamist Sayyid Qutb focused on demonstrating that his critique of modernity's ra-tionalist epistemology and moral neutrality is as incisive and recognizably political as the critiques of Marx, Weber or Rousseau, even though Qutb's critique emerged from a form of expression that is distinctly Islamic.[10] Indeed Euben is, in some places, sensitive to the danger that the repeated use of the paradigm of familiarity may in-terpret the agenda of Islamic fundamentalists in terms of "our" concerns, or in terms of their accessibility to Western worlds of meaning.[11] "Nonetheless," in the words of one analyst, Euben's analysis "tends to remain focused on drawing attention to 'parallels' between the ideas of various Islamic thinkers and contemporary Western debates about the 'crisis of modernity,' a focus that obscures the varied and rich di-alogues taking place within the Islamic setting."[12] In the absence of detailed explo-rations of the contrary, such analyses unfortunately reinforce, rather than challenge, the presumption that other traditions have addressed the same kinds of questions that Western political theory has aimed to address (albeit in different ways). They also suggest that what is most valuable about examining these resources is precisely their ability to replicate the concerns and preoccupations of Westcentric theorizing.

Similarly, the exploration of topics such as "the Chinese conception of distributive justice," "Chinese conceptions of the state," or "Islamic democracy" imply not only that other traditions are interested in asking the same kinds of questions we are, but that the conceptual categories and frameworks that animate and organize our inquiries are the same ones that animate other traditions. Many scholars neglect to make explicit the concepts and frameworks that motivate the queries in the non-Western traditions they study, as well as how these differ radically from those in the Westcentric tradition. Approaching a non-Western text with a presumptive conceptual framework tends to neglect the question of what categories and motivating inquiries have been used to organize political theorizing in other traditions.[13]

For example, Joseph Chan attempts to answer the questions: "Does Confucianism contain the concepts of distributive justice and social justice? Are there ethical principles governing the distribution of resources in Confucianism?" While these are worthy questions, the particular manner of undertaking the exploration can lead to the sort of unexamined presumptions that I pointed to before. Chan begins his analysis by exploring the conception of justice in its classical Platonic, as well as modern, individual-oriented formulations, asking whether similar concepts exist in Confucianism. He concludes that Confucianism has a concept of justice similar to the Greek one that forms the basis of the Westcentric notion, in its distributive, individual-oriented, and moral character.[14] Based on the fact that Mencius and Xunzi understand society in the way that modern Western thinkers do, he posits the existence of a rudimentary formulation of a Confucian perspective on social justice.

Indeed Chan's formulation is well grounded in close readings of these Confucian texts. But his inquiry suggests that what matters is the Western framing of the question of distributive justice, rather than a commencement of an investigation through the preoccupations of the Confucian thinkers themselves. As Chan himself fleetingly acknowledges, Confucian thinkers did not frame issues of society's distributive impact on people's well-being as a concern of justice.[15] But this begs the question of how exactly Confucian thinkers might have framed such questions, and what foundational assumptions might have motivated their inquiries into such matters. Indeed, it seems likely, in Chan's own account, that rather than framing the inquiry in terms of justice, Confucian thinkers may have been concerned with the foundational importance of *ren* or humaneness as the motivating premise for inquiring into political life. Why not begin, then, by centering the concerns that preoccupied Confucian thinkers—namely, people's abilities to attain goodness or humaneness or virtue, however defined—and working forward from those motivating assumptions? But by framing the entire inquiry through a category that was not explicitly in use within Confucian reflections on the issue—namely, Platonic, Rawlsian and/or individualist Westcentric conceptions of distributive justice—Chan unintentionally perpetuates the notion that our method of organizing inquiry must be appropriate, even when reading a thinker whose manner of framing inquiry into that matter differs radically from our own. So too for Azizah al-Hibri's essay "Islamic Constitutionalism and the Concept of Democracy," which seeks to analyze the position of Islamic constitutionalism on democratic governance. Al-Hibri explicitly states that her inquiry will be conducted "from a Western constitutional vantage point . . . in other words . . . study the Islamic system of governance in light of principles basic to Western democracies,"[16] rather than centering her inquiry on the preoccupations about rulership and political authority emerging from within the Islamic tradition.

What might be considered problematic about the presumptions I have just identified? It is easier to dismiss the first evaluative and exclusivist claim—exemplified by Parekh and Passmore—that non-Western resources, in order to be considered worthy of investigation, must look recognizably like "political theory" to *us*. Such a claim rests on some singular understanding of what political inquiry in the West constitutes, which proves to be something of a fiction. Political theory as practiced in the West can hardly be defined in an uncontested manner; it is characterized by an irreducible plurality of assumptions, preoccupations, methods and objects of inquiry. It is, as Timothy Kaufman-Osborn reminds us, "a miscellany of inquiries absent a core."[17] The desires to assign value to some modes of inquiry as legitimate but others as not, to define political inquiry as this kind of scholarship but not that, rely on some conception of the "political" or of political inquiry that is not shared even within the EuroAmerican West, much less across civilizational boundaries.

But even the more implicit presumption that other traditions *do* conduct political inquiry as we do, unwittingly reinforces a West-centered conception of political theorizing if it implies that certain texts must be worthy of investigation *because* they display preoccupations or modes of argument that are recognizable to us. The reference to what constitutes political inquiry within our own sets of practices is a problematic point of departure for the turn toward non-Western intellectual resources if it assumes that the criteria of merit are equivalent to our own highly specific conventions. (Of course, the more radically exclusivist position conflates the specificity of our own theoretical conventions with independent criteria of intellectual merit, thus naturalizing the former.) My argument here is *not* that we should not recognize Confucius, Gandhi or Sayyid Qutb as perfectly legitimate theoretical resources and objects of inquiry and continue to focus on their works. Rather, I wish to problematize the assumption that their appropriateness is due to the fact that their explorations line up with our own understandings of what political inquiry must look like. The point, then, is not that all CPT is necessarily limited by specifically Westcentric frames of theorizing.[18] Rather, the failure to make explicit how other frameworks, categories and motivating inquiries are often different from the ones organizing Westcentric scholarship leaves much of CPT vulnerable to such a lack of awareness. Indeed, much of the best work in CPT is precisely the kind that pointedly makes the reader aware of these differences.[19] But the relative lack of explicit reflection on the matter may lead to a concurrent neglect of those facets of these very same thinkers that actually challenge our understandings of the political. It may also allow scholars to continue producing work that leans un-self-consciously toward making the treatment of non-Western texts "fit" the existing Western categories of inquiry, rather than problematizing them altogether.

How might we proceed instead? In contrast to these arguments, a cosmopolitan political thought should avoid beginning its inquiries from the locus of one's own conventions and seeking analogous things elsewhere, taking for granted the defining nature of these practices. It should willingly engage with ideas that defy settled understandings of "the political," and make explicit the resulting challenge to accepted presumptions about what constitutes political theory. As a result, the kinds of arguments political theorists make about *why* something is valuable and worthy of analysis—whether it is Gandhi's political writings, the various modes of Koranic exegesis, or contemporary constitutional debates in India—require reenvisioning. That is, we no longer approach these resources because they mirror our understandings of what constitutes political inquiry; rather, we study them precisely because we seek a disruption and reenvisioning of those understandings.

THE CANONICAL LENS

I wish to argue that such disruptive ends are best served by beginning through an immersion in the modalities of inquiry located *within* other traditions, rather than from the vantage point of location within the West's conventions and practices of political inquiry. One might argue that what constitutes valuable resources for political inquiry are what people in any given tradition say are valuable resources. They are to be determined by the members of a tradition and by their accounts of the concerns, preoccupations, beliefs, practices, texts, categories and modes of existence and inquiry that they consider to be valuable and worthwhile. This approach has the advantage of implicitly empowering members of a tradition to recognize the merits of and assign value to these resources according to standards that are *internal* to their tradition, rather than allowing the external Western observer to make choices based on his or her standards. As I have indicated, much existing scholarship in CPT points promisingly to such a direction, but if a cosmopolitan political thought is to avoid reproducing Westcentric practices, it requires more explicit reflection on this.

What might it mean to locate one's investigations within the modes of inquiry of another tradition? One could argue that this requires adopting a *canonical* lens— that is, conducting one's investigations in terms of units such as "Chinese political thought" or "Indian political thought," or "Islamic political thought," as many CPT scholars tend to do.[20] This view privileges the "civilizational" character of theorizing and sees civilizations as geographically and culturally distinct entities displaying unique theoretical traditions. Implicit in this approach is the idea that each of these traditions are seen as the source of important influence on the texts, thinkers and practices that follow, respecting the distinctiveness of a given tradition, the continuity that characterizes the relationship among its constituent elements, and their impact on members of the tradition.[21]

Of course, such as view can stem from a well-meaning desire for a noninvasive approach to otherness that preserves its uniqueness and highlights its underrecognized contributions. It allows members of the tradition to identify the sites of civilizational value. But we also know that when adopted uncritically, a canonical lens can conflate internal authority and agency with an artificially constructed image of coherence and continuity. Rather than acknowledging that intellectual traditions are often characterized by *ways* of knowing and understanding, a sweeping canonical lens can equate traditions with particular individuals whose ideas one can then pinpoint as "distinctly" or "uniquely" Chinese, Indian or Islamic. It also implies that the history of the tradition can be viewed in a holistic manner, and that a continuity of preoccupations can therefore be found. Sometimes, such a view also conveniently masks the porousness of boundaries between (and within) civilizations, leading to a neglect of crucial inter- and intra-civilizational exchange, borrowing and synthesis.[22]

The problem of essentializing discourse, inherent in the sweeping "civilizational" lens, is further compounded by the relationship of canonicity to imperialism.[23] In tracing the history of Orientalist British Indology, Ronald Inden claims that

Indologists have not only taken Hinduism to be the essential religion of India; they have viewed it as the exemplification of the mind of India . . . the essence of that mind was its "feminine" imagination . . . She was an inferior substitute for the West's masculine, world-ordering rationality. In the end, Indians were seen as concerned more with the renunciatory quest of the individual for mystic absorption.[24]

For centuries, the grand Orientalist narrative of Indian thought emphasized mysticism and renunciation over worldliness and rationality,[25] while dissenting strands of atheism, instrumental rationality, empiricism and critical challenge were routinely ignored and thus even more marginalized in Indians' own internalized self-understandings of their intellectual heritage.[26] Only recently have any narratives—Indian or Western—begun to dissent from this construction, suggesting a renewed emphasis on the nonmystical, materialist, rationalist and deliberative currents in the Indian tradition.[27] A canonical lens cannot easily be equated with the location of agency to assign value internally within a tradition. This becomes complicated when such agency is itself colored by external constructions of value that have already shaped the notion of a heritage through configurations of power.

Even the terms "canon" and "canonical" must be apprehended with some caution, for they are far too disfigured with specificity to have much resonance with traditions outside the West. The very use of the word "canon" is implicit with inevitably Western and often biblical connotations, with roots in ecclesiastical and juridical traditions that rarely carry the same meaning outside these contexts.[28] Uncritical usage of a canonical lens obscures the extent to which many non-Western traditions, rather than being reducible to particular thinkers or texts, may be characterized by modes of knowledge production, knowledge reproduction, knowledge transmission and knowledge reception; and by certain methods of studying, reason giving and inquiring.

A REHABILITATION OF THE CANONICAL LENS

The solution to this dilemma is clearly not the wholesale endorsement of a sweeping canonical lens employed in an uncritical manner. But neither, I argue, is it the wholesale jettisoning of the notion of a "tradition" of political thought as a myth. Cultures may not be hermetically sealed monads or reified entities with settled boundaries, but the converse is also true: in our rush to deconstruct all boundaries and categories and decry them as "essentialist," we may mistakenly destroy the somewhat meaningful ones. As Clifford Geertz reminds us, civilizations are meaningful entities, porous and fluid though their boundaries may be.[29]

How, then, might we preserve the value of traditions while remaining vigilant about what their constructions suppress? The challenge here is a dual one: avoiding ethnocentric reference to our own specific practices, without acquiescing simply to canonical constructions that paint traditions in essentialist terms. I propose an approach that would differ from the simple civilizational or canonical lens in several crucial ways and would require three critical interventions in order to do so:

genealogical investigation; internal investigations of power and dissent; and finally, scholarly, vocational practices surrounding the treatment of intellectual resources.

The first critical intervention centers on the necessity of genealogical investigation. A rehabilitated canonical lens must pay attention to tracing the history of the construction of value within any given tradition. In the case of Chinese political thought, for instance, canon construction has much to do with the internal workings of political dynasties, their varying fortunes, and the political imperatives emerging from specific historical moments. The canonization of a body of classical texts declared authoritative often proceeds by political, ecclesiastical or literary fiat.[30] The collection of writings now known as the Confucian canon, for example, was mostly a group of "ill-sorted and fragmented ancient writings," eventually presented as coherent and canonical because of a series of political upheavals in the late third-century BC. John Henderson's detailed study of Chinese canonical history highlights the crucial role of councils and kings in the establishment of an official Confucian "canon" during the Han era (202 BC to AD 220).[31] The story that Henderson and others tell of the Confucian canon is that of a disjointed and incoherent assortment of writings reconstructed through various political and historical occurrences, as corresponding to universal moral, cosmological, historical order— and seen eventually as based "in the nature of things," dehistoricized through an artificially created "timelessness."[32] Such investigations need not focus narrowly on the political or institutional aspect of canonization at the cost of throwing into doubt the intellectual merit of these texts. Yet they are invaluable for the purposes of an informed genealogy that recognizes the intellectual merits of a tradition's narratives without falling prey to the essentialist myths that perpetuate the influence of such narratives.

The second critical intervention centers on questions of power and hegemony *internal* to the construction of value within the tradition. We have already seen the influence of *externally* imposed hegemony on the construction of value. But the scholar interested in a cosmopolitan political thought must also ascertain what (if any) are the *internal* sources of plurality, dissent, marginalization and exclusion. How are privilege and marginalization reified and sustained through an emphasis on the value of certain ideas or texts, and a minimization or negation of others?

These questions take on particular importance in the case of postcolonial civilizations. A canonical approach seems to have the advantage of respecting the voices of formerly oppressed peoples by empowering them to identify value for themselves.[33] But this "empowering of the collective other" can be a double-edged sword. The collective other is rarely an undifferentiated entity, and empowering one segment of a society often comes at the expense of marginalizing, silencing or ignoring another. If it is to engage in a genuine empowering that is not simply a nod to the elite voices in a tradition, a canonical approach must display a genuine sensitivity toward the manner in which intrasocietal power dynamics are reflected in the construction of value.

As an example, any understanding of the Indic tradition of political thought must have a keen sense of the suppression of non-Vedic, non-Brahminical knowledge that resulted from the predominance of the Vedic narrative in the Indian intellectual tradition. The singular narrative of the Vedic texts as foundationally representative of the Indic tradition indeed owes much to Orientalist essentializing of the Indian or Hindu "mind," but it seems equally prevalent among Indian scholars of the tradition. Dissenting narratives that highlight the artificiality of this story are by now increasingly visible; the cosmopolitan scholar of political thought would do well to acquaint herself with the interplay of such competing narratives.

For instance, intellectual dissent from non-Brahminical sources by members of the former untouchable caste, known as *dalits*, constitute epistemic, moral and political challenges to the dominance of Brahminical thought.[34] Dalit dissent against the patriarchy and hierarchy of Brahminical Hinduism was motivated primarily by the moral and political reformism of thinkers like B. R. Ambedkar (India's first president, born a *dalit*), Jyotiba Phule and E. V. Ramaswamy Naicker, a.k.a. Periyar. It utilized not only the classical resources of Buddhism and its objections to Hinduism, but also nonhierarchical and nonspiritual folk practices, along with the resources of secular rationalist humanism. Dr. Ambedkar's turn toward Buddhism explicitly rejected the so-called eternal and infallible truths of the Vedas and Upanishads, replacing them with an experiential and empiricist epistemology in which only one's own experience was to be trusted.[35] He called for a wholesale rejection of Hinduism by the dalits, symbolized by his public conversion to Buddhism and his call for all dalits to follow suit, bringing about a shift in the practices and self-understandings of a marginalized population.[36]

Certainly dalit thought is neither coherent nor monolithic in itself, and dissonant voices can be found within. But the trend toward the rejection of Brahminical textual—and subsequently political—authority is an important theme around which these thinkers cohere. The tactics used by these thinkers were both hermeneutic and historiographical, resulting in a useful and creative opposition to the structures of Brahminical domination. Valerian Rodrigues tells us that a majority of dalit thinkers use commentary on the significant texts of the tradition (as well as its popular practices) in order to produce subversive interpretations that expose the hollowness and depravity of Brahminical hierarchy.[37] Historiographic reinterpretation constructed an alternative history that valorizes the non-Brahminical, non-Aryan Dravidian heritage of the dalits as indigenous, ethnically distinct, and morally and politically more progressive.[38] This dissenting strand of thought has come to be tremendously influential among the *bahujan* political activists of India, yet remains relatively under-theorized as an important component of the Indian intellectual tradition. Any scholar attempting to gain a robust understanding of the Indian tradition must remain sensitive to the manner in which attempts to solidify a monolithic self-understanding have in turn suppressed or marginalized others.

Our third critical intervention focuses on the scholarly practices and discourses surrounding the treatment of intellectual resources. Here, one asks: is there a lively tradition of discourse surrounding these resources, and if so, what are the protocols and conventions of that discourse? Are there particular ways that scholars internal to the tradition comment on, classify and participate within discursive practices? Where are the attempted points of fixity, where are the points of openness, the points of resistance to closure, what remains live and negotiable? Answering these question requires the scholar to develop familiarity with the internal commentaries, judgments of political/philosophical works, normative statements about the relevance and validity of the works, and their suitability for use (if at all) in teaching curricula. In the exploration of scholarly or vocational practices, one asks scholars and academics what they read, study and comment on, how curricula are organized, how public discourses about the relevant texts and ideas are conducted, and what the practices of disciplinary formation are.[39]

But this critical intervention expands the focus of investigation beyond simply canonical texts and thinkers. It targets the preoccupations of a tradition, as well as its practices of knowledge production, knowledge transmission and knowledge preservation. It goes beyond those classical or scholarly modes of inquiry recognizable in the West, to folk, noncanonical or popular modes. A scholar interested in the South Asian tradition would indeed study the canonical and classical texts of the "great" traditions as organized within recognizable disciplinary formations such as universities, religious institutions and scholarly research organizations. But s/he would extend her or his investigation into other modes of knowledge transmission that specifically reject and sometimes subvert the premises of canonical or scholarly learning.

One such example is the practice of *bhakti* poetry as an alternative method of knowledge production. Various movements between the seventh and thirteenth centuries in India cohere under the umbrella term of *bhakti*, a movement led by poets, saints and other religious/spiritual reformers.[40] Originating as a revolt against Brahminical orthodoxy and caste-based ritualized patriarchy, the bhakti movement symbolized cultural resistance to the patriarchy of feudal privilege, caste and gender hierarchies and inegalitarian marital norms by giving voice to women and subordinated classes. Medieval mystic poet-saints such as Kabir and Mirabai not only rejected the elitism of the canonical Vedic texts, they explicitly disavowed scholarly learning and identification with any one scriptural tradition, focusing instead on daily practices of devotion (*bhakti*) that were emotive and instinctual, yet provided profound insights into the human condition.[41] The bhakti movement thus sought to transcend the boundaries of organized religion and inculcate a mystical, universal and egalitarian mode of participation in ultimate knowledge. It emphasizes individual choice and responsibility in spiritual and religious matters, calling for a practice of devotional recitation requiring no mediation by scholarly or spiritual authority. Knowledge of the divine, of cosmic matters, and ultimately of spiritual liberation is available to all regardless of religion, caste or gender. This knowledge was revealed and transmitted through the recitation of folk-style devotional poetry and hymns, in contrast to rigorous canonical scriptural study mediated by priestly or scholarly authorities. Thus, it was communally structured, egalitarian, and open to participation by all individuals. In addition to a historical study of bhakti movements, modern-day equivalents of these bhakti practices and communities would be an important complement to the scholar's investigations on scholarly discourses and disciplinary conventions in South Asia. Such investigations will reveal both *political-theoretic* content through discourses on egalitarianism and resistance to hierarchy as well as *methodological* insights into alternative modes of knowledge transmission.

Such interventions proceed by locating oneself within the traditions and communities where such knowledge is produced and reproduced. One inserts oneself into the discourses that preoccupy these communities, absorbing their practices about knowledge and its production. Leigh Jenco suggests that such expertise is made available not simply by studying these localized modes of knowledge production from afar, but by participating in them with a willingness to "be disciplined by" foreign communities of scholarship.[42] Such a study requires the ability not simply to travel to the worlds of indigenous intellectual production where such knowledge is produced and reproduced. Rather, it requires a long-term and more in-depth knowledge of the conditions of such production, such as its institutional (or noninstitutional) modes of organizing scholarship, its modes and sites of training, and its various constitutive practices, as well as its target audiences.[43] It requires therefore a literal and metaphorical dislocation of the self from the comforts of disciplinary home and training, from settled practices of intellectual production, and from settled vantage points about such production. From the outset, then, a cosmopolitan political thought requires of its proponents and practitioners a willingness to self-dislocate, not simply by finding themselves physically located in worlds of intellectual production alien to their own, but also by participating in those worlds and by imbibing their practices of scholarship. This self-dislocation requires an attendant ability to historicize and denaturalize the conventions of one's own disciplinary home.

EXEMPLARS OF DENATURALIZING CRITICAL INTERVENTIONS:
HUMANENESS, SAGEHOOD, KORANIC EXEGESIS AND ASCETICISM

What might be the result of the critical interventions I have proposed? As I have suggested, these interventions might illuminate how the preoccupations and animating inquiries of this tradition, as well as its modes of investigation, differ crucially from our own. It might suggest new modes of knowledge that displace conventional understandings and traditional objects of political inquiry. But these interventions will differ from previous ones which have sought to redefine the boundaries of political theory's identity. Unlike the interventions of other literatures that have broadened the boundaries of political theory by challenging accepted standards of inquiry—such as deconstructionism, feminism, or psychoanalytic theory—a cosmopolitan political thought will conduct its challenge through the contributions of *specifically* cultural and civilizational alterity. Rather than an attempt to gate-keep in order to solidify an elusive sense of self-definition, a cosmopolitan political thought explicitly embraces the stretching of its boundaries, inviting messiness and challenge. It invites self-reexamination precisely through the provocations of civilizational alterity as seen, presented and studied from *within* the very civilizations that confront us with their otherness.

I now provide examples to illustrate what sorts of displacements and denaturalizations may result from such interventions. Older generations of CPT and comparative philosophy scholarship occasionally demonstrate an uncritical acceptance of Westcentric presumptions about what constitutes political theorizing. However, newer modes of scholarship have already begun to demonstrate potential moves toward critical displacement. In some cases I will focus on excavating the denaturalizing interventions implicit in this kind of scholarship; in others, I will point to potential new directions to be explored.

One result of such an intervention might be a self-conscious centering of inquiry on the concerns of another tradition, with explicit reference to how such preoccupations denaturalize the preoccupations of Western political inquiry. Take for example Brooke Ackerly's article examining the possibility of a nonliberal Confucian way of thinking about democracy. Ackerly starts by raising a question—"Is liberalism the only way toward democracy?"—that problematizes the West's very way of seeing a particular political phenomenon. In so doing, she locates her question within the conceptual framework that animated Confucian inquiries, namely that of humaneness, or *ren*. Rather than begin by finding commonality in Western and Confucian values, or excavating Confucian values that could sustain respect for liberal-democratic norms, Ackerly seeks to develop these ideas "from *within* the value system [of Confucianism], not merely borrow decisive features from it."[44]

Thus, Ackerly's investigation begins not by centering the preoccupations of Western liberal democrats, but rather by elaborating the core values of Confucian thought. Among the most central of Confucian preoccupations, she argues, is a concern with *ren*, interpreted variously as humaneness, as the heart/mind of human beings toward other human beings, a way of being human, or the overarching virtue of a perfected human being. Related to this foundational preoccupation are inquiries into human nature and Confucian debates about whether the purpose of cultivation in the path of ren is to develop humans' essentially good character or to counter their essentially bad one. These are accompanied by reflections on what kinds of social and political criticism may be encouraged by ren.

Of course, one might respond that the Confucian and neo-Confucian preoccupation with ren was perhaps no different from the ways in which ancient Western thinkers like Plato and Aristotle discussed the question of what it meant to be human. Both Plato and Aristotle grounded their visions on basic principles of human nature, which in turn defined the human condition, as well as the crucial issues of political life and order. While the *content* of the concept of humanness has shifted radically over the course of the Western tradition, thinkers from Kant to Mill to Rousseau have all struggled with and built their visions of political life on these questions, what kinds of beings humans are, and what kinds of capacities or predispositions are in their nature?[45] Surely the centrality of this preoccupation with humanness is as central to the Western tradition as the idea of ren is to the Confucian one. But further investigation immediately reveals how problematic it is to assume that Confucian debates about ren map neatly onto the Western preoccupation with what it is to be human.

Stephen Angle, for instance, acknowledges that Confucianism shares something with Aristotle if we see classical Confucianism as preoccupied with ren in the sense of stressing the seeking of a good and complete human personality.[46] But Angle also reminds us that ren is widely understood by Confucian scholars to be used in two different senses, both as a specific virtue and as a broader term signifying the attainment of all the interrelated virtues.[47] For neo-Confucians, ren is both a specific virtue related to basic feelings like love, concern, empathy and care; and the manner in which these feelings are linked to a particular way of perceiving one's life and experiences.[48] Zhu Xi calls ren "the coherence of love": that is, love experienced as part of the valuable and intelligible way that all (relevant) things can fit together. The early neo-Confucian Cheng Hao states: "The humane (*ren*) person regards all things in the universe as one body; there is nothing which is not a part of him."[49] Thus, Angle claims, full-fledged ren is not just caring or sympathy, but a warm and compassionate concern that extends, in organic fashion, to all related and relevant aspects of one's context. For neo-Confucians, it is critical that this concern is human concern, first nurtured in intimate family relations and then extended outward. The concept of humaneness, in this view, expresses the necessarily felt human interconnection with all aspects of one's environment and is not reducible to how the concept of human nature has operated in the thought of Western thinkers such as Aristotle, Mill or Rousseau. My point here is that work such as Angle's and Ackerly's should inspire cosmopolitan scholars to highlight the ways in which the preoccupations and categories of other traditions explicitly differ from those we find familiar, rather than falling prey to the temptation to reduce these to fit familiar understandings of political inquiry.

Another important result of such critical interventions is displacing the centrality of Westcentric modes of knowledge production and reproduction. As an example, I turn to Michaelle Browers' analysis of Koranic exegesis among contemporary scholarly communities in the Arab world.[50] Browers examines how contemporary Muslim intellectuals across the Arab world are employing various interpretive strategies toward Islam's main texts such as the Koran, the *hadith* and the *sunna*. The construction of a new hermeneutics for Koranic exegesis, she shows, is part of a project of reform for these intellectuals, in which the "the increasingly textual quality of Islam—that is the focus on (re)reading religious texts as a method of religious reform—seems to open the doors of *ijtihad* [independent interpretation] fairly wide by contributing toward an increase in the plurality of hermeneutical strategies."[51]

The most urgent mission of Islamic reformist thinkers in the modern period, Browers argues, has been to refute the Islamic doctrine that asserts the claim of tradition to govern interpretation.[52] Among the reigning orthodoxies of Sunni Islam is the assertion that the Koran is not a created text, but rather the uncreated, unmediated word of God. In direct challenge to this orthodoxy, contemporary reformists like Muhammad Shahrour, Nasr Hamid Abu Zayd, and Hassan Hanafi textualize and contextualize the Koran, developing new hermeneutic approaches that depart altogether from this orthodoxy. These approaches, for which each of these thinkers has been persecuted, center on the questions of the Koran's historicity, the importance of historical context in interpretation, and a recovery of original meanings through placing commandments within their historical contexts, or through privileging metaphorical interpretations over literal ones.[53] In different ways, each thinker calls for a direct return to the text that privileges the individual reasoning of the interpreter and a break with religious authorities.

Browers' analyses are deeply situated in the intellectual communities of the region she studies. She pays careful attention to the (contentious) plurality of discursive conventions and methodologies prevalent in these communities, identifying the lines along which the orthodoxies of dominant narratives are solidified and those along which dissent and contestation break through. Her work highlights the diversity of both religious and political writings in the Arab world, showcasing the idea that even a tradition represented as monolithically in the West as Islam is internally plural and rife with dissent. As such, it represents the best kind of immersion in the preoccupations, concepts, categories and concerns of another tradition, as well as its ways of knowing and modes of reasoning. Browers analyzes not merely the conventional textual resources that are so prevalent in Westcentric inquiry, but also the nonacademic discourse of intellectuals and activists. Looking beyond strictly scholarly discourse, she uses as her sources public discussions at academic conferences or other forums such as the speeches of mullahs and imams at religious gatherings, in addition to books, journals, newspapers and pamphlets.

Moreover, work like Browers' is also an invaluable reminder that immersion in such categories and preoccupations can cause us to reenvision what constitutes recognizably political inquiry. Scriptural interpretation and hermeneutic debates over the status of religious texts are not commonly thought to be part of political inquiry in the Westcentric tradition. But the eliding of the political and the theological in Islam gives the interpretation of religious texts a specifically political import in a way that is distinct from the conventions of Western political thought. Analyses like Browers' underscore the need for more work centered on the primary political preoccupations and concerns of other traditions. Such work can highlight the narrow specificity of Westcentric definitions of what appropriately constitutes political inquiry. Taking seriously a tradition's own account of its theorizing leads to the possibility of broadening our understandings of recognizably political phenomena.

Of course, as we have seen, the notion of "the political" is elusive, both in our tradition and in others. But the solution is not simply to say therefore that anything goes, and that every kind of inquiry is therefore "political" theory. As Timothy Kaufman-Osborn points out, if the political is everywhere, then it is nowhere.[54] Rather, the task is to outline what sorts of concepts and categories might productively challenge our own understandings of the political from a foreign vantage point. What precise sorts of interventions would constitute such a challenge? One alternative is to show that something that we may not have considered "political" can indeed be reconsidered as such through an encounter with another tradition's resources. Another is to show that such encounters could explore seemingly familiar political questions in ways that reveal the specificity of the West's own understanding.

An example of such work would be Gandhi's view of the centrality of asceticism (*brahmacharya*) to a nonviolent and just political action. For Gandhi, nonviolence is connected to the most fundamental human task, which is truth-seeking. The spiritual quest for truth served as the driving purpose for all other realms of life, especially for the political.[55] Moreover, the pursuit of *ahimsa* or nonviolence was crucially connected to this quest for truth: Gandhi repeatedly suggests that while truth is the end, *ahimsa* or nonviolence is the means. Nonviolence was understood in an expansive sense. Beyond just noninjury, it referred to a complete absence of ill-will and goodwill toward all life.[56] The pursuit of this ahimsa was an entire way of life wherein constant self-examination and rigorous discipline are combined with the systematic cultivation of virtues such as humility, sincerity and selfless service to others in all aspects of daily life.

How does asceticism fit into this search for truth through nonviolence? The individual's ability to see the truth is strengthened by conscious, disciplined self-suffering, also understood as austerity and self-control. Here, Gandhi appears to rely on the classical Hindu understanding of suffering as a tool of connection with the truth, which purifies consciousness and moral vision.[57] Bodily penance, according to Gandhi, is a "remedy to get rid of untruth."[58] The search for truth therefore requires controlling and disciplining the senses in all realms of life, through the monastic virtues of renunciation and austerity, which withdraw attention from the senses and focus the mind and moral vision on the goal of truth. Gandhi was known for his adherence to a strict form of asceticism called *brahmacharya*, which he defined as control over all the senses in thought, word and deed. He imposed the strictest standards of austerity on himself, standards that were applied to the realms of diet, celibacy, spiritual practice, economic life, and nutrition, none of which Gandhi believed were exempt from the requirements of total ahimsa. The variety of self-disciplinary attitudes and strategies that went into Gandhi's own pursuit of ahimsa—particularly in the realm of celibacy—are well-known, and his lifestyle has been described as "sometimes obsessive" in its relentless pursuit of austerity. We have heard, of course, of Gandhi's many fasts unto death, which were ostensibly undertaken for political purposes and were often performative in character. But in Gandhi's own writings, fasting is more than simply a tool of political pressure or expression, it is a spiritual practice that controls the mind, and allows the truth-seeker to withdraw from sense pleasures and desires, purifying her moral vision. So too with more quotidian elements of life such as diet, nutrition, sexuality, hygiene, and medicine. His struggles with them, he repeatedly emphasized, were intimately related to nonviolence understood in the broadest sense, as a method of seeking truth through asceticism and ascetic practices.[59]

But more broadly, Gandhi understood the ascetic quest to be central to a nonviolent and just politics. His obsessive focus on this question went beyond the causal relationship between self-control and truth-seeking. Gandhi also made a point of publicizing every minute (and potentially distasteful) detail about his bodily self-discipline in a confessional manner.[60] Gandhi seemed to suggest that it was only in scrutinizing and publicly confessing the most primordial aspects of sensual life, that he could impose upon himself the discipline that would lead him to pursue ahimsa.[61] The various explanations for this preoccupation with asceticism rely on the emphasis given to ascetic activities in traditional Indian/Hindu accounts of political action and political power. In different ways, each of these analyses suggests that the Indian tradition had influenced Gandhi to see a connection between the sphere of the political and the ability to control personal corporeal desires. As Lloyd Rudolph and Susanne Rudolph point out, in contrast to Westcentric understandings of political power as restrained by mainly external and institutional factors, the Indian tradition emphasized the importance of inner over external restraints on those who wielded political authority: "The belief that private morality had public consequences reflects the emphasis in traditional Hindu thought on ethical as against institutional restraints."[62] In this view, those who are able to practice internal self-restraint are better able to compel the external environment. For Gandhi, "The practicioner of *tapasya* (austerities) accumulated special powers ... many Hindus believe that men are endowed with a certain amount of life-force, which if used up in passionate, lustful or self-seeking endeavours, will no longer be available for higher purposes."[63] Bhikhu Parekh similarly suggests that Gandhi's quest for ascetic control reflected the Hindu view that personal purity and political success were deeply interrelated.[64] Indeed, as Parekh suggests, Gandhi's vision of independent India involved a few score *brahmacharis* (celibate practitioners of asceticism) who would "possess the enormous physical, psychic and spiritual energy required to 'ignite' the Indian masses and to 'fire' them with enthusiasm. Being unmarried and without private attachments, they would also be able to 'rise to the height of universal love' and to give their undivided attention to national regeneration."[65]

Joseph Alter takes this explanation even further, suggesting that for Gandhi, the political strength of the nation depended quite directly and literally on the micropolitics of bodily self-discipline. "Gandhi's concern with his body," Alter asserts, "cannot simply be understood as an obsessive compulsion to exercise self-control ... nonviolence was, for him, as much an issue of public health as one of politics, morality and religion ... Gandhi embodied moral reform and advocated that reform's embodiment in terms of public health, which was inherently political, spiritual and moral."[66] Gandhi was involved in a larger campaign that connected political engagement and self-discipline with the conscious public monitoring and self-surveillance of visceral, primordial urges.[67] His advocacy of bodily self-control, through intricate discussions of nature cures, mud packs, hip baths, breathing exercises, and recipes for encouraging celibacy, suggests an intimate relationship between the ascetic control over corporeality and the ability to successfully pursue just and nonviolent politics.

Parekh's reference to "universal love" suggests yet another explanation for the specifically political import of asceticism in Gandhi's thought. Gandhi seems to identify the sexual desire of the male-female dichotomy with the violence, aggression and other-appropriation inherent within the sexual duality. He compared this appropriation to the violence and other-denial often embedded within political conflict. Transcending the sexual dichotomy through control over the senses would allow an interaction of the sexes in which the opposite sex no longer remained an "other" to be manipulated, dominated, appropriated, or possessed.[68] In turn, it is suggested that transcending this conjugal desire would allow men and women to see and love each other as human beings, rather than as objects of lust, conquering the subsequent dominance that inevitably follows. Thus, it is ascetic self-control that facilitates the transition from sexual love to love of nation and eventually love of humanity.[69] In this view, the transcendence of desire and the corresponding ability to transcend sexual duality is linked to the ability to transcend the conflicts that divide humans from one another, and thus to attain a kind of universal goodwill toward fellow citizens and all of humanity.[70]

Asceticism is a prime exemplar of a concept or category that has not conventionally been seen as "political" by Westcentric standards. In contrast to much of Western political thought which has relegated corporeal and sexual desire to the private realm of the household, Gandhi reminds us that we may need to reexamine our concept of "the political" to reintroduce the treatment of desires and corporeal needs. Indeed, Gandhi is not alone in seeing the body, its desires, and pleasures as sites of political exchange, action and contestation. The emergence of the late modern feminist movement, in particular Foucauldian and and/or poststructuralist feminists[71] and the attendant politicization of gender brought about a blurring of boundaries between public and private. What was once within the realm of the biological or the *oikos*—bodily needs and desires, family relations, reproduction, sexual interaction— is now ineluctably in the realm of the public, or the *polis*. But Gandhi's emphasis on asceticism as a crucial component of political life goes beyond merely challenging the public-private dichotomy so prevalent in Westcentric political inquiry. Rather, it aims to show that the body is necessarily an *instrument* of a certain kind of political action and exchange, and that a just, nonviolent and humane political life must include the scrutiny, management and eventual transcendence of certain corporeal desires. The concept of the "political" may thus be reenvisioned from the perspective of immersion in another tradition's categories. In this Gandhian reenvisioning just offered, the category of the political may no longer be autonomous; rather, it may be understood as relationally placed with respect to other categories, such as the corporeal, or the inner world of sentience and spiritual seeking. The body, long relegated to the realm of the private, or acknowledged as a site of political contestation due to the categories of gender and sexuality, could perhaps be understood as an important instrument of politics in a new way, challenging the predominant dichotomy between reasoned speech/discourse and violent bodily conflict as the primary means of political engagement. The categories of asceticism and bodily desire, not usually employed as political in most Westcentric inquiry, could become new loci of inquiry on this view, because of the reexamined relationship between the body and political life.

And, in this view, Gandhi becomes an important resource for investigation, *not* simply because his ideas of nonviolence resonate with the liberal humanism that underlies much of Western political thought, but rather because his preoccupation with brahmacharya (asceticism) and the scrutiny of bodily desire as a form of political action challenge Westcentric understandings of "the political." Joseph Alter points out that the paradigm of liberal humanism has "swallowed Gandhi whole."[72] It is easy for those who come out of an intellectual tradition rooted in the Enlightenment to find in Gandhi's teachings a kind of faith in the human spirit that fits well, if not perfectly, with the principles of philanthropy and socialism, among other virtues of liberal humanism.[73] In contrast, this reading of Gandhi brings to light how his thinking, particularly about the body, stands in direct contrast to much Westcentric thought, unsettling conventional paradigms of what counts as "political" life and "political" action in contrast to "private" life and action.

CONCLUSION

An objector could argue that it is the elasticity and fluidity of the very notion of the political that allows us to extend it beyond its conventional boundaries. Given the discipline's eclectic and mongrelized nature, the West's understanding of what counts as political is quite expansive. As such, it could easily integrate the concepts of Koranic exegesis, ren, or brahmacharya within it, as recognizably political modes of inquiry. Wendy Brown, Timothy Kaufman-Osborn and others remind us of the ever-shifting, dynamic and pluralistic nature of the enterprise of political theory, along with the openness and flexibility of the concept of the political.[74] Of course, conceptual and categorical overlap between traditions, combined with the fluidity of our own understandings of the "political," can make concepts like Koranic exegesis, brahmacharya or ren ultimately recognizable to us. But the point is precisely that prior to encounters with other traditions' resources, such concepts or categories *did not* exist as recognizably political. Rather, it takes an encounter with a foreign tradition to broaden and stretch conventionally established notions of political phenomena and categories.

The emphasis on the displacement of Westcentric categories I have just provided may suggest that a cosmopolitan political thought must be centered on the expectation of radical alienness in every case. It may suggest a consequent denial of the possibility of commensurability with texts or practices from other traditions. This is hardly the case. For sure, certain modes of Koranic exegesis are similar to interpretive and commentarial practices in Western religious hermeneutics and political thought. The political writings of Kautilya, Sayyid Qutb or Gandhi may bear many points of resemblance to an Aristotle, a Rousseau or a Plato. Moreover, we can perhaps only understand the nuances inherent in the concept of ren or brahmacharya by calling upon equivalent concepts, categories and preoccupations implicit in our traditions. More fundamentally, as we have seen, all traditions owe intellectual debts to one another in a process of cross-cultural fertilization that spans millennia. Islam's debt to Aristotle and the Greeks is widely acknowledged, as is contemporary Indian thought's debt to Islam, while Buddhist logic is highly indebted to Vedic literature. Indeed, the reason/revelation dichotomy was a dominant theme in medieval Islamic thought and is a problematic in Western political thought today, at least in part because of the way that Islamic thought influenced Aquinas. A cosmopolitan political thought need not emphasize alterity to the neglect of these powerful, preexisting currents of intercultural hybridizing which make other resources eminently recognizable to us.

But a cosmopolitan political thought must also take note of the central dilemma presented by such encounters, namely that texts and concepts from other traditions are often placed at the complex intersection of alienness and familiarity. Moreover, this alienness and familiarity may not map neatly onto the ways in which our "own" thinkers are both alien and familiar to us; Gandhi is alien to us in a different way than Machiavelli is, and Plato's works may present us with a sense of familiarity that is entirely different from that which we feel when we encounter, say, Confucius. Seen through either Western or non-Western lenses, the encounter with otherness is rarely utterly mystifying or entirely comprehensible, and for the same reason, civilizational representation and cross-cultural resonance are hardly mutually exclusive. The challenge is precisely the delicate balance between seeking to subsume all otherness by explaining it in terms of the familiar, or insisting that the otherness of the other is recognizable only to those embedded in its context and that transcultural recognition is therefore impossible.

Indeed, the facile assumption that such transcultural recognition is always available to be unearthed rests on the unexamined prejudice that an underlying familiarity is the ground on which all otherness can be made comprehensible for us. This issue becomes all the more complicated with the increasing influence of modernity. It is especially tempting to find familiarity in otherness as modernity causes a confluence of norms across traditions, because many modern thinkers from non-Western traditions are at least familiar with, if not educated in, a Western idiom. Much of what they have to say is woven through with Western influence, even when their goal is to be harshly critical of this very influence, as in the case of many postcolonial thinkers. The placement of such thinkers at the confluence of various traditions seems, on the one hand, to make it (misleadingly) easier to attribute a certain familiarity to them. But on the other hand, it makes it more difficult to grapple with their situatedness within a non-Western tradition. In the case of someone like Gandhi, it is easy to assume that the message of nonviolence is a universal one, precisely because Gandhi writes in English, using references, concepts and idioms that are an inevitable result of his immersion in the English language, his placement as a colonial subject educated in Britain, and his resulting absorption of some Enlightenment ideals.[75]

To assume, however, that this alone makes crucial elements of his thought easily recognizable across cultural boundaries would be a mistake. The messages of ahimsa (nonviolence) and *satyagraha* (civil disobedience) may be universally recognizable, and certainly Gandhi himself may have intended for them to be so—this in itself is not a terribly novel claim to make. But any decontextualized assumption that ignores how deeply these messages are situated within the Vedic language of *dharma*—an ancient Vedic concept for which there is no exact equivalent, variously translated as force of moral order, duty, role, religion, or law—would lead to only a partial understanding of Gandhi's thought. In the next chapter, I will argue that Gandhian nonviolence can scarcely be understood without at least a basic familiarity with the hermeneutic struggle over the meaning of the term *dharma* as it appears in the *Bhagavad Gita*.[76] Gandhi becomes an important figure for investigation because he brings to our attention the preoccupation with political action as a form of dharma. In fact, his insistence on dharma as the central pillar of moral and political life suggests that certain non-Western understandings of the "political" may emerge out of preoccupations for which no real equivalents exist in Western thought.

The point, then, is not that one should choose to study certain kinds of texts and not others. Rather, even when we are presented with ideas that seem familiar, we might look deeper for the ways in which these ideas dislodge our modes of understanding. Instead of resting easily with texts or ideas which call upon no discomfort in questioning the boundaries of one's own enterprise, we need to look deeper for those *aspects* of intellectual resources that throw into question traditional understandings of "the political," or of "political theory." Gandhi's ideas of nonviolence may strike us as deeply familiar to the humanism of the Enlightenment. But a deeper investigation of Gandhi will reveal that his concept of brahmacharya and the preoccupation with dharma emerge from his placement within the Vedic Hindu tradition, providing a vision of the political that challenges in many ways the Westcentric one.

In the end, of course, Gandhi is neither utterly alien to us nor utterly familiar. Nor is his work easily categorized as utterly situated or utterly transcultural. It is this dilemma that lies at the heart of a cosmopolitan political thought. But grappling with this paradox will allow us to break through and get past the binary formulations of West/non-West and self/other that characterize much of political theory. A cosmopolitan political thought that seeks to break through and move beyond such oppositional framing requires deep and sustained engagement with this paradox. It is precisely such a paradox that creates a field of understanding in which all things can at once be at play—the binary *and beyond* the binary. To immerse oneself within the otherness of foreign modes of knowledge production and transmission is the necessary route to moving past the oppositional frames that otherize them so starkly.

INTERPRETING THE OTHER

The Hermeneutics of Comparative Political Thought

THE HISTORY OF political theory is liberally sprinkled with tales of misreceptions, mistranslations, and distortions. In fact, such mistranslations are part and parcel of the "West's" construction of its founding moments, such as the Enlightenment. Fania Oz-Salzberger tells us that seminal moments in the intellectual history of eighteenth-century Europe involved epoch-making translations of texts, because many of the works conveying Enlightenment ideas could only be written in local languages. Since Latin had disappeared, Europe had no universal language, and translation was indispensable for the diffusion of Enlightenment texts and ideas. Voltaire's quotations from Locke in his *Lettres Anglaises* (1734), Johann Lorenz Shmidt's important rendering of Spinoza's *Ethics* (1744), and Kant's awakening from his "dogmatic slumbers" by a German translation of Hume are some of the most famous examples. By the eighteenth-century, Descartes and Locke were being translated into other languages, and philosophers such as Hume and Rousseau reached new audiences through translation. Moreover, de-Latinized Europe's assembly of new ideas into a cosmopolitan discourse offers a fascinating range of what Oz-Salzberger calls "mistranslations, from simple mistakes, via unwitting shifts of tone or meaning, to conscious textual manipulations [which included] restructuring of original grammar, semantics and style, as well as shifts of authorial sense by translators . . . broadly acknowledged and often permitted, even required, by many authorities."[1] Most Enlightenment theorists and practitioners actually approved of wide-ranging adaptation of works into the host language and to the tastes of the host culture. Indeed such mistranslations and distortions have often been seen as productive and creative, as sources of new knowledge and new ways of understanding the thinkers, texts or conceptual schemes being analyzed. Studies of mistranslation and misreception, Oz-Salzberger tells us, need not assume that the receiving language and culture necessarily "lost out" by misunderstanding the original words, concepts and intentions. Arguing for instances of "creative misreception" or "creative misunderstanding," Oz-Salzberger, Margaret Leslie and others reveal that misreadings can often lead to intellectual stimulation and conceptual enrichment.[2]

But the project of comparative political theory seems particularly susceptible to such instances of mistranslation, and the implications of such misreception are not insignificant for the task of a cosmopolitan political thought. Placed in the context of the West's representations of its civilizational others, distortion carries a historical weight inseparable from the appropriations and misappropriations that have accompanied Orientalist readings of otherness. Particularly in the colonial context, distortions of "native" texts and practices by European colonial interpreters have gone on to form the bases of misrepresentations of civilizations and peoples. They have permeated and solidified Western representations of otherness, often misconstructing non-Western self-understandings. The British codification and canonization of legal codes for Hindus and Muslims in colonial India fixed relatively fluid identity categories into rigid ones. It transformed personal law from a vast body of texts and locally variegated customs into a rigid, codified body of legal rules that recognized a specific set of religious texts as ultimately canonical for each religious community (Brahminical *Shastric* texts for the Hindus and *Sharia* for the Muslims). The very categories of "Hindu" and "Muslim" are themselves constructs of a colonial interpretive lens, and what is now called personal law in contemporary India is the result of a broad colonial misreception and even distortion of the role of India's classical literature in everyday legal practices.

More recently, much work in comparative philosophy focuses on correcting the mistranslations that have long colored Western translations of non-Western texts and concepts. Stuart Gray demonstrates that Western scholarship on Brahmanical-Hindu political thought has often prematurely "(referred) to or (relied) upon non-Indian assumptions, concepts, ideas."[3] It has attempted to find equivalences between Western and Indian political ideas, inappropriately employing anachronistic modern European terminology while explicating ancient Indian political ideas, and often failing to adequately employ Indian concepts, terms and categories. The result is the misinterpretations and distortions of these ideas, and a "pervasive domestication of fundamental differences."[4] According to Gray, ignoring the tremendous diversity of the Sanskrit language and the differences in interpretive nuances between Vedic and classical Sanskrit, ignoring the chronological challenges that lead to changes in terminology, and neglecting to examine the genre in which such terminology arises, has caused scholars of Brahmanical political thought to consistently misinterpret key categories within the Vedic lexicon. These include *dharma* (moral law or duty or role), *rta* (cosmic order), and, most importantly, *matsyanyaya* ("law of the fishes" in which the stronger swallows the weaker in the absence of an overarching law). The concept of matsyanyaya, Gray shows, has long been misinterpreted as a chaotic "state of nature" by most Western scholars, analogous to the vision provided by Hobbes or Locke. Gray takes into account the sacrificial, ritualistic and cosmic nature of the terminology used to explain the concept of matsyanyaya, rather than the purely political, administrative or institutional ones which are often erroneously used. In so doing, he reveals that the concept refers to a far more drastic and harsh dissolution of the fundamental cosmological order of the universe, entailing a wide-scale cosmic destruction involving all forms of life—human, animal, plant, gods, and so on.[5]

The pervasiveness of such routine mistranslations is hardly restricted to South Asian intellectual resources. Irene Bloom reminds us that the precise meaning of the Chinese term *liang* in the writings of Mencius and Confucius is difficult to estimate, and Western translations all too hastily tend to mistranslate it as "innate" in the sense of the "essential nature of something," or something inherent in a living organism from birth. A more appropriately nuanced understanding of the term, Bloom claims, would avoid an important metaphysical notion of an "essential" or "original" nature, recognizing that *liang* requires no disjuncture between the biological and the cultural, and that capacities are both given as well as potentially developed or fulfilled, lost or destroyed.[6]

The practitioner of a cosmopolitan political theorizing would be nothing if not keenly aware of the legacy of such misreceptions in the West's engagement with cultural alterity. A crucial task for the scholar turning to foreign resources, then, will be to undertake the interpretation of texts and the analysis of ideas; that is, to study, interpret and understand the scholarly resources within a given foreign civilization. In Western political theory, the interpretive task now encompasses a wide variety of activities such as intellectual history, phenomenological hermeneutic methods or text-driven conceptual analysis. It may be tempting to begin with the assumption that interpreting any text or idea in political theory—even those from other civilizations—is simply a matter of finding one's methodological lens: Foucauldian, Straussian, conceptual, intellectual history, deconstructionist, and so on. But, I argue that the existence of Western interpretive techniques is often insufficient to understand well the ideas from other civilizations, given the unique challenges they pose. In fact, the tendency to view non-Western conceptual apparati in terms that are intuitive to Westcentric thought[7] means that a cosmopolitan political theory needs to explicitly problematize Westcentric interpretive techniques as adequate tools for this hermeneutic task. Shedding light on the particular challenges of such a task and providing a preliminary account of their methodological significance are the purposes of this chapter.

I argue that these interpretive methodological interventions have some bearing on reenvisioning the task of political theory in a more cosmopolitan fashion. My argument is in several parts. First, I outline the evolution of three hermeneutic moments that characterize the encounter with a text or idea from beyond the Western canon.[8] Each of these moments involves confronting a particular methodological issue, as well as a proposed solution to the challenge. Taken together, these three moments are designed to provide the vision of a more self-consciously developed approach to comparative political theory. This vision includes a struggle with the dual imperatives of what I call adherence and scholarship, which characterizes the move from the first to the second (and eventually third) hermeneutic moments. A good comparative political theorist—indeed, one who aims toward a cosmopolitan theorizing—will have to alternate between internal immersion in the lived experience of the text and an external stance of commentary and exegesis of the text. In the end, I argue, struggling with the conflicting imperatives of these moments is precisely the task of a more complex approach to political theorizing. The comparative political theory I describe will call on methodological capacities that are often far removed from what we think of as the political theorist's toolkit and, as such, will involve the reenvisioning of the political theorist's task. But the picture I seek to provide is more than simply a blueprint for the development of comparative political theory. It argues that comparative political theory stands in a particular relationship to the evolution of political theory's self-understanding as a whole, and how we envision its methodological challenges has implications for the development of a more genuine cosmopolitanism in the field of political theory. My contention here is that existing understandings of cosmopolitanism in political theory fall short in several ways. A more genuinely cosmopolitan political thought is one that will directly confront the challenges presented by the encounter with other texts and ideas, while also highlighting how such encounters may disturb our familiar understandings of politics. And instead of restricting our understandings of cosmopolitanism to the categories contained mainly within a Western framework, as most analysts do, a newer and more genuine understanding of cosmopolitanism should link it explicitly to self-dislocation. That is, comsopolitanism should be linked to existential immersion in the unfamiliar, to the imperative to make intelligible this existential experience of unfamiliarity, and finally to the theoretical illumination that this experience brings forth. The picture I provide, then, suggests that these methodological challenges are inevitably implicated in a potential (and long overdue) reconstruction of political theory's self-image.

THE FIRST INTERPRETIVE MOMENT: THE HERMENEUTIC
OF EXISTENTIAL UNDERSTANDING

I begin, then, by defending the choice of an interpretive method I call existential understanding and illustrating its effectiveness with the case study of a South Asian text. The choice of such a method illuminates the idea that the comparative political theorist's first hermeneutic task lies in bringing oneself as close as possible to the "world" of the other text, or concept or category, taking into account the perspective of the text's (or concept's) own cultural framework and a subsequent shrinking of the distance (both literal and metaphorical) between the reader and the text. In this first hermeneutic moment, the reader enters an entirely new world, traveling outside one's own subjectivity and learning to read the text from within the cultural framework of the text itself. Such a hermeneutic suggests that texts, or the ideas within them, cannot simply be understood by an analysis of the concepts in the text itself. Rather, the operation requires a praxis-oriented existential transformation in which the reader learns to live by the very ideas expressed in a text.

An existential hermeneutic stands in direct contrast to an objectivist method which sees texts as "objects" of inquiry to be approached in a neutral, scientific manner. It calls for the reader to recognize the deep alterity of the text and eradicate his or her "subjective" concerns.[9] In contrast, an existential method requires precisely that the reader *not* see oneself as separate from the text or concept, and that the subject *not* gaze at the object from a distance, attempting to achieve a scholarly objectivity in one's understanding. Understanding, on an existential view, is achieved precisely by *becoming* one with the ideas in the text, by reducing any sense of separateness between the knower and the known. Texts and ideas are not objects to be known or explicated in some purely scholarly sense, but rather truths that must become absorbed into the being of the reader through action. Experience, rather than abstract knowledge, is the only way of achieving such understanding.

An existential hermeneutic also has advantages over several other Western approaches.[10] In principle, an existential hermeneutic seems based on phenomenology. For phenomenological thinkers, subject and object are already connected to one another, and this very connection provides a necessary starting point for interpretation. Setting aside one's own subjective concerns to enter the world of the object is thus not only impossible, it implies a mistaken view of the process of interpretation. The subject-object dichotomy is a deeply mistaken notion of how we come to understand things, because we always already have some relationship to the very thing that we are trying to understand.[11] However, the phenomenological method, while rightly recognizing the misguidedness of objectivism, also raises a potential problem for the comparative political theorist. It asserts that the text and its interpreter are already bonded to one another because the subject has some "prejudices"—understood, in the Gadamerian sense, as presuppositions based on immersion in the concepts and categories of our own tradition—about the object she encounters.[12] And, approached in the right way, this presupposition aids us in making sense of a text or an idea. Thus the interpreter's subjectivity is brought into focus as unavoidably important, rather than something to be repressed or battled in the quest for a mythical "objectivity." The danger here is that the interpreter's subjectivity, when tied to her immersion in her own tradition, might lead her to misunderstand a text from another tradition. The comparative political theorist needs to take seriously the otherness of a text as well as of the tradition in which it is embedded. The phenomenological approach rightly reminds us of the importance of the reader's subjectivity, but also of the extent to which it is tied to categories and frameworks that may be entirely alien to the text one is encountering. In encountering a non-Western text, the notion of prejudice may be a more likely obstacle than a resource. Absent the sort of immersion in a tradition that allows prejudices to be a creative force, relying on these prejudices may contain potential for misunderstanding. Because prejudices operate in relation to those things that are familiar, using them as the lens through which one encounters otherness suggests that one may try to understand the unfamiliar by assimilating it into our own interpretive categories.[13]

Let me turn to Hindu thought in order to illustrate. The Sanskrit term *dharma* is complex, often translated as moral law, or force of cosmic order. It has both a general and particular meaning: generally, to live *dharmically* means to align oneself with the supreme Truth of the divine force which sustains the cosmos. On a particular level, it means to live according to the righteous and sacred duties appropriate to one's station in life.[14] The concept appears in (among other texts) the *Bhagavad Gita*, the sixth book of the epic *Mahabharata*. The setting of the *Gita* is the battlefield where war is about to begin, and the text is a dialogue between the protagonist warrior-prince Arjuna and his companion and teacher Krishna (eventually revealed to be God himself). Arjuna feels only sorrow at having to fight a fratricidal war for the sake of political power, and in a series of revelations spanning eighteen chapters, Krishna counsels the despondent Arjuna, urging him to perform his duty as a warrior, so rightful political authority can be restored.

What initially seems like a solution that condones political violence for the sake of maintaining rightful authority through a *dharmayuddha* (a just war) turns eventually into a series of revelations about the nature of the human self, the illusory quality of the material world, the necessity of performing one's dharma without attachment to the fruits of action, and the eventual transcendence of the human soul to the divine. Krishna commands Arjuna to fight, not simply on the grounds that it is his sacred duty to do so, but also because all beings are destined to perish, and in doing our duty without attachment to the fruits of our action we are playing our required role in the cosmic spectacle of creation and dissolution. In so doing, we come to understand the importance of detachment and disciplined action. In the end, Krishna seems to say that Arjuna must fight, not simply because his clan must restore rightful political authority, but rather because he must perform his dharma without regard for consequences. The Western scholar attempting to understand the *Bhagavad Gita* is faced with making sense of this text, of its ethical and metaphysical assertions, and their consequences for political life.

One way in which the idea of a divinely ordained moral code is familiar to the Western tradition is through the terms of Aquinas' natural law. When confronted with the concept of dharma, this may be the way in which we are naturally led to think if we rely on prejudices emerging from our own tradition.[15] Thus, the scholar may be led to imagine that Krishna's advice to Arjuna is given in terms of duties to be performed according to a discernable set of principles that determine the reasonability or justice of certain actions, so that they conform to a divine will. The right performance of dharma, the scholar might speculate, could mean something akin to rationally guiding oneself to the right path of action, based on a set of moral principles, a rational hierarchy of human ends, or a knowable "order" of the universe determined by the divine. But this would not quite do justice to the term, or to the texts where it is used. Dharma has none of the connotations of divine rationality associated with natural law, nor does it specify the ways in which human laws, hierarchies and moral codes must be structured in order to mirror divinity. Nor is Krishna's advice to Arjuna simply based on a notion of the universe as ordered in a certain way, or Arjuna's duty to conform to a certain hierarchy. In its most general sense, dharma goes far beyond the differences of established religions, parochial ties and social conventions.[16] The notion of dharma is infinitely fluid across varying interpretations of different texts and rarely tied to any single concept of moral order or set of principles. To act dharmically is most often accepted as the goal of Hindu life, yet the question of what precisely constitutes dharmic action is contentious. Much of the complexity of this concept would be lost in attempting to explain it through the familiar categories of natural law.

The concepts of natural law also give us no insight into the larger interpretive dilemmas in the text. For instance, does Krishna's insistence that Arjuna fight suggest that a good understanding of dharma necessitates participation in violent politics? The nationalist B. G. Tilak claimed that message of the *Gita* was to justify participation in a modern kind of politics, "the politics of violence and 'tit for tat,' politics as a game of 'worldly people' and not of spiritual people." Its maxim was to "return wickedness for wickedness."[17] But Gandhi held to the view that the message of the *Gita* was *ahimsa*, or nonviolence, that the language of battle was not to be taken literally when contemplating the meaning of dharma. "In trying to enforce . . . the central teaching of the *Gita* . . . one is bound to follow . . . *ahimsa*."[18] How, then, does a text that appears to condone political violence later become the theoretical foundation for Gandhian nonviolence? In these debates, what precisely might it mean for a human being to perform his or her dharma? What are the political implications of these debates for our understanding of dharma?

This illustrates the problem presented by the divergent subjectivities of the internal and external reader: if the speaker and the hearer must share the language of their discourse, then the aim of a cross-cultural hermeneutic must be to allow the speaker and hearer to share as much as possible. An existential hermeneutic allows for precisely this sort of sharing. To elaborate on its requirements, we may turn to the writings of Mahatma Gandhi.[19] I turn to Gandhi for a number of reasons: the project of engagement with a non-Western text suggests we rely on a hermeneutic approach that emerges from the same tradition as the text itself. But the choice of Gandhi is more than a result of his substantive immersion in the Hindu tradition of thought: Gandhi provides insights about method that transcend his own substantive conclusions about the meaning of certain texts, extending beyond the specifics of South Asian texts.[20]

The right understanding of the meaning of any textual truth required, in Gandhi's view, a "spiritual experience" of the text, "a well-cultivated moral sensibility and experience in the practice of [its] truths."[21] Scholarly learning was necessary but not sufficient and interpretation required, above all, experiencing the ideas, insights and virtues elaborated in the texts.[22] It is existence itself and the experiencing of—even identifying with—certain states of mind that impart the knowledge of the truth of the text, on this view. Understanding, in other words, requires adherence and belief. Bhikhu Parekh suggests that the very moral and political authority that Gandhi derived from the rigor of his truth-seeking lifestyle gave him an interpretive authority over the Hindu textual tradition that was distinctly superior to that of pure textual scholars such as *pandits* and *shastris* (various kinds of Sanskrit scholars).[23] In fact, Parekh suggests that Gandhi claimed this interpretive prerogative from within the very parameters of the Hindu tradition itself.[24] Describing Gandhi's interpretive disagreements with orthodox Hindus over the issue of untouchability, Parekh suggests that Gandhi appropriated some Vedic hermeneutics. Using terms such as *atma-darsan* ("a vision of the highest") and *satyano sakshatkar* ("seeing" or "realizing the truth"), Gandhi asserted that interpreting ancient texts required "qualifications other than textual scholarship . . . only a man who had undertaken the spiritual journey himself was equipped to decipher the deeper meaning of a . . . work."[25] Implicitly characterizing the *sanatanist* (or orthodox) scholarly interpreters of the texts as learned but "dissolute," Gandhi made it clear that he found pure scholarly understanding of a text to be of little value, in the absence of experiential understanding.[26] Rather, he quite deliberately based his interpretive authority squarely on praxis rather than exegetical scholarship. Although he never directly said so, unlike many of his commentative predecessors, he was "a *mahatma* who had sincerely tried to live by the central values of his tradition. He therefore claimed the *adhikar* [authority] to understand it better than the 'mere pandits' and to disregard their interpretations and protests."[27]

Certainly, Gandhi is not the only non-Western thinker to suggest the perspective of adherence as the appropriate hermeneutic method for textual exegesis. Leigh Jenco has reminded us that neo-Confucian thinkers in the Chinese classicist tradition such as Wang Yangming and Kang Youwei similarly advocate what I have called an existential hermeneutic.[28] In this second hermeneutic moment, the scholar focuses on the role of the adherent, paying attention to the subjectivity of what some scholars of religion have called the "native exegete,"[29] rather than of the external reader. But we might object: does the religious language of such a hermeneutic require belief in a text? What interpretive prerogative can then be given to scholars who are (most often) not members of an adherent community? And does Gandhi's specific rejection of scholarly knowledge imply that exegetical and scholarly competence is not necessary? It should be clarified that an existential hermeneutic does not suggest that interpretive competence requires membership in a community of adherents, or that it specifically precludes a scholarly or exegetical grappling with the text. Rather, it suggests that one's scholarly understanding of a text be enriched by the perspective of adherence, and that crucial additional knowledge can be gained through *replicating* the perspective of adherence and immersing oneself in the adherent's world.

Existential understanding suggests, then, that a text from a radically different culture may best be understood by penetrating the consciousness and lived experiences of those who live by the ideas expressed in a text. Such immersion involves the scholar's ability to penetrate a whole worldview, to produce a description of the adherents' own self-understanding in relation to the text, and to do so *in terms of* their own language, practices and ideas. It would call for the scholar to go beyond the ideas in a text and access ways in which they may be lived out by their adherents.[30] An existential hermeneutic makes no claim about the necessary privileging of an "insider's" perspective. It does claim, however, that any attempt to detach the texts or ideas from the social and cultural setting out of which they have come is a recipe for misunderstanding. An existential hermeneutic draws heavily on *verstehen*, a method that famously focuses on the intentional ferreting out of the material from which individuals craft their meaning making. Hugely influential in fields such as anthropology and in the development of methods such as participant-observation and ethnography which focus on lived experience, *verstehen* seeks understanding not only from the perspective of the actor in the situation, but also from within frameworks (traditions, practices, etc.) that shape the experiences and perspectives of the actors.[31] We might expect, then, that in seeking to gain an existential understanding of the text in this second hermeneutic moment, the scholar will gravitate toward the sorts of hermeneutically oriented anthropological and ethnographic methodologies that shed light on lived experience.

Existential understanding also relies on the premise of self-dislocation articulated in the previous chapter. The crucial importance of travel to the task of comparative political theorizing, Roxanne Euben argues, involves a kind of dislocation into modes of thought that are "strange and estranging rather than familiar or confirmative: the capacity for imagination, reflection and judgment is cultivated not by reading to affirm what one knows but by exposure to what disturbs, provokes, and dislocates."[32] Indeed, this suggests that existential immersion will draw upon the self-dislocating capacities we articulated previously: intellectual *and* existential activities that require the scholar to self-consciously exit the parameters of Westcentric political thought; to situate herself, spatially and otherwise, in the worlds she is trying to understand, and to struggle with the challenges that its alterity presents. This self-dislocation involves a necessary disconnect from the disciplinary and substantive home located in the parameters of a Westcentric study of political thought, and a resituation in another, an immersion in its attendant practices of knowledge and its systems of meaning. This suggests, in turn, that gaining knowledge of alterity requires something more than an imaginative dislocation; it requires an actual, physical movement away from the comforts of home and hearth.

What does this imply for our preceding example? How does a self-dislocating existential hermeneutic contribute to our understanding of the *Bhagavad Gita*, the concept of dharma, and the interpretive dilemmas described? When applied to interpretive analysis, self-dislocation calls for the scholar to not only immerse herself intellectually in the practices of knowledge production that characterize a tradition, but also in the practices and life-worlds that characterize adherence to specific texts and concepts within that tradition. Thus, the existential interpreter is called upon to understand the concept of dharma in the *Bhagavad Gita* in a praxis-oriented fashion, living the virtues described in the text. Such an interpreter might investigate experientially the dharmic life Gandhi instituted at his *ashrams* (community of followers), where readings of the *Gita* are conducted in the context of a way of life characterized by constant self-examination and a rigorously disciplined lifestyle geared toward the total cultivation of ahimsa. In pursuit of such a lifestyle, Gandhi believed one was truly able to access the knowledge contained in the *Gita*. The meaning of dharma therein was, on his view, completely tied to ahimsa or nonviolence. In its most minimal formulation, ahimsa means a refusal to do harm: "in its negative form," Gandhi acknowledges, "it means not injuring any living being, whether by body or mind."[33] However, we may recall from the previous chapter that in the more expansive interpretation that Gandhi gave it, ahimsa came to mean more than simply noninjury or harmlessness: "In its positive form, ahimsa means the largest love, the greatest charity."[34] It is this latter broader definition of ahimsa that came to be identified with Gandhi's interpretation of dharma. Recall also that for Gandhi, the pursuit of ahimsa was an entire way of life rather than simply a conceptual commitment; it involved constant self-examination, scrutiny, and a rigorously disciplined lifestyle, along with the cultivation of virtues such as humility, sincerity, and selfless service to others. It was in the pursuit of such a lifestyle, Gandhi believed, that one was truly able to fulfill dharma.

Existentially, then, sustained adherence to ahimsa was the fulfillment of man's highest dharma or duty.[35] The list of vows established at Gandhi's Sabarmati ashram[36] included, for instance, vows of truth, celibacy, control of the palate, non-thieving, non-possession, self-reliance, and fearlessness. Such vows, observed through daily practice, became the manifestation of ahimsa, in its various different forms.[37] The scholar attempting to gain the fullest possible understanding of the *Bhagavad Gita* might spend time at Gandhi's Sevagram ashram in Wardha, India, participating in the daily schedule of prayer, meditation and labor, examining how daily readings of the *Gita* are combined with the practice of dharmic virtues. A recent visit by a journalist to Sevagram revealed that current-day Gandhian residents adhered strictly to this vision of pursuing ahimsa. The daily recitation of the *Gita* was combined with the lifestyle requirements outlined above, such as meditation, labor and the taking of vows. The residents of the ashram call their environment a "laboratory for Gandhian values."[38] In *Mahatma Gandhi and His Apostles*, Ved Mehta revisits different Gandhian communities of social, political and environmental activists to retrace the ways in which the emphasis on ahimsa was lived by various adherents of Gandhi in different contexts. In *Moved By Love*, Vinobha Bhave, a political activist and famous follower of Gandhi, discusses the establishment of various ashrams that he calls "laboratories for living," communities in which the study of the *Gita* may be combined with the lifestyle requirements of *ahimsa*.[39] The researcher seeking an existential understanding of the text may find herself in a series of any such contexts and communities. She may insert herself into conversations with and among community members who claim to live by a certain understanding of dharma and access their understandings and implementations of dharma. She may employ methodologies used by anthropologists, ethnographers, or scholars of comparative politics (such as participant-observation, interviewing, or case analysis) in order to assess how dharma is understood by these individuals.

It is likely, then, that the scholar who visits such communities will find that the interpretation of the *Bhagavad Gita* employs an interpretation of dharma that is tied to ahimsa or nonviolence. The picture of dharma that emerges from her existential exploration is likely to demonstrate that the language of battle and violence in the *Bhagavad Gita* is to be taken poetically, rather than literally. As Gandhi postulates, "The [*Bhagavad Gita*] depicts for all time the eternal struggle that goes on daily between the forces of good and evil in the human breast and in which thought good is ever victorious."[40] Krishna's advice to Arjuna is not necessarily an advocacy of a violent politics. Rather, the battle depicted in the text is meant to represent the battlefield of the human mind, and its struggle to overcome desire with detachment and disciplined action.[41] It is precisely an existential approach that should shed light on such an interpretation of dharma as linked to ahimsa: the existential details gleaned from the lives of adherents—ashram-dwellers, community members, other social and political activists—and their own understandings of dharma should shed light on the fact that dharma is not simply the warrior's duty to fight. As the theorist struggles with these interpretive dilemmas, an existential approach is likely to provide a richer and more nuanced understanding of the text than a mere exegetical understanding of it, allowing one to grapple with the interpretive issues in the text more fully. In this hermeneutic moment, then, the researcher is required to establish an existential connection with the context in which the text is interpreted by its own adherents. She uses methodological skills that are anthropological or ethnographic in nature and calls upon imaginative and empathetic capacities that focus on penetrating the lived experience of the text.

THE SECOND HERMENEUTIC MOMENT: THE RECONSTRUCTED CULTURAL ACCOUNT

But what might the subsequent methodological implications of this hermeneutic be for the task of scholarship, particularly that of political theorists? One conceptualization of the task of comparative political theory suggests that the encounter with non-Western texts remain centered in the existential hermeneutic moment, avoiding the speech and articulation-centered models of Western thought, which often do violence to the substance of existential insights.[42] But what if we conceive of the task as bringing into articulation and analysis the lived experience of the "other" text? If, as I have argued, the ultimate task of a cosmopolitan political theory is to allow the insights gleaned from unfamiliar resources to dislodge settled Western understandings of political theory, then the task of political theorizing must be seen as making unfamiliar texts comprehensible to Western audiences, *precisely* in order to foster such challenges. This in turns raises a series of questions that place the existential imperative of adherence potentially in tension with the task of scholarship and of "theorizing." An understanding of the task of comparative political theory that sees as necessary the step of "translating" the lessons of lived experience into textual, commentative form will give rise to the next hermeneutic moment.

The second hermeneutic moment emerges in the project of textually "representing" existential immersion and attempting to put forth a cultural account that captures the experiences that shed light on the text. If the purpose of immersing oneself in a set of practices is ultimately to make a text comprehensible, is not some form of such representation necessary? This suggests that the ideas in the text not only have to be brought back into writing for a certain kind of audience (likely an audience outside the tradition being investigated), but also that the researcher's reconstructed account of the "experience" of the text plays a crucial role in this process of translation. But the very process of entering the native exegete's consciousness raises methodological issues, particularly when it is followed by the imperative to "represent" their world as a source of textual meaning. First, it raises the possibility that the scholar may continue to consider herself as the "representative" of the true or authentic experience of the text, as somehow able to correctly divine the inner worlds of the others she is studying. It leaves much potential representative authority in the hands of the scholar, presumes the age-old model of the scholar "representing" the world of the natives to her colleagues, and, in so doing, employing the very tools of the observing external "gaze" and "voice" that inscribes, reports and comments. It assumes that there are native "points of view" that can accurately be reported and redescribed, native voices that can easily be respoken. It also points in the direction of a dangerous reification of that world, and the all-too-tempting assertion that there is, for instance, an authentic essence of the *Bhagavad Gita*'s meaning that can be grasped only through a definitive experience. Moreover, "experience" and "existence" are fraught categories, perhaps no more easily accessed, translated and made articulate than the text itself, nor any more free of power constructs and what Gayatri Spivak has called the "epistemic violence" of Orientalist knowledge production.[43] Can existential understanding access the "truth" of an experience any better than that of a text? And can it avoid being similarly implicated in power relations?

In positing cultural accounts of lived experience, the political theorist is unavoidably implicated in the project of representation, a project that is no doubt both epistemically and politically problematic. Spivak reminds us that the "native consciousness" often remains silently, blankly beyond the reach of Western researchers' ability to access it, subject it to the scholarly gaze, make it transparent, and redescribe it.[44] Postcolonial theorists have also pointed out that attempts to access the native consciousness are often guilty of further "production" of otherness for

Western consumption, a production that is as problematically laden with power relations as the textual analysis that Edward Said famously described in *Oriental-ism*. And experience, we have increasingly discovered, is rarely transparent, easily explained, or epistemically authoritative.[45] But newer generations of political scientists, anthropologists and ethnographers sensitive to and trained in postcolonial theory also point to the possibility of scholarly cultural accounts that are phenomenologically aware and self-reflexively immersed. Good representation is no longer seen, as it once was, as the project of making the native's experience transparent, and good scholarly accounts are no longer expected to be authoritative or accurate in the manner of an utterly objective participant-observer. Producers of cultural accounts are now keenly aware of the role their subjectivity plays in co-constructing these accounts, and of how power relations and their own positionality affect these constructions.[46] They are also aware of the partial, multiple, and often somewhat fictitious nature of these accounts: rather than aspiring to capturing "authentically" the entire native consciousness, they aspire to multiple, specific instances of experience and discourse.[47] Rather than seeing themselves as authoritative representatives who give voice to otherwise silenced others, they see themselves as co-creators of meaning, inserting themselves into specific instances of dialogue with "native exegetes" and allowing their cultural account to be a result of their participation in these dialogues, rather than a result of their wholly "authentic" scholarly gaze.

To return to our previous example, any good researcher will immediately recognize that the Gandhian ashram is hardly the only context in which the *Bhagavad Gita* or the concept of dharma can be studied existentially, and that the Gandhian interpretation of dharma is often contentious. Any good representation of the existential understanding of dharma must account for the existence of multiple, conflicting experiential voices. The Indian political theorist Meera Nanda offers an account of dharma that is existentially and anthropologically grounded, connecting its textual bases to social conventions, beliefs and ways of life.[48] Nanda argues that in contrast to neo-Gandhians who interpret the *Gita* as nonviolent and antihierarchical, modern-day Hindu nationalists have produced interpretations of Vedic texts such as the *Gita* that emphasize rigid caste-based hierarchy and violent politics. For instance, Nanda conducts an analysis of public political discourse to show that India's development of the nuclear bomb in 1993 was distinctly packaged in the idiom of dharma, with many Hindu nationalists seeing in the text's imagery a cultural and religious justification for the development of nuclear weapons.[49] Moreover, dharma, she argues, is seen as rigidly tied to concepts of *varna* (caste) and *karma* (past actions): that is, one's duties are clearly dictated by one's station in life, which in turn is a result of one's past actions and misdeeds. Caste-based hierarchy, then, becomes the defining lens through which dharma is determined, and any deviation from this strict understanding becomes a recipe for disturbance in the moral order of the universe. Nanda follows the existential understanding of a lower-caste woman who associates her own dharma with her low station in life, explaining the "uncleanness" of her own caste as the result of past karmic debts and considering it her dharma to be "humble, obedient and discreet."[50] It seems clear, then, that middle-class Hindu nationalists, right-wing politicians, and lower-caste peasant workers have very different experiential understandings of dharma, which may seem entirely at odds with the understandings of the neo-Gandhian activist we encountered earlier.

However, this need not be an obstacle to the task of existential hermeneutics. The best kind of fieldwork recognizes the multiplicity of these positionalities—Westerner, fieldworker, ashram-dweller, subaltern villager, middle-class political activist, etc.—and pushes ahead with the work of translation. More complete, richer and fuller understandings of dharma and of its role in the *Bhagavad Gita* will be accompanied by good, self-reflexive, ethnographies and fieldwork-filled accounts of how certain populations experience the term and the text. None of these will aspire to authenticity, facticity or complete truth; rather, they will acknowledge their own incompleteness, the positionality of their authors, and the polyphony of the voices and experiences they are trying to capture, from different sites of analysis. Nor should the insights about the viability of "representation," and the problem of making "the native speak" suggest a paralyzing caution in the task of bringing the experiential basis of an idea into written exegesis and commentary.[51] The language of partiality and invention should not raise empiricist hackles, nor should the awareness of positionality and co-constructed meanings suggest that such "representation" must therefore be impressionistic, idiosyncratic or free of any meaningful connection to the lives of the others that they wish to illuminate. The awareness of the researcher's positionality and subjectivity in constructing cultural accounts need not mean that all cultural accounts are nothing other than *our* constructions of others' experience, or that phenomenologically informed empirical work is invariably "inauthentic" because it produces only a self-absorbed account of the researcher's prejudices and projections.[52] Newer research in political science that takes its cue from the "interpretive turn" embraces the postcolonial and anthropological insights about partiality and positionality, while showing how gratuitous subjectivity and idiosyncracy in representation can be checked. Researchers' analyses are constrained by various practices: the attitudes of doubt and "testability" embedded in review processes serve as controls on the more obvious "non-objective" practices of phenomenologically informed research.[53] And we now know that phenomenologically oriented methodologies do contain evaluative criteria that ensure one's representations can be recognizable to the people one has studied ("informant feedback" or "member checks"), and that researchers check their own meaning-making by searching for evidence that would challenge their own subjectively constructed representations of otherness ("negative case analysis").[54]

CONCLUSION: TOWARD A COSMOPOLITAN POLITICAL THOUGHT

Finally, I want to explore the implications of this hermeneutic for the tasks and self-understandings of political theorists. I have suggested here that fieldwork, underlined by a commitment to existential understanding, enriches a merely scholarly understanding of the text. But now I want to argue that the choice of such a method is also closely tied to what I have called a cosmopolitan political theory. I wish to offer, then, an understanding of comparative political theory that requires the theorist to ultimately move toward a third and final hermeneutic moment, in which one struggles to reconcile the conflicting imperatives of adherence and scholarship. If the second hermeneutic moment was about representation of the experience of adherence, the third, I argue, will require the theorist to move back toward the scholarly imperatives of speech and discourse, and the theoretical articulation of experiential engagement. This struggle to reconcile the second and third moments is precisely what will be involved in the turn toward a cosmopolitan political thought. But in making this claim, I also wish to offer an understanding of cosmopolitan political theory that distinguishes it from the sort of cosmopolitanism that has recently been the focus of normative interest in political theory. In contrast to these existing treatments, I wish to offer an alternative understanding of cosmopolitanism, one that turns the lens onto the practice of political theory itself. I will call this a cosmopolitan political thought, and I argue that its development is intimately linked to the methodological questions about comparative political theory that I have raised here.

I return now to a distinction I made in the introductory chapter, between *cosmopolitanism* and a *cosmopolitan political thought*. The former, as we have seen, is a body of literature with a particular set of normative claims about structuring our moral commitments and our political, legal, social or institutional structures; the latter, I argue, is a way of thinking about the practice of political theorizing itself. Discourses on cosmopolitanism, as plural and multifaceted as they are, remain underutilized—I have argued—by political theorists, who have ignored in particular their promise for reenvisioning modes of practice and inquiry within political theorizing. Rather than producing newer and more variegated forms of abstract discourse *about* cosmopolitanism—fragmented or cohesive, situated and embodied or abstract and ideal, historical or presentist—political theorists require an integration of these formulations into discussions about the larger point and purpose of the comparative political theory project, and the practices of inquiry that constitute it.

Philosophy, Scott L. Malcomson suggests, is of limited use in thinking about cosmopolitanism, and the cosmopolitan's challenges are not in theory but in practice.[55] Rather than turning to Kant or the Stoic cosmopolitans then, I suggest we turn our attention to the very practices of a cosmopolitan mode of political theorizing.

A central component of such cosmopolitan practice, I submit, will entail a necessary return toward the scholarly imperatives of speech and discourse, and the theoretical articulation of experiential engagement. I have argued that cosmopolitan political theorists need to grapple with the discomfort of encountering alterity, engaging with it existentially through a self-dislocating movement that resituates them in alien worlds of disciplinary and existential practice. But a cosmopolitan political theory is also one in which theorists struggle with the demands of bringing these dislocating insights into one's own familiar contexts and of articulating these insights within the discourse of familiar theoretical terms, precisely so that they may challenge the self-understandings that define these terms.[56] Of course, the recent emergence of comparative political theory constitutes an admission that a reexamination of the strictly Western content of political theory is necessitated by the turn toward cosmopolitanism. But the sort of cosmopolitan political theory I argue for has methodological rather than merely substantive implications: it would require CPT to be practiced in a certain *way*, ultimately moving beyond the existential hermeneutic and toward the speech and discourse-centered imperatives of scholarship, despite the difficulties of this task. If we see CPT as the project of articulating alternative ways of understanding the political world, then the existential knowledge gained by the scholar must be brought into discourse. The comparative political theorist is thus implicated in the task of making a text or idea "speak" through the voices and experiences of its adherents. The articulation of the insights of lived experience through the creation of cultural accounts must lead to a final hermeneutic moment in which the adherent or fieldworker turns back into a theorist, by articulating how these insights challenge our theoretical understandings. And this, in turn, is precisely what is involved in a more cosmopolitan political thought: CPT must move beyond the perspective of adherence and fieldwork, if political theory is to engage ways of understanding the political world that question settled Western ones. Self-dislocating existential engagement alone cannot complete the task of a comparative political theorist: it must be followed by the project to disturb familiar modes of knowledge through speech and discourse.

What does this mean in a concrete sense? To return to our previous example, the researcher who has undergone an existential engagement with the concepts of dharma and ahimsa must now revert to a theoretical discussion of these concepts and how they may illuminate our political life. What do the multiple existential understandings of dharma—understood, either in the Gandhian sense as the moral imperative to live a certain kind of lifestyle, or in a more orthodox sense as caste-based hierarchy—tell us about politics? And how, in turn, might this dislocate our familiar understandings of politics? This will not be easy. In addition to the methodological pitfalls described above, it also requires the perspective of commentary and analysis, a "standing outside" of adherence and an exegetical stance in deep tension to the imperative of an existential hermeneutic. The phenomenological component of an existential hermeneutic suggests that the scholar insert oneself into the happening of an experience, becoming a participant in an event, rather than an observing, reporting subject. Yet, the commentative and exegetical components of scholarship (indeed, specifically Western models of scholarship) require that the scholar transcribe, comment on, and eventually evaluate such modes of existence, reverting to a position of observer and commentator. Does not such scholarship, understood traditionally as the imperative to analyze the meaning of a text, imply precisely the sort of dispassionate stance that treats the existential insights of the text as objects of analysis? Furthermore, the speech and writing-centered imperatives of Western scholarly communication stand in danger of violating the substance of expressions contained in experiential insights, precisely because existential understanding captures truths that may be too sublime, complex or praxis-based to be adequately captured in words.[57] In fact, Jenco claims that the very imperative toward speech and discourse betrays a Eurocentrism that renders silent forms of knowledge that are not easily expressed in speech and discourse.

Certainly, we have to be sensitive to the risk that some subtleties of existential "truth" may be lost in the attempt to make ideas speak to us, and that the project of representing them to outsiders carries both epistemic and political baggage. The alternative, however, is to continue with a political theory where ideas from non-Western civilizations remain contained within their own traditions, speaking only to and for their adherents. If CPT is to take place not at the margins of, but rather *within* the core of political theory itself, then explorations of neo-Confucian thought or the *Bhagavad Gita* cannot remain tucked away in corners of interest only to classicists, postcolonial scholars, comparative political theorists or area-studies "types." The self-contained study of these ideas is a recipe for their ghettoization: it suggests they may be at best superfluous or marginal to the "real" study of political theory (which is what we in the West do). It also suggests that such works have significance only as the manifestation of some other culture or civilization. In contrast, a cosmopolitan political theory would be one in which we might bring the ideas of Gandhi or Confucius to bear on our discussion of freedom or justice, in the same way that we would use Rawls, Marx or Hobbes. Doing this well, however, calls on us to grapple with the tough issues involved in "representing" these ideas in our discourse, attempting to bring them to life without violating the existential insights they provide, nor assuming an authority or authenticity to our representations. Thus, a truly cosmopolitan political theory must—somewhat paradoxically—be both geared toward, yet accompanied by a healthy skepticism about, the project of making ideas "speak" to us.

Indeed, the methodological dilemma of CPT is that the pitfalls involved in "representing" other texts and ideas stand in tension with a more cosmopolitan understanding of the task of political theory. But the right response to this is a reenvisioning of CPT as balancing the competing demands of scholarship and adherence in the push toward genuine cosmopolitanism. Given the choice between a political theory that allows ideas from the non-Western world to remain relatively unexplored because of the methodological pitfalls potentially entailed, and one which self-consciously grapples with the admittedly difficult task of bringing ideas into discourse, I suggest we choose the latter, precisely because this choice is deeply implicated in the evolution of our self-understanding as political theorists. Thus, a genuinely cosmopolitan field of political thought will require both a substantive turn beyond the Western canon, but also a methodological commitment to grappling with the most troubling yet ultimately fulfilling challenges of the existential hermeneutic.

But why should this sort of cosmopolitanism be tied solely to the particular existential hermeneutic I have described? It is worth exploring whether other approaches—such as, say, Straussianism or the Cambridge school—might equally implicate the interpreter in the sort of cosmopolitanism I envision. However, I argue here that these alternative methods imply a task and purpose to political theorizing that is antithetical to the sort of cosmopolitan political thought I envision. For Leo Strauss, the purpose of interpreting ancient texts is to mine them for transhistorical, universal truths about political order that can address our—specifically Western—contemporary moral crisis. The text is a self-sufficient, autonomous object of inquiry, existing independent of the preoccupations of the interpreter, whose task is to access the (often esoteric and mystical) universal meaning of the truth of the text.[58] For Quentin Skinner and other theorists of the Cambridge school, the purpose of political theory is to understand thinkers of the past exactly as they understood themselves, while the meaning of the text is to be understood through a recovery of the author's intentions, which requires, as far as possible, a neutralization of the influence of the interpreter's circumstances.[59] Skinnerians agree with Straussians on the dangers of misunderstanding by the isogesis—or "reading in" to the text—of the reader's own (usually modern) presuppositions, calling instead for a careful understanding of the author's intentions, and the conventional and linguistic context of the utterances. For Strauss, however, this study of intent and context can be transcended, leading to the discovery of universal and timeless truths. The Cambridge school, meanwhile, is deeply critical of the Straussian idea of "perennial truths," insisting that political theory is a historically contingent and circumscribed activity, and criticizing the impulse to find anything more "timeless" in a text emerging from a particular time and place.[60]

But discussions about interpretive method inevitably imply a position on what the purpose of that interpretation is and what the task of the political theorist might be. Ultimately, neither the Straussian method (which sees texts as a source of timeless values, and thus political theory as the search for universal knowledge) nor the Cambridge method (which sees political theory as deeply contingent, contextual and historicist, with the past having nothing to say to the present) contains the resources for a cosmopolitan reenvisioning of the task of political theory. A Straussian view would suggest that non-Western texts could only be read if they served as legitimate sources for transhistorical truths about moral order, independent of the specific contextual concerns of their readers. And, in the absence of such moral relevance, it would suggest that such texts cannot speak to us. A Skinnerian or Cambridge view, on the other hand, would suggest that these texts are interesting only as historical or cultural relics, with no relevance for our time or place. Neither of these interpretive methods allows for the sort of challenge and dislocation that the existential—and, ultimately, theoretical—encounter with alterity should bring forth. A cosmopolitan political thought, rather than seeking universal values in these texts, or rejecting the possibility of any present-day knowledge in any "other" ideas, should see new political insights as potentially emerging from any set of resources, present or past, "our" traditions, or "others." The cosmopolitan political thought I have identified holds out the possibility of a dynamic relationship between texts and their readers. This relationship neither ties the text rigidly to a contextual situation devoid of any cross-temporal or cross-cultural insights, nor, equally rigidly, insists on moral universals detached from the concerns and perspectives of particular readers. A cosmopolitan political thought should not be wary of finding answers to political problems across borders, by suggesting that texts can speak only to or for their own contexts or audiences. On this view, Confucius' *Analects* or the *Bhagavad Gita* could be seen as objects of contextualized inquiry *and* potential sources of politically relevant knowledge across time and space.

Notice, then, that this third hermeneutic moment embeds the scholar in yet another important paradox. A cosmopolitan political thought requires both an extreme historicism and an ahistoricism at different moments in the encounter with alterity. The self-dislocation I have described in the first hermeneutic moment aims to understand texts and ideas in a historicist way, tying their interpretation entirely to their context. Meanwhile, the creative reinterpretation of such texts and ideas in the third hermeneutic moment—which I will elaborate on in the next chapter—will be ahistorical, seeking to make these ideas speak across cultural boundaries. Nor is any reconciling required among the historicized and ahistorical interpretations of texts and ideas that would emerge from these complementary and mutually inter-constitutive processes. Indeed, as I will soon demonstrate, creative reinterpretation has co-existed comfortably with context-specific inquiry. Throughout history and in a variety of traditions, thinkers and texts have been read as both relevant to a particular context and as speaking across boundaries to other contexts. Ultimately, a political theory that aspires to cosmopolitanism must take seriously both the situ-atedness *and* transcultural movement of ideas. That is, it neither strictly ties them to a context, nor makes them travel in a way that seems inappropriate, contrived or disrespectful of the tradition from which they originate. Moreover, these nodes of situatedness and transculturality require recognition at different moments of en-gagement with alterity. That is, there are moments in a cosmopolitan investigation when it is imperative to emphasize the situatedness of Gandhi's thought within its Vedic home, its placement within a particular "center" of family resemblances. Yet, there are moments when it may be appropriate to break Gandhi's thought free from this connection to home and family center, allowing it to speak to problems and contexts beyond its own.

This understanding of cosmopolitanism may require eventually that all compara-tive political theorists engage in fieldwork of some kind. But why not dispense with fieldwork altogether, if good cosmopolitan political theorizing is about the ability to imagine otherness and articulate its insights? Such dislocating insights, it may be argued, are easily accessed through imaginative encounters with travel, encounters that may be had without requiring the physical dislocation involved in the existen-tial hermeneutic. Surely there is no dearth of existentially informed anthropological accounts that shed light on the lived experience of many non-Western ideas.[61] Why then demand fieldwork of political theorists? Why not rely simply on phenomeno-logically aware and existentially immersed translations of anthropologists or ethnog-raphers to complement our readings of political texts? Asked another way, why not let theorists be theorists and leave the perspective of adherence to the comparativists or anthropologists? But the visceral and physical exposure to unfamiliarity is quite different from reading about it or imagining it. The sorts of dislocations experienced by the physical traveler often elude what Euben calls the "armchair" traveler: phys-ical encounters are more likely to "put at risk the 'deepest issues that give our lives the purposes' we think they have [and] enact a dislocation that unsettles, disturbs and even frightens."[62] Moreover, it is the requirement of fieldwork that should allow the comparative political theorist to bridge the competing demands of scholarship and adherence. The student of the *Bhagavad Gita* who has been required to under-take several instances of lived experience (in a Gandhian ashram, among *pandits*, or among middle-class Brahmin politicians) is more likely to be able to grapple with the conflicting demands of representing its ideas, bringing them into discourse in the West, while remaining sensitive to all the concerns outlined above. My suggestion here is that the requirement for immersion in the perspective of adherence via fieldwork strengthens the comparative political theorist's mandate of scholarship. And, absent the necessity to struggle with these conflicting imperatives, the cosmopolitan political theorist can remain an armchair traveler, protected from the most difficult risks of dislocation and from the challenges of articulating those risks to her compatriots and colleagues.

The requirement of fieldwork also underscores that existential immersion is mutually implicated with linguistic immersion. An objector might argue, based on the Sapir-Whorf hypothesis of linguistic relativity, that how we see the world is determined by the overt and covert structures of our native language.[63] Language determines thought to a greater or lesser extent, and cultural concepts inherent in different languages effect the cognitive classification of the world such that speakers of different languages think differently. Understanding another's worldview is in turn nearly impossible without the confounding influence of language, which itself requires translation. Thus, the semantic space of "the political" in Chinese is determined by the fact that the concept is expressed in that language. From such a standpoint, can scholars whose native language is English grasp and assimilate the way in which Chinese authors think about politics, not to mention communicate it to their readers? Consequently, how much confidence can we have that translators of Chinese texts or ideas are really able to "get at" the concept or experience of the "political," as expressed in the original language?

More stringent versions of this deterministic view may throw into doubt the possibility of accurate cross-linguistic translation of *all* ideas, and thus the very project of cross-cultural interpretation and theorizing. But weaker versions of the Sapir-Whorf hypothesis recognize that learning another language can make possible access to the cognitive classifications of the experiential world that arise from that language. We know that languages are in fact highly translatable and only in select cases of poetry, humor and other creative communications are ideas routinely "lost in translation." Indeed, most early work on comparative philosophy is based on the intuition that cultures have been communicating across linguistic barriers for millennia, and that there is enough overlap among human languages, as well as a variety of linguistic mechanisms both within and across languages, to ensure that they do not remain completely unrecognizable to each other.[64] Matters of translation and interpretation are wedded permanently, Henry Rosemont tells us, to matters of beliefs, assumptions, attitudes and intentions. What follows from this is that "we must presuppose that we share some beliefs, assumptions, attitudes and intentions—not an unreasonable presupposition, considering that we are both human—before either of us can begin to interpret any of the other's sentences."[65] Moreover, "if there are no wholly different human languages . . . wholly cut off from all other human languages, then there can be no wholly different human views of the world."[66] On this argument, existential immersion is effective because it necessarily includes a linguistic component, which makes comprehensible to outsiders the experience of certain worldviews, beliefs and conceptual structures. Studying Chinese will therefore be an indispensable part of understanding what is meant by *ren* in various Confucian and neo-Confucian texts, so that the experiential world arising from the use of that terminology can be replicated. The requirement of fieldwork further reinforces this connection between linguistic and experiential immersion, and underscores the fact that the former is a necessary and crucial component of the latter.

In the end, then, how we think about the comparative political theorist's methodological struggles has deep implications for how we reconceive of our understanding of cosmopolitanism, as well as of political theory. Conversely, to seek a genuine turn toward cosmopolitanism in political theory involves more than simply the mandate to read beyond Western material; it calls upon the comparative political theorist to approach the methodological issues involved in that encounter in a certain way. In this chapter, I have argued that in a cosmopolitan political thought, those who engage in the reading of texts from outside the Western canon must struggle with the conflicting imperatives of scholarship and adherence. On the one hand, they are called upon to be part anthropologist or part ethnographer, developing an existential connection with the communities within which the text is read and immersing themselves in the lived experience of the text. On the other hand, they must revert to the stance of external observer and commentator, constructing cultural accounts in order to represent the experience of the text and articulating how these insights may be used to illumine our political life. The former imperative calls for a deeply historicized and contextually based understanding of intellectual resources, while the latter leads toward an ahistorical and transcultural reading of these same resources. Thus, good comparative political theorists must reconcile methodological imperatives that seem at odds with one another. But a cosmopolitan political theory, I have argued, is one in which precisely such struggles and complex encounters with otherness are increasingly available to disrupt our settled understandings of political life. In the next chapter, I turn to the methodological issues inherent in the imperative of transcultural borrowing, which seeks to bring foreign normative commitments and frameworks to bear upon West-centered problems.

4

"OTHER" TEXTS, OUR CONTEXTS

Western Problems and Non-Western Solutions

THE COMMITMENT TO radical self-dislocation raises questions of what is to be done with the new knowledges and experiences thus gained, and what their implications might be for our understanding of political theory. Few theorists have been clear on what set of intellectual activities is subsequently possible or necessary for the scholar who has immersed herself in foreign traditions of political thought. Even fewer have made any claims about what the subsequent possibilities imply for our understanding of political theorizing itself. The few existing accounts imply one of two things. Some suggest that the logical conclusion to the deep immersion in otherness and the attendant recognition of the hegemony of Eurocentric categories is to remain detached from a Eurocentric disciplinary home and immersed in another tradition of political inquiry. Alternatively, others suggest that the form of disciplinary inquiry we call political theory in the West is already inherently "comparative," and therefore the study of most non-Western texts can simply occur under its existing rubrics. These analyses suggest that the scholar who has engaged in a self-dislocating study of otherness is faced with two quite conflicting choices.

The first scenario suggests that immersion in foreign practices of political inquiry must be so radically dislocating, that it will ultimately produce critical doubt about the very disciplinary initiative we call political theory in the Western world. This view suggests that the hegemony of EuroAmerican political theory is so thorough in disciplining how questions are framed and how knowledge is produced, that any decentering of this hegemony must occur as a "recentering" or semi-permanent relocation of one's scholarly practices within another tradition's epistemic communities.[1] This recentering should in turn cast fundamental light on the parochialism of Western modes of political inquiry, and its result may be a rejection of the Westcentric discipline of political theory as we know it.

The other alternative suggests that treatments of most non-Western texts and ideas can unproblematically be integrated into the existing canons and methods of the Westcentric disciplinary framework of political theory. The practice of political theory, this view holds, has always been "comparative" in some sense, for we are usually separated from the ideas and thinkers we study by some degree of spatio-temporal distinction. The alienness one may encounter through self-dislocating engagement with non-Western texts need present nothing particularly new as a case of radical difference.[2] This is especially true given the hybridity and synthesis that make it even more implausible to draw strict lines of distinction between civilizations. And, even if non-Western texts can present challenges to our existing views, they must excite the imagination of political theorists situated in the frameworks of the dominant Western problematics and categories. Thus, Gandhi can be studied and taught alongside Plato and Machiavelli within an enlarged discipline of political theory, without any rethinking of the categories of inquiry that structure our treatment of these texts.

Left unsaid is what set of options remains open to the scholar who does not see existing categories of Western political inquiry as unproblematically "comparative" enough to subsume the differences presented by unfamiliar resources. Nor, simultaneously, does she see semi-permanent immersion in non-Western disciplinary traditions as the antidote to the hegemony of Eurocentrism. The second option leaves intact the existing structures, methods and disciplinary practices of political theory, rather than problematizing them.[3] It intimates that the ways in which political theory has thus far conducted its comparative inquiries are satisfactory to the task at hand, and that existing methods are well structured enough to subsume new kinds of distinctions. This position also suggests that the focus should be on making the treatment of non-Western texts fit the categories of Western inquiry and its preoccupations, rather than on problematizing those categories and preoccupations altogether.

The first option, meanwhile, also leaves our scholar unsatisfied. It suggests few, if any, possibilities for intervention into Eurocentric modes and categories of inquiry through the introduction of new insights gleaned elsewhere. Leigh Jenco speaks of the possibility of changes beyond simple additions to the canon or providing "disparate voices" and "case studies" as reminders of our specificity. Instead, she claims, we may allow historically excluded traditions, debates and modes of knowledge processing to discipline *our* reflections on and definitions of political life, through *their* standards, goals and concerns.[4] But how can we provoke new ways of inquiry unless we inject these newly disciplined reflections into our disciplinary home, the parochialism of which is now revealed even more starkly?

The cosmopolitan scholar of political theory cannot be satisfied with either of these alternatives. One need not see the utter disavowal of and disconnect from the EuroAmerican disciplinary home as the only antidote to its Eurocentrism. Nor should one seek to "bring knowledge back" simply to be included with EuroAmerican knowledge. The scholar must follow up with what I call a "self-relocation." This self-relocation allows one to resituate oneself within familiar debates with a reconstituted vision that brings new methodological and substantive insights to bear on them. This self-relocation is a return that sees one's disciplinary home through new eyes, seeking to implement new visions within it. These relocations need not be physical, for I commend the vision of EuroAmerican scholars immersing themselves in other traditions of inquiry as participants rather than as external observers or witnesses. Rather, such relocations can target intellectual interventions toward the Eurocentric disciplinary home, while remaining spatially and geographically anchored within another tradition of inquiry.

A cosmopolitan political thought must be replete with investigations in which alterity presents a concrete possibility *for us*, such that we may use these texts and authors as lenses through which we view our own models of political life. One not only imagines "oneself living differently"[5] but confronts the very real challenges that this reenvisioning presents. This requires that the normative insights obtained from the epistemic and existential immersion in otherness now be brought to bear on research problems and questions, at least in a scholarly manner, if not ultimately an existential one. Such contributions must be self-critical and transformative in scope, excavating the creative possibilities for problem solving inherent within otherness. I will refer to this process as one of transcultural learning, borrowing or application.

But this is a theoretical and practical minefield that raises crucial methodological issues. Here, I will explore two possible models of transcultural learning, showing that each is implicated with a set of complex concerns and assumptions. I present these two models not necessarily to demonstrate that one is superior to the other, nor to suggest that they represent a perfectly dual typology. Rather, I use them as heuristics that illuminate the issues involved in the process of normative transcultural learning, how existing analyses of transcultural borrowing have approached the topic thus far, and what important *aporaie* are evident in these analyses. Ultimately, I argue that transcultural learning requires a necessary continuity between self-relocation and the prior processes of epistemic and existential dislocation. The cosmopolitan scholar's ability to navigate the complexities of self-relocation emerges from prolonged placement in the foreign epistemic communities and practices of adherence. It arises from what we might call a cultivation of "insider" status and from the kinds of creative license that such status confers. Self-dislocation and relocation are thus mutually implicated and complementary processes in a cosmopolitan political thought. The former makes the latter more compelling, and, taken together, they represent the effective potential for disturbing Westcentric political theory's settled categories and presuppositions.

I. POLYVOCALITY AND CREATIVE REINTERPRETATION

One model of transcultural learning starts by assuming a commitment to texts and authors as polyvocal, and ideas, practices and ways of life as correspondingly mobile across geospatial boundaries. Proponents elaborate the view that texts and ideas take on different meanings in response to the concerns of different interpreters and communities, evolving accordingly. Intellectual resources are thus seen as inexhaustible in meaning, potentially connected to multiple transcultural "worlds" even while remaining connected to and rooted in certain specific socio-historical realities. Authors and texts can therefore address themselves unintentionally to multiple communities of interlocutors, with multiple meanings subsequently emerging. The meaning of a text is not a changeless property of an object but always reaches beyond what the author intended.[6] And, readings of texts and thinkers that transcend their boundedness, no matter what their "original" intent, can be a source of conceptual enrichment.

But this in turn raises many issues for our scholar. Does this view of texts and authors as polyvocal reject the idea of interpretive "authority" as rooted in any single set of meanings or practices, and thus require a commitment to creativity, synthesis and hybridity as methodologies for transcultural borrowing? Adherence in many traditions is often predicated on some form of creative reinterpretation and innovation; in the Western tradition of political thought, those whom Sheldon Wolin calls "epic theorists" have often taken creative license with key texts in their own traditions, refusing to view either the text or its tradition as static and sedimented.[7] Moreover, such a view is hardly exclusively Western. For instance, creative innovation as an important mode of receiving and transmitting the authority of canonical texts is amply in evidence in the Indic tradition. While Vedic authority may be continuously invoked throughout Indian history, the precise reception of the Vedas within various genres of discourse, along with the variety of exegetical strategies therein, demonstrates an astounding plurality.[8] A variety of dissenting and creative interpretations of Vedic texts, K. Satchidananda Murty claims, have been in place since ancient times.[9] The ritualist or Yajnika school took the Vedas as mainly a source book for the performance of rituals; others, such as Venkata-Madhava, took them as guidance for worshipping the Vedic gods; and still others have interpreted the Vedas as essentially monotheistic and mystical.[10] Commentators such as Durgacharya not only acknowledge but also advocate the possible reinterpretation of textual meanings driven by the subjectivities, motivations and varying contexts of different exegetes.[11] In the *Nirukta*, a celebrated treatise on etymology, Yaska writes that the reinterpretations of ordinary men who ponder the meaning of ancient texts not only permits them to find in it something new, but also that such contextualized reinterpretations are as valid as the original contemplative interpretations of the sages (*rsis*).[12] In his commentary on the *Nirukta*, Durgacharya writes: "from these mantras as many meanings as possible, all of them indeed, may be derived; there is nothing wrong in this."[13]

As we have seen, modern Indian thinkers have exemplified these creative strategies for reinterpretation across the ages. Gandhi may have relied explicitly on the Vedic tradition, but the interpretations he produced of the *Bhagavad Gita*, we may recall, were considered highly unorthodox and contentious, rejected by many traditional scholars precisely for the creative license he claimed.[14] He in turn, rejected the scholarly "authority" of these traditionally trained priests and Sanskrit scholars, claiming an exegetical and interpretive authority of his own based on praxis rather than scholarship.[15] Anthony Parel reminds us of the radically differing interpretations of the *Bhagavad Gita* produced by three Indian political thinkers of the twentieth century: Gandhi, Tilak and Aurobindo. While Gandhi's interpretation suggested an activist and nonviolent engagement with the political world, the nationalist B. G. Tilak claimed that message of the *Gita*, as we have seen, was to justify a worldly, modern and perhaps Machiavellian kind of politics, devoid of spiritual or higher aims. Tilak embraced the need for a politics of retaliation and mutual deterrence through violence, all of which he claims was embedded within the *Gita*.[16] Sri Aurobindo, meanwhile, produced a mystical and other-worldly interpretation that rejected politics and political action altogether, emphasizing instead an ascetic withdrawal from worldly affairs and a complete disconnect between spiritual and political action.[17] Each of these three interpretations has communities of adherents in contemporary India, and none can claim uncontroversially to be a more "authoritative" community of belief. Should a cosmopolitan political thought recognize, remain committed to or privilege this kind of hybridity and creative reinterpretation, rejecting the notion of singular determinate meanings, or legitimate cultural contexts?[18]

Furthermore, can *trans*cultural hybridity across cultural borders be seen as simply an extension of the *intra*cultural dissent and synthesis demonstrated by thinkers like

Gandhi or Aurobindo? Creative license and reinterpretation may be a somewhat different proposition *across* cultural borders from *within* them, and transcultural hybridizing may carry different baggage from intracultural dissent and multivocality. In other words, should internal dissent *within* a tradition about the meaning of a concept or practice provide unproblematic license for a scholar to creatively import and hybridize *across* borders?

Moreover, is the view privileging trancultural hybridity implicated with a piecemeal and fragmentary understanding of traditions and their cultural products? Rather than seeking to import entire traditions, ideas or doctrines across cultural boundaries, should a cosmopolitan political thought aim toward a series of fragmented models of thought? And, on such a view, will the units of transformative analysis and transcultural learning not be piecemeal, nonholistic and discrete components of ideas or texts, rather than coherent or organic totalities? With few exceptions,[19] there has been little self-consciousness about the units of analysis in cross-cultural learning. Will the focus of analysis be on a text, a thinker, on the history of an idea within a tradition (or within a thinker's works), or on comparisons among ideas across traditions? How will these units of analysis be brought to bear on one another? I propose here a distinction between "micro-level" "mid-level," and "macro-level" entities. Macro-level entities would be the largest units of analysis, usually encompassing entire traditions (say, the Islamic, the Indic, or the Chinese)— units that are holistic in scope and subsume under their umbrella a broad sweep of thinkers, ideas and texts united by geographic or cultural continuity. Mid-level entities may refer to the entire corpus of a thinker (say, Gandhi or Rawls); entire texts (such as the *Bhagavad Gita* or Confucius' *Analects*); thematic ideas (dharma within the Indic tradition, *ren* within the Confucian tradition); or doctrines or schools of thought (e.g., the *maqasid-al-sharia* tradition of argument within Islamic jurisprudence, deliberative democratic theory within the Western tradition, or dalit political thought within the Indian tradition). Finally, micro-level entities would be the smallest units of analysis, specific ideas and/or normative commitments of a given thinker or text. Examples of such micro-level entities include Gandhi's idea of *satygraha* (nonviolent political action), the Rawlsian original position, or Aristotle's "mean" of action. Indeed, this taxonomy may be far from perfect and its internal boundaries perhaps blurred. But one might argue that in a cosmopolitan political thought committed to polyvocality and hybridity, transcultural normative challenges would occur in a piecemeal fashion, between discrete "micro-" or "mid-level" entities, rather than between entire traditions.

Certainly, entire traditions of thought or systematic doctrines often have historically traveled across boundaries to find themselves transplanted in new social and cultural contexts that are utterly unlike those of their origin. This is hardly a new phenomenon. Islam has found many non-immigrant American adherents (many of whom are converts) in the African-American community,[20] while Martin Luther King's civil disobedience movement was an application of Gandhi's satyagraha in a different cultural context. The theory and practice of *yoga*, despite having originated in a specific context—the North Indian Vedic one of Brahminical texts and ideas— has taken on a life of its own by traveling to the West, embraced by many Westerners without the slightest familiarity with Sanskrit or the Vedic tradition.[21] However, these transcultural applications rarely travel in a way that preserves the integrity of an idea or set of texts in the precise form that it took in its original context. Rather, these ideas often end up mutating in a piecemeal manner, maintaining certain characteristics that connect them to their original context and acquiring new forms in connection with their new context.

Rather than comparing the normative value of entire traditions or systemic wholes, this view suggests that the critical thrust of a cosmopolitan political thought will be pluralistic and nonhegemonic, fractured and disaggregated. It would examine the confrontation between mid-level or micro-level entities such as specific thinkers, texts, or ideas, rather than bringing entire traditions, doctrines or ideologies into relief with respect to one another. This emphasis on piecemeal and discrete interactions ensures that the normative contributions to problem-driven research are laden with specificity and particularity, and often fragmented rather than whole. It would involve dissected bits and pieces of ideas, rather than a wholesale imposition of an entire system of thought upon another.

Notice that this creative importation does not necessarily involve a careful re-creation of the idea within its context. Rather, it requires a nuanced ability to see what kinds of evolution are possible as an idea travels beyond its own context. The normative challenge described in this model will not occur between distinct models of thought remaining separated by the boundaries of time and geography, or being compared in their historical or cultural holism. Rather, it will have a transformative element, requiring that an idea or a text evolve through traveling outside its context and interacting with the new context in which it is transplanted. It will most likely result in hybrid, synthetic models of thought and action that are the "pure" result of neither one context nor another. The cosmopolitan scholar's task will be precisely to make the transition between deep existential immersion in a particular context, and the importation of its cultural products into another, often radically alien context. This process of creative importation would require a sensitivity to distinguish between what is necessarily tied to originary context and what transformations seem both possible and necessary as the ideas or texts travel beyond their origin for application in transcultural ways. It separates what is uniquely tied to the epistemic and existential context of an idea from the ways in which it may evolve in other ones.

An Example: Gandhi's Theory of Nonviolence or Ahimsa

To illuminate this polyvocal and piecemeal approach to transcultural learning, I will explore a micro-level normative challenge in which Gandhi's understanding of nonviolence, or ahimsa, can be brought to bear on a specific problem: namely, a method for arbitrating competing truth claims in a multireligious polity.

There are many senses in which Gandhi's concept of ahimsa or nonviolence is attached to a specific web of meanings, beliefs and practices emerging from its originary context. First, it is rooted in deeply Vedic metaphysical assumptions about human nature and epistemology. Following the Vedic Hindu tradition of *advaita*, or non-duality, Gandhi sees the cosmos as a divine whole within which human beings participate and the task of human life as ultimate reunification with this divine consciousness, through which one comes to know the Absolute Truth or God. However, most human beings are in practice deeply limited in their ability to see the Absolute Truth, which is complex, pluralistic and fluid in nature.[22] Absolute Truth is so multifaceted that it cannot adequately be captured by any one mind, or manifested entirely in any given human life. Thus, any one person's grasp of knowledge about the moral world is necessarily incomplete, and the totality of Truth remains, for the most part, elusive to any individual person or set of people. The challenge of politics, as with any other realm of life, is constant vigilance to ensure that even as one is epistemologically limited, one's worldly actions accord with the seeking of truth.[23]

Violence in politics is thus unjustified, Gandhi claims, "because man is not capable of knowing the absolute truth and therefore not competent to punish."[24] The problem of authority is inextricably tied to this metaphysical pluralism, as well as to the problem of epistemic limitation—it is because of our difficulty in coming to know the Truth that certain kinds of political action become unjustifiable. Thus, the Gandhian doctrine of nonviolence is a response to both a fluid and pluralistic view of the universe, as well as to the limitations of moral knowledge on human understanding. As critical as Gandhi may have been of much of Hindu orthodoxy, his view of nonviolence relies heavily on assumptions about perfectionism in human nature, metaphysical pluralism and epistemological limitation—ideas that are in turn situated within distinctly Vedic metaphyics and epistemology.[25]

Second, as I have already argued, Gandhi's notion of ahimsa, or nonviolence, relies heavily on the Hindu concept of dharma, often translated as moral law or force of cosmic order, but more generally indicating an alignment with the divine force that sustains the cosmos. Acting dharmically—that is, according to dharma—necessitates living according to the righteous and sacred duties appropriate to one's station in life.[26] Gandhi not only wholeheartedly embraced the Hindu idea that dharmic action was the goal of life, he also posited a rather specific answer to the question of what precisely constituted such action. As we have seen, Gandhi tied the fulfillment of one's dharma or sacred duty to the imperative to follow ahimsa, and defined ahimsa not minimally—as simply a refusal to do harm—but more expansively, as a way of life involving an all-encompassing and rigorously disciplined search for truth. The meaning of dharma was thus connected to the overall pursuit of ahimsa, and sustained adherence to ahimsa, as I have argued, was the fulfillment of one's highest dharma or duty.[27]

Third, this duty of comprehensive truth-seeking for Gandhi allows for no separation of spiritual seeking from other realms of worldly action. In contrast to many modern or Western views, the "political" for Gandhi was not an autonomous sphere of human life, guided by its own set of assumptions and principles. Rather, it was no different from any other realm of human action, and was to be guided by the ongoing quest for truth. The political aspect of human selfhood was therefore inseparable from the rest of one's being.[28] The interconnectedness of different realms of activity leads to the idea that each of them must be informed by and reflect the same central purpose or concern.[29] For Gandhi, the spiritual and the ethical quest for truth—that is, the dharma of truth-seeking—serves as this driving purpose for the other realms of life, and quite especially for the political.[30]

Thus, rather than referring to political actions or beliefs that are detached from an overall search for truth, Gandhi imagines ahimsa as a way of being, a commitment to the duty of truth-seeking in the most comprehensive sense. Recall that ahimsa for Gandhi refers to the fullest pursuit of total moral virtue, a whole way of life, along with the total commitment to all the philosophical and metaphysical assumptions underlying the practice. From chapter 2, we also recall that this ahimsa understood as pursuit of virtue and truth-seeking includes the important component of conscious, disciplined self-suffering or *tapas* as a spiritual tool that purifies consciousness and moral vision. This self-suffering then becomes the key expression of a comprehensive and nonviolent search for truth.

This Gandhian view of nonviolence, when detached from its context and from some of the meanings therein, can be brought to bear in creative ways on problems beyond its original context. I have argued elsewhere that we can extract from Gandhi's ahimsa a secular doctrine of political action that speaks to certain contemporary problems of pluralism in multireligious or multicultural societies, without relying on the metaphysical assumptions of Hinduism as Gandhi does. After all, Gandhi's model of political action, one might object, would be far too dependent on the stringent requirements of right-living. Precisely because Gandhi sees no separation of the almost saintly aspirations of spiritual seeking from worldly political concerns, it may be that his view of nonviolence demands an intensity of spiritual commitment that seems impractical for transcultural learning. This idealization of ahimsa, an objector might contend, makes this mode of political action the exclusive privilege of some, unavailable to those who subscribe to neither its metaphysical commitments nor its teleological requirements. In order to address the contemporary problem of conflicting moral claims in multireligious societies, we may go beyond the limits of the virtue-based model that Gandhi has provided by excavating a model of moral and political arbitration shorn of the Mahatma's religious/metaphysical framework.

In order to so, however, we must creatively reinterpret ahimsa as a "civic" virtue; that is, as a secular virtue that does not rely on the on the metaphysical assumptions of Hinduism and perfectionism. Nonviolence described as total moral virtue resembles what Gandhi calls a creed or a religion. He also refers to nonviolence as a "law of life," or a life-force,[31] emphasizing its spiritual components. However, Gandhi also makes the following distinction between a creed and a policy: "A particular practice is a policy when its application is limited to time and space. Highest policy is therefore fullest practice."[32] Gandhi sometimes suggests that nonviolence can *only* be practiced in this manner, as a creed or a way of life, but also accepts the possibility, at other points, of something less than the fullest pursuit of nonviolence.[33]

Thus nonviolence as a civic virtue, I argue, can be isolated from the creed-like elements of ahimsa.[34] Anthony Parel tells us that we can think of ahimsa in terms of something like a civic virtue; he calls this the virtue of the citizen versus that of the monk. So if we think of ahimsa as a civic virtue, we think of it as something that can be at work in the public realm, the virtue of the citizen or the statesman, appropriate for political life, with no basis in any particular metaphysic. I call this civic ahimsa. This civic virtue of ahimsa, I argue, can be seen as the potential basis for a public philosophy in multicultural or multireligious democracies where conflicting truth-claims constitute the core of many public debates. Taken together, the requirements of the civic virtue of ahimsa can be used as a public standard for the justification of and arbitration among political views and actions.

It is necessary, then, to identify exactly what is meant by civic ahimsa and what exactly it can be asked to accomplish in a multicultural or multireligious society. I have argued that Gandhi's ahimsa can be seen as a public standard for moral and political arbitration, not in the sense of mediating a conflict, but rather as a method of adjudication that allows people to use their judgment to make moral and political choices in consonance with the truth as they see it, as well as to present those choices in public discourse and provide public justifications for action. It is in this sense that ahimsa arbitrates—it allows one to *pass judgment on* the worthiness of an action, and it could apply to either the political actors who are themselves parties to a conflict (in that they would use the criteria to judge their own actions), or to observers attempting to make sense of, and judge the truth claims involved in a conflict.[35] This civic ahimsa can also serve as the public standard for engaging in political discourse and action related to conflicting truth claims in multireligious or multicultural democracies. It allows citizens to present their metaphysical views in public discourse and action, while acting in ways that express their deepest convictions as political actors and participants. When in the position of an observer, spectator, or judge, it allows them to assert their insistence that these discourses and actions adhere to certain criteria. Civic ahimsa allows citizens of a multicultural polity to say, "You may certainly bring your truth-seeking into public discourse, but here are the criteria by which you may do so." Accepting civic ahimsa as a standard of public justification calls for a collective commitment to this ethic.

What does this mean? Civic ahimsa, I submit, can be thought of as a way to allow and assess the use of metaphysical arguments in public debates designed to influence policy, using the criteria of adherence to a method. Assessing the adherence to the criteria of this method can serve as a public norm that adjudicates which party's moral claims may be considered permissible in such debates. In this sense, civic ahimsa is not necessarily a method of conflict resolution, for it need not directly adjudicate the resolution of conflicts at a policy level. Policy decisions about the validity of competing moral views can continue to be made as they have been: in courts, in legislative bodies, or through electoral processes and referenda. Decisions about constitutional limits on marriage in California, for instance, could continue to be made either through electoral referenda, such as the recent Proposition 8, or through judicial processes that might override the validity of the proposition in the courts. These decisions, however, are often preceded by public discourse and activism. Civic ahimsa can serve as a standard for judging and justifying public discourse and political action over controversial issues involving foundational truths. The criteria of civic ahimsa subject the discourses and actions involved in these processes to scrutiny, as citizens attempt to influence one another or the judicial or executive mechanisms of policymaking. It tells us what sorts of arguments, ideas, speech and action claiming to be based on truth might be permissible in public discourse and activism, particularly when parties are pleading for a policy outcome based on a moral or metaphysical claim. Thus, civic ahimsa is not necessarily a method of deciding competing truth claims or resolving conflicts based on these claims: instead, it is a recommendation for ascertaining which kinds of actions and speech based on truth claims are justifiable in public discourse and which kind are not.

What are the criteria involved in this practice of civic ahimsa? I submit that it involves three requirements based roughly on three components of Gandhi's comprehensive or dharmic search for truth. But these requirements are detached from the overall virtue-based truth-seeking that Gandhi himself insists on, as well as from any necessary metaphysical assumptions.[36] They would be seen as constraints on the truth-based arguments of any member of the polity attempting to influence policymaking. The first requirement is that of epistemological humility and self-scrutiny. This requires that one who presents metaphysical views publicly can do so only after subjecting her or his position to great scrutiny and acknowledging the potential fallibility of one's own grasp of the "truth." It also requires considering the possibility that an adversary may have a better grasp of the "truth." Practically, this requires political actors to give serious consideration to the viewpoints of their adversaries and not dismiss them without a fair hearing. This demonstrates respect for the adversary as a fellow human being engaged in the search for truth, to whose position one owes at least some presumptive respect until proven otherwise. In judging the actions of each party, we ask which (if any) party had demonstrated such humility and respect in good faith, through either their actions or public discourse.

Second, the Gandhian method requires that one adhere strictly to the requirements of moral persuasion through discourse and attempt to convert an adversary to one's own moral position as the initial step in political conflict. Parties to a conflict must engage in rigorous persuasion through negotiation and discourse, while arguing respectfully and humbly for the moral superiority of their position. Only when such persuasion has failed should they attempt to use nonrational (yet nonviolent) means of persuasion. By requiring all political actors to engage their adversaries' moral position, Gandhi wants to underscore the point that politics is a search for the truth, rather than simply a struggle for political advantage or victory in arguments. Actions that aim to gain only political advantage without engaging the adversary's moral position and arguing for the de facto superiority of one's own moral position are not to be granted credibility. Those who want to stipulate their beliefs and attempt to have them gain advantage in the political realm, simply because these beliefs are their *own*, are not adhering to the requirements of nonviolence. Only those who have arrived at their position after confronting persistent doubt and self-scrutiny can convert others to their position. Conversely, those who engage in such discourse must also be willing to be persuaded: "while he carries on his own persuasive activity, he allows the opponent every opportunity and indeed invites him to demonstrate the correctness of his . . . position, and to dissuade him of his own position."[37]

Finally, the activist must be willing to suffer nonviolently, undergo punishment, and invite legal sanction if necessary, without harming others. Here, rather than arising from any attachment to a *yogic* view of *tapas* as a method for truth-seeking, the final step of undergoing suffering serves as the test of true political conviction. It allows the activist to draw on his or her fundamental convictions regarding the ultimate meaning and purpose of life, in a way that demonstrates (1) the relevance of this conviction in a particular instance, (2) the strength of this conviction, and (3) the acknowledgment of the position's potential fallibility. If one believes so strongly in the validity of a truth as the basis of a political position, then one should be willing to suffer for it, in a way that harms only oneself. Such action could take the form of civil disobedience; long marches in harsh conditions; deliberate law breaking with intent to invite the full sanction of the law; or simply a dramatic act such as fasting publicly, "sitting-in" or other prolonged discomfort.[38] Notice also that this dramatization would be a means of last resort, only after genuine moral persuasion through discourse had been exhausted. Nonviolent suffering is not to be trivialized as a mere political stunt; that is, those who strike, boycott, fast, or break the law without having engaged in moral discourse would not be granted validity.

Because political action is but one way in which she seeks the truth, a political agent acts nonviolently, understanding that her vision of the truth may be mistaken and her adversary's more complete than her own. This implicitly acknowledges the possibility of error in any one person's understanding of truth at any given time: if we are mistaken, we alone suffer the consequences of our mistakes.[39] It also reinforces the notion of politics as an effort to seek the truth. Through nonviolent suffering, the nonviolent political actor hopes to engage an adversary in a joint examination of their respective truth claims. An adversary, then, is not simply someone whose moral or political "truth" is mistaken and therefore overthrown by force. Rather, it is because we keep ourselves open to the possibility that her "truth" may be valid that we treat her as an equal partner in the search for truth and demonstrate to her our conviction in terms that do not threaten her. In a strategy of nonviolent political action, suffering also operates to break through the rational defenses of the opponent when the appeal of reason has failed. It dramatizes one's moral position through a sort of "shock treatment," demonstrating the activist's strength of conviction and representing her sincerity by the willingness to suffer for her moral position.

Notice that in claiming to "evaluate" certain political truth claims, citizens and policymakers need not profess to ascertain the validity of an entire belief system. Rather, they can assess the truth status of a particular political action or project based on adherence to the three criteria of the nonviolent method.[40] Notice also that in claiming to "evaluate" truth claims, the standard of public adjudication or justification mentioned here can pertain only to specific *actions* rather than to moral or metaphysical *belief systems*. Indeed, the convictions underlying these actions or discourses are always brought to the fore in the course of political action. But civic ahimsa allows us to decide whether to grant legitimacy to the *actions* and *decisions* of the parties to a conflict by asking whether the parties have adhered to the requirements of civic ahimsa. Instead of focusing simply on the reasons given for a particular position, the requirements of civic ahimsa shift the focus of justification to the actions that go along with these reasons. Reason giving continues to be important—after all, we come to the truth of a matter by weighing the reasons given on each side of an argument.[41] However, civic ahimsa adds an additional component to the evaluative process, by subjecting the public discourse and actions accompanying the reasons to scrutiny. To return to the example of Proposition 8, when assessing the validity of constitutional limits on same-sex marriage, civic ahimsa does not necessarily allow judges, elected officials or fellow citizens to judge the truth claims about the metaphysical meaning and status of marriage underlying either side's arguments. What it would do, however, is give them a way to assess the validity and viability of the truth-based arguments, actions and discourses that were brought into the public realm in arguing for one position or the other. One might object that policy decisions about arguably metaphysical matters such as abortion or same-sex marriage should *require* an honest evaluation of their very truth status, rather than be based on an assessment of their proponents' or opponents' method of argumentation. Shouldn't judges or citizens decide these issues based precisely on the truth of the matter, rather than on *how* they are being argued for (or against)? But using civic ahimsa as a standard reminds us that even metaphysical contemplation of policy decisions rarely occurs in a vacuum devoid of public reasoning and activism, and that policymaking outcomes are also deeply intertwined with the quality of public argumentation.

Certainly, it might be argued that making a public truth claim does not automatically make one a genuine truth-seeker, and that the imposition of one's own truth claim is often a thinly veiled desire for the exercise of power, rather than for the sincere desire for politics to be based upon truth as one sees it. One might say that opponents of same-sex marriage are simply seeking the preponderance of Christianity in politics rather than seeking truth, or that immigrants seeking the right of women to wear veils or to conduct arranged marriages are simply staking a claim to power. But the Gandhian criterion of disciplined and conscious self-suffering ensures that those who want to make truth claims in politics are held to their stated goal, and that sincere truth-seeking, rather than power seeking, is rewarded in those cases. The criterion of suffering trumps measures such as lobbying, advertising, coercive measures and other kinds of arguments that depend on economic or physical power. Public discourse about constitutional measures against gay marriage would be conducted and judged not on grounds of the amount of money spent on advertising campaigns, but rather on the self-suffering involved in the political actions of its proponents or opponents, thus guarding against bad faith attempts at political persuasion. Certainly, civic ahimsa privileges the perspective of those political actors who seek the truth—but only if they seek to make policy based on truth, and only if they can demonstrate the sincerity of their desire through conscious, disciplined self-suffering. Nor should the method of civic ahimsa require the moral stance of a truth-seeker in politics in general; as we have already said, civic ahimsa is not a method for resolving all policy conflicts, and not all conflicts need to be resolved on the grounds of their truth claims. Instead, civic ahimsa sets standards for the public behavior and argumentation of those who seek to incorporate a metaphysical view into their political argumentation. It both allows for such truth-seeking in certain instances, yet sets limits and constraints on it.

There are, of course, many other issues that may arise in the model of civic ahimsa I have just proposed, and much more may be said about its potential merits and pitfalls.[42] For now, however, let us concern ourselves with how civic ahimsa can serve as an exemplar for our cosmopolitan scholar's project of transcultural learning. Notice that the project of normative engagement I have described here will require reinterpretation and importation, and as such, will assume something resembling "creative license." This creative license in turn requires a piecemeal and fragmentary understanding of Gandhi's thought, for such reinterpretation would : (1) import the idea of nonviolence or ahimsa into new contexts and for new purposes, both of which differ greatly from the ones Gandhi originally ascribed to it; (2) detach it from its philosophical (if not cultural or geographical) context and from the Vedic metaphysical assumptions this involves; (3) detach it from its overall spiritual context of dharmic truth-seeking. Such creative license would allow Gandhi's nonviolence to speak polyvocally in response to problems and questions from a new context, transforming and evolving in response to this relocation, and taking on different meanings in response to the concerns of different interpreters. This creative license would also treat Gandhi's model of nonviolence in a piecemeal and disaggregated way, a synthetic model of political action that need not be the "pure" result of either the Gandhian/Vedic context nor the Western liberal one, but a hybrid that emerges from its interaction with both contexts and their attendant concerns.

We can also see how this creative piecemeal treatment of Gandhi's nonviolence brings ideas from non-Western traditions to bear on specific problems and normative issues. In this case, we are afforded a potentially new answer to a question we have grappled with in Western political thought; namely, how we might construct a tolerant and egalitarian political order that allows for truth-seeking and makes space for truth claims as the basis for political beliefs and actions, yet privileges no single set of truth claims over others. Indeed we could say that the secularized dharma of nonviolence—i.e., the duty for our moral and political beliefs and commitments to be circumscribed by the civic requirements of nonviolence—allows us to preserve stability and fair cooperation in a multireligious or multicultural yet free and equal society, without jettisoning the search for truth. We might ask our citizens to "embrace the dharma of ahimsa," understanding that the meanings of both dharma and ahimsa have evolved in their relocation in a new context and in response to a new question. Here, to speak of nonviolence as dharma would no longer have the meta-physical connotations that it traditionally is attached to. It no longer refers to spiritual laws that relate to the upholding of cosmological order, or to the fulfillment of one's specific righteous and sacred duties and roles. Nor would ahimsa need to mean the rigorous truth-seeking lifestyle in the sense that Gandhi required, involving strict vows and rigorous self-scrutinizing discipline. The nonviolent self-suffering required under civic ahimsa would have no necessary connection to the Vedic understanding of tapas as a tool for clearer moral vision. Rather, the dharma of ahimsa (or the duty of nonviolence) can be creatively reinterpreted for the secular liberal or Western context to mean a set of civic actions or duties that circumscribe one's ability to act or speak politically, a set of requirements that both constrain and expand the political possibilities. It constrains political possibilities by the limits it places on the actions that are allowed in political persuasion, but it expands the range of possibilities because it allows metaphysical argumentation into the mix.

2. HOLISM AND INTEGRITY

We have seen how one model of transcultural learning affords our scholar the opportunity to bring new foreign ideas to bear on old problems and questions in a creative, syncretic and piecemeal way. But one might argue that a cosmopolitan political thought needs a methodological grounding that is more than a mere imitation of empirical realities. So what if Islam has traveled across geocultural boundaries to evolve and take on new forms in each new context? So what if the Western practice of yoga or of Islam involves modes of creative evolution that allow their precepts to transform in new existential contexts? These factual realities alone cannot provide our scholar with the intellectual grounds for creative and nonholistic reinterpretation and importation.

An alternative model for transcultural learning is provided by Leigh Jenco who uses the example of neo-Confucian "Western Learning" theorists Zhang Shizhao, Yan Fu and Tan Sitong. These scholars suggest that when seen as holistic exemplars, wide-scale imitation of foreign models can lead to reproduction of cultural constructs and continuation of entire traditions in new foreign contexts. Faithful reconstruction of these exemplars, this view suggests, should be the precondition of the cultural portability of entire traditions, for superficial engagement cannot yield meaningful answers, and extracting particular elements would belie the internal holistic complexity of societies.[43] Each entity or tradition is self-sufficient and can ask and answer its own questions independent of contributions from other cultures. In contrast to the fragmentary and hybridizing tendencies that were emphasized in our previous model, Zhang, Yan and Tan argue that the political and its forms do not exist in isolation from wider society, culture, values, and mores. Foreign borrowing should therefore be seen as a strategy for learning a system of interconnected, society-wide practices, rather than select ones. Ideas remain patently holistic, not only in the sense that they rely on a wide array of extra-institutional attitudes and behaviors to make them work, but also because their components can be pried apart only at the risk of dissolving completely the institution itself. Conversely, Tan claims that imitating rituals, acts, observable practices, institutions, and other material manifestations of knowledge will have no purpose without the right kind of *dao*, that is, the deeply interconnected systems of meaning that enable the existence of particular practices and institutions at particular times and places.[44] Thus meaning or *dao*-making is not keyed to ethnic background so much as "specific, but replicable, learning processes," pointing to the enormity of cross-cultural borrowing as "an institutional, society-wide event."[45]

An objector committed to such a view might argue that the only appropriate method of importing ideas across cultural boundaries is a holistic one, namely one that faithfully preserves the idea or text in its organic nature. This method maintains the connection of the text or idea to all contextual factors, and allows it to travel only by attempting to replicate the entire webs of meaning within which it takes its shape, thus maintaining its uniqueness and integrity. On such a view, for instance, one might insist that the only acceptable way of allowing Gandhian nonviolence to travel beyond its original context would be to faithfully replicate his understanding of ahimsa as situated within Vedic metaphysical categories, as well as within the imperative toward truth-seeking and dharmic action in politics. Indeed, Gandhi himself may have intended the concepts of ahimsa and satyagraha transculturally— i.e., for all times and places—but what is less clear is whether he intended for them to be detached from their dharmic, Vedic metaphysical context. Gandhi's own views on the potential applicability of his ideas across cultural contexts are neither clear nor uncomplicated. On the one hand, he claimed no necessary cultural context for the practices of ahimsa and satyagraha, and strongly insisted that they transcended religious affiliations. He exhorted members of all faiths to not only join his political movement but also to embrace the truth-seeking lifestyle he advocated. His ashrams were models of interfaith interaction where Hindu, Muslim and Christian prayers were recited daily, and no belief in the Hindu tradition was required for any participation in a Gandhian moral-political lifestyle. Existentially, then, Gandhi had no cultural or metaphysical limitations on participation in nonviolence. Epistemically, however, it is a different story. Gandhi casts his ideas strictly in terms of their connection to certain Sanskritic/Brahminic worldviews, emphasizing their connection to certain highly specific epistemic and ontological assumptions. While ahimsa seems existentially open to believers of all kinds, it seems epistemically tied to the Vedic tradition, a tie that Gandhi, while not affirming explicitly, seemed loathe to sever.

On this view, the Vedic understanding of dharma clearly forms the epistemic context within which Gandhi places political action, and to detach it from this context would be to assume a creative license that violates the holism and integrity of Gandhi's ahimsa. One might be tempted to insist that the only way for us to import Gandhian nonviolence into new contexts is to faithfully recreate not only its internal complexity, but also the very web of interconnected meanings and practices within which it takes shape. This would include metaphysical and epistemic grounding in Vedic assumptions about human nature, knowledge and pluralism; the centrality of the dharmic imperative; the pursuit of a particular lifestyle involving rigorous vows and penance; and so on.

But this alternative view is hardly uncontested, leaving our scholar with no less controversial a methodology on which to build an approach to transcultural borrowing. The commitment to holism and integrity of exemplars, as Jenco acknowledges, soon becomes implicated with the highly fraught categories of authenticity and accuracy. Zhang and Yan suggest that the reproduction of foreign models must be not only holistic but also "authentic," and that the very success of transcultural learning depends on the authenticity of its reproduction. Jenco claims that Tan's notion of authenticity "chastened" by a recognition of its limits "does produce something meaningful, even if necessarily partial."[46] Western Learning thinkers point, she claims, to the need to engage communities rather than individuals in the search for cross-cultural knowledge, and to "society rather than the individual as a site for transformation."[47] Authenticity, according to Tan, offers a way for entire communities to replicate foreign ways of life by pointing to external practices and standards, rather than the inscrutable interpretations of individuals, that sustain meaning and intelligibility.[48] The process calls into being a collective rather than merely individual sense of how a given institution functions, providing a "profound insight into the collectively sustained nature of political institutions, values and practices."[49] Its goal, Jenco claims, is be converted to a new way of thinking that implies a series of interconnected and embedded networks of meaning, rather than discrete concepts held in isolation from one other and from the matrices that give them meaning.[50]

But this commitment to a chastened version of authenticity still does not get us around the following problem: any view of a cultural construct that sees it as an organic unity will have trouble accounting for its internal fissures or the pluralities of its manifestations. We must still grapple with the question of which particular version of the institution or way of life is to be reproduced. Is there a more "authentic" or "accurate" version of Gandhian ahimsa in the Indian tradition, for instance, and what is our scholar to do about the dissonant voices within this tradition that seek to recreate it in different ways? Should Gandhi's life and writings serve as the only exemplar, under the assumption that only Gandhi himself could have reached the state of perfected virtue that he equated with nonviolence? Which communities, ways of life, or institutions can be said to embody ahimsa most fully? This in turn could easily authorize a dangerous return to essentialism, suggesting that we can identify some singular expression of an institution as the "accurate" one, or that only one monolithic understanding of the web of meanings, practices and ways of life can serve as its supporting framework.

Here, too, our scholar would need to tread carefully, because it remains unclear what the basis of her commitment to holism and integrity should be. Nor is it clear that such a commitment would be without internal contradictions. Thus far, the commitment to holism expressed by Zhang, Yan and Tan appears to be an intellectual one concerned with the nature of the relationship between traditions and their cultural products. It suggests that ideas or texts have meaning and come to life only in the context of communities of adherents, within a supporting web of meanings, practices and ways of life. But left unsaid by our Chinese interlocutors is the fact this intellectual concern for holism is not easily separable from a related but different concern. This is a moral or political concern about the violence done to the cultural products of formerly colonized civilizations. Postcolonial and/or subaltern scholars may worry that the act of creative reinterpretation and importation is easily implicated with a form of distorting appropriation, doing violence to the meaning and placement of an idea, or turning it into an instrument purely for the West's self-centric purposes.[51]

As we have seen, those who care about the alterity of non-Western ideas have good reason to be concerned if creative reinterpretation occurs *across* cultural borders rather than just *within* them. This sort of objector may be concerned with the following issue: how do we guarantee that transcultural hybridity and creative license do not indicate a disrespect or distortion of the alterity of the ideas in question? This "epistemic violence," in Gayatri Spivak's words, could come in several forms. First, any reinterpretive engagement with a text can turn into an appropriation characterized by manipulation or distortion, an appropriation of otherness for one's own purposes, and an exertion of hegemonic control over the text or its adherents.[52] A second form of epistemic violence involves seeing all non-Western cultural products as valuable only as instruments of utility to Western concerns and preoccupations. This set of objections is grounded in moral and/or political worries about the violence to individual and collective self-understandings that have been the result of historical disparities in power. But here too our scholar would encounter methodological paradoxes: different strands of postcolonial and subaltern literature contain competing imperatives. Those concerned with guarding against the epistemic violence of appropriation often identify reductionist and essentialist treatments of alterity as implicated in such violence. They seek instead to preserve the fragmentary and nonessentialist nature of its cultural constructs as an antidote to this possibility.[53] Can the preservation of holistic exemplars accomplish such goals if it is committed to singularity, authenticity and accuracy?

But the focus on alterity as the crucial feature of transcultural learning now opens the door to another series of challenges. These arise not necessarily from a subaltern commitment, but from a more general conundrum about the status of alterity and of its contributions to normative theorizing. Any detailed encounter with the alterity will recognize the internal plurality of traditions. It will also acknowledge that the orthodox doctrinal center of a tradition often presents the scholar with alien, morally distinct and autonomous views, while the more pluralistic, hybrid and nonideal type views radiate outward, away from the tradition's orthodox center. In other words, the closer one moves toward doctrinal orthodoxy at the center of a tradition, the more likely one is to encounter deeply distinct substantive moral commitments, and mutually incompatible sources of authority. Meanwhile, the further one moves away from the center, the more likely she or he is to encounter plurality, synthesis, and the increasing familiarity of hybridized views, rather than the radical alienness of orthodoxy.[54] But this in turn raises another dilemma for the *normative* contributions of alterity: if the goal of self-relocation is for West-centered scholars to learn from ideas or texts that speak from beyond our traditions, then, as Andrew March reminds us, we *require* a confrontation with their radical alienness, rather than with familiarity. But conversely, it may be the case that the ideas most likely to present us with this deep distinction are also *least likely* to be able to speak to familiar dilemmas. In other words, the more alien, unfamiliar or orthodox the position, the less amenable it may be to transcultural importation. Doctrinally orthodox texts or thinkers are likely to be attached to the internal concerns of their tradition, and less likely to provide guidance on normative issues beyond their traditional home.[55]

Let us take the Brahminical formulation of Hindu caste hierarchy as an example of a central, orthodox doctrine. This hierarchy divides human forms of life into four classes or *varnas*, based on natural superiority or inferiority, and past *karmic* credit and debit.[56] Interpersonal social, professional, and religious interaction among Hindus was long said to be heavily regulated by rigid injunctions in the *Manusmriti* (*The Laws of Manu*), which prescribes all ritual behaviors and social intercourse from birth, including marriage, occupation, and so on. Many orthodox Hindus cite the *Manusmriti* and its rigorous codification, ritualization and stratification of Hindu life as the most central of doctrines. It may be the case that an orthodox text like the *Manusmriti* provides a more challenging expression of a normative problem. It may challenge the commitment to absolute free and equal status of human beings in a democratic society, because the Hindu tradition calls into question the dominant liberal Western view. But for the same reason, it is unclear whether the deeply distinct and morally autonomous doctrine of caste could provide any transcultural insights. The stratification of social and political life through the caste system seems to have little ability to speak beyond the concerns of its own context. (Indeed, the entire principle of caste-based social hierarchy has been repealed in India, at least constitutionally, but less so in practice.) It is difficult to see how an encounter between such interlocutors would be anything other than a face-off between the most simple basic doctrinal commitments of the given views, bringing into relief their most fundamental moral—and metaphysical—commitments. The result of any such confrontation would seem to be an impasse at which one determines that the core commitments of the two traditions are incompatible. What precisely would be interesting about such a result, and what transcultural learning or normative transformation could it lead to?

It may be the case that the most interesting and relevant guidance on normative matters across traditions comes not from the orthodox doctrinal center of a tradition, but from thinkers and texts that dissent from orthodoxy. Such thinkers usually formulate hybrid and synthetic doctrines that lie at the blurry intersections of boundaries between traditions. Good, rigorous and interesting theorizing often involves the ability to grapple with the intricacies of a normative commitment, and to struggle with the ways in which its applications might vary according to a given context or problematic. This in turn requires openness to unusual interpretations and understandings that are fluid, rather than an entrenchment of the most fundamental commitments. For instance, Gandhi was hardly orthodox or ideal-typical as a representative of the Hindu tradition of political thought. Moreover, his capacity to provide challenging insights on an interesting normative question was hardly a result of his centrality, orthodoxy or representativeness within that tradition. Rather, it arose precisely at the point of hybridized contact between the porous boundaries of traditions that had already been somewhat intertwined with one another. His metaphysical and epistemic views may have relied on Vedic claims about the status of humans in relation to the divine, while the role of self-suffering in nonviolent political action was influenced by the Hindu concept of *tapasya*, elaborating the purifying effects of ascetic discipline.[57] But these were also fused with a commitment to the human capacity for moral reasoning, and a role for the autonomy of the human conscience, both of which were clearly influenced by Western Enlightenment ideals. His reading of the *Bhagavad Gita* celebrates the individual's moral autonomy while deliberately rejecting some of the communitarian, hierarchical and caste-based implications that other thinkers take from the same text.[58] This, combined with the influence of liberal Enlightenment views on freedom and equality in political life, made Gandhi's social and political thought a creative fusion of early Vedic/Brahminical metaphysics, later folk political practices, and modern Western liberal influences. Moreover, the capability of Gandhi's thought to provide meaningful normative insight through what I have called civic ahimsa is a result not only of Gandhi's ability to reinterpret the orthodoxy of inherited doctrines, but also of our own ability to reinterpret Gandhi himself.

I return to the example of Gandhi not to argue that it stands in as a proxy for all possible encounters with alterity. It may be the case that Gandhi's own placement as a transcultural subject makes his work uniquely amenable to the sort of normative transformation I describe. It may also be the case that there are other thinkers, texts or concepts across a variety of traditions that can be both radically alien in their deep orthodoxy, yet provide transcultural normative insights. I use Gandhi's example to illustrate that the commitment to self-relocation must be more carefully grounded in the question of which precise concerns it is motivated by. On the one hand, if the key motivation is to preserve the uniqueness of alterity, then a scholar may have to choose those thinkers and texts that represent more orthodox, doctrinaire, or radically distinct normative commitments, but in turn sacrifice more interesting normative insights. On the other hand, if the goal is transcultural learning capable of probing the Westcentric context in a relevant way, then she may find herself wading through the theoretical fracture and disaggregation that underlie traditions and their cultural products. She may then have to compromise on the quality of alienness or distinction, and this may in turn call into question the commitment to integrity and holism, in order to deliver interesting results for normative transformation.

CONCLUSIONS

I mention these challenges not to argue for any particular approach *tout court*, nor to demonstrate the implausibility of any of them. I seek to shed light on the care with which the scholar of cosmopolitan theorizing must tread. Self-relocation into the disciplinary home raises questions that are neither simply navigated nor easily resolved. We need to think carefully not only about which texts or ideas we choose to introduce as reframing devices in the process of self-relocation, but also about which, if any, of the above concerns should be paramount within the process. Scholars will need to navigate often conflicting impulses that lie at the heart of the enterprise of transcultural learning. Will the contributions of alterity occur as a result of holism and integrity, rather than piecemeal and discrete understandings of the tradition? On what level (micro, macro) can ideas and texts travel across boundaries? Does it matter whether we import them wholesale or piecemeal? How important is integrity for the process of transcultural learning? Relatedly, will they require some creative reinterpretation, recognizing the necessity of piecemeal hybrid fusions, and seeing the transcultural hybridity as an extension of the intracultural dissent and hybridity? Or will we need to recognize some notion of "authenticity" or "accuracy" in order not to do violence to the very meanings we have studied?

Nor, it should be clear, are the models described here meant in a dichotomous or mutually exclusive fashion, representing two poles of a dualistic choice. Rather than providing definitive binary responses to the dilemmas of self-relocation, these models point to the fact that the self-dislocation involved in epistemic and existential immersion is one's best guide to grappling with these dilemmas. Self-relocation cannot be driven by general methodological principles or conclusions. It must proceed inductively and from the ground up, through the very act of immersing oneself in the specifics of ideas, authors, texts and traditions, on a case-by-case basis. In each possible instance, the perspective of immersion in the concerns and perspectives of the tradition where one has existentially engaged will allow the scholar to address carefully the merits of the available approaches. Said otherwise, only the scholar who has taken seriously the self-dislocating activities previously outlined can engage in the self-relocating task in a way that carefully navigates all of the dilemmas outlined above. This scholar has undergone a process that provides scholarly credibility, for it locates one at a positionality that makes his or her relationship to a set of texts or ideas stand up to the scrutiny of fellow members of that intellectual community. It is not merely that it puts one beyond the reach of Orientalist or Eurocentric reproach and thus provides a "stamp" of insider approval, but rather that it gives a scholar the tools to treat a subject matter that travels across boundaries with the requisite sensitivity and care. This prior effort of participation in a set of activities and ways of life might confer something akin to an "insider" status. Creative license is something that implies a permission or authorization to engage in an act that might otherwise seem problematic, absent this authorization. This replication of "insider" status, then, acts as our scholar's license to import ideas across boundaries, not in a blindly arrogant or appropriating way, but with the requisite methodological understanding to ensure that such importation occurs with care for the nature of the ideas and texts involved.

In a cosmopolitan political thought, then, self-relocation and transcultural learning work best when they are preceded by an immersion in and surrender to otherness. When preceded by such a dislocating operation, the cosmopolitan political theorist can proceed toward transcultural importation having cultivated a deep respect for the texts, ideas and their multiple adherents in all their alterity. Such respect comes not from the careful and distant respect often afforded a fragile but ultimately strange and dangerous "other." Rather, it is akin to the instinctive care and regard one might offer to one's fellow community members with a shared sense of "cultural ownership" over a tradition and its products. The visceral experiencing of existential dislocation in the process of immersion allows one to speak or to write authoritatively about how such dislocating insights can be brought to bear on one's own context. A cosmopolitan political thought relies on a multipronged process in which the operation of self-relocation and transcultural importation depends crucially on the experience of prior epistemic and existential dislocations. In turn, this underscores the necessary multiplicity of methodological tasks and purposes—along with the deep continuity amongst these tasks—that characterize such a cosmopolitan political thought.

Finally, not every author or text one encounters in the course of studying alterity will provide potential transcultural normative insights: some of them may strike us unattractive, disturbing or even immoral. The Indian political theorist Meera Nanda rightly points out, for instance, that Vedic texts (including the *Bhagavad Gita*) contain impulses toward exclusion, violence, hierarchy and intolerance. How might a cosmopolitan political thought assess which texts are ripe for transcultural importation, and which ones require evaluative critique? Andrew March reminds us that a political theory that turns beyond its own parochial EuroAmerican borders must involve something more than uncritical sympathy that valorizes all non-Western ideas as an apologetic act of rehabilitation. In fact, treating non-Western traditions and their cultural products with respect, he claims, often means holding them to the same standards of eligibility for critique and rejection that their Western counterparts face.[59] The multiple methods I have described here should be worthwhile in providing a sound basis for such critique. The perspective of adherence contained in an existential hermeneutic, rather than exclude our capacity to make evaluative judgments, should provide a method for making such judgments more credible. Precisely because the history of evaluating "otherness" is so closely tied to the politics of imperial practice, we need a perspective for evaluation that self-consciously detaches itself from the vantage point of presumptive authority and immerses itself in the world of the believer. Evaluative judgments must emerge from the perspective of one who has attempted genuinely to gain entry into the consciousness of adherents to another tradition, and to replicate the perspective of an "insider." Such judgments may be on much firmer moral and political ground than those that purport to know or to judge alterity from a distance. The use of an existential hermeneutic ultimately lends more weight to an external interpreter's claim that certain Hindu nationalist interpretations of the *Bhagavad Gita* emphasizing caste-based hierarchy and violent politics may be problematic—not just politically, but morally and ultimately existentially. The final advantage of this multipronged process of self-dislocation and relocation, then, is the strong warrant it provides for those scholars concerned with possibilities for evaluating the ideas one encounters in non-Western traditions. Self-relocation need not require that every encounter with alterity result in the understanding of all ideas as eligible for transcultural importation. Rather, in conjunction with self-dislocation, it provides scholars with the capacity for discriminating judgment— to distinguish between foreign resources that present potential for transcultural learning and those that require critique and thus must be rejected as candidates for such learning.

5

DESTABILIZING EUROCENTRISM AND REFRAMING

POLITICAL INQUIRY

POLITICAL THEORISTS WHO study non-Western modes of inquiry often cite the destabilization of political theory's Eurocentric bias as a predominant imperative. But the view of self-relocation put forth in the previous chapter may continue to garner further scrutiny from those committed to this imperative. In particular, it may attract critique from those who call for a semi-permanent immersion of scholars in foreign traditions and epistemic communities. Recall that proponents of such a view insist that the only logical conclusion to the rejection of Eurocentric categories is to remain detached from a Eurocentric disciplinary home and immersed in another tradition of political inquiry. A committed advocate of "recentering" political theory around foreign scholarly communities may find the relocation process suspect as a potential source of disrupting Western political thought's Eurocentric bias. One may insist that it remains deeply enmeshed in Eurocentric entrapment. Cosmopolitan political theorizing would do well to attend to the nature and shape of such critiques, because the ability to respond to them will be equally crucial to articulating its mandate.

Even when engaged in the process of dislodging Western normative insights, such critics might object, are we not targeting preoccupations that are mainly Western in nature? Are the problems to be solved and the questions to be answered not dictated by concerns that emerge mainly from the West? In fact, some might object that making Western audiences and disciplines the target of one's interventions is itself an indication of Eurocentric preoccupation.[1] This is true especially if we are conducting our investigations in Western languages and publishing in English for the Western academy. Furthermore, doesn't the very project of bringing non-Western texts into the discourse of Western problematics betray a utilitarian, self-referential relationship to otherness?

This view suggests that the centrality of the project of dislocating Eurocentrism may be incompatible with a cosmopolitan political thought, if the latter is a series of investigations conducted in English or other Western languages, within Western academic venues, for the purposes of Western scholars' edification, and within the auspices of the discipline we call political theory. If anything, one might argue, the project of self-relocation underscores the very entrapment of a cosmopolitan political thought in the web of Eurocentrism. It suggests a return to the institutional infrastructures and demands of an academy that reproduces the dominance of Western categories, by speaking in the languages and forms of discourse supported by those categories. Indeed, one might even argue that we cannot claim to be doing "political theory" if we want to deconstruct Eurocentrism, for is the discipline of political theory itself not a Eurocentric construct? This view suggests that the central dilemma that should animate political theorists' approaches to the study of otherness is the choice between viewing traditions as only meaningful to their own members in their own languages, or acknowledging that any attempt to speak about ideas across traditions will be Eurocentric. This is because it will rely on some standards of commentary, analysis and scholarship learned within one particular tradition, in our case, the Western one. Eurocentrism is a trap that awaits any scholar who attempts to study otherness, and the only solution to one's entrapment is to disengage entirely from one's disciplinary home and locate oneself permanently in the other tradition one is studying.

In this chapter, I engage critically the idea that the dilemma of Eurocentrism conceived in this way should define the task of a cosmopolitan political thought. I argue that the choice provided by this view is narrowly construed and asks the wrong kind of questions. It misconceives both the imperative to deconstruct Eurocentrism, as well as the resources and opportunities available to the cosmopolitan political theorist who seeks to engage in self-relocation. Indeed, proponents of immersion in other epistemic communities are right to suggest that simply finding new kinds of answers to Western political theory's animating dilemmas is hardly sufficiently destabilizing. They are right to insist that decentering its hegemony requires a fundamental reframing of questions, and a reconstitution of premises about knowledge production and organization. It requires the introduction of competing frameworks that displace altogether the terms of existing debate, rather than simply "include" non-Western knowledge.

But the choice outlined above misconceives the imperative to dislocate Eurocentrism because it assumes a kind of entrapment in Western categories that can be overturned only at the cost of complete withdrawal from them. It imagines that there exists somewhere a space for the scholar to hide away completely free of the clutches of such categories. Meanwhile, this animating dilemma also misconceives the available resources and opportunities because it assumes that such resources only inhere in sites of "pristine" non-Eurocentric discourse. It ignores the possibilities for the radical reframing of political inquiry that open up once we recognize the pervasiveness of Eurocentric assumptions *within* the very non-Western traditions we investigate and learn to locate the sites of resistance to Eurocentrism in new ways.

A shift in thinking about these misconceptions will reconstitute the relationship between a cosmopolitan political theory and the deconstruction of Eurocentrism. A cosmopolitan political thought can be something other than a purely utilitarian relationship with otherness that only serves Western targets and preoccupations. It can clearly engage in the destabilization of Westcentric preoccupations through insights and frames of inquiry gleaned from other traditions. In so doing, however, it must move beyond a notion of deconstructing Eurocentrism as simply the flight away from modes of political inquiry thoroughly infiltrated by Eurocentric assumptions and the recovery of those that have resisted them. The cosmopolitan project requires not simply grappling with the inevitable "trap" of Eurocentrism. Rather, it reframes and answers a series of questions about what resources are available in a tradition *despite* its pervasiveness, and how these resources may challenge Eurocentric modes of knowing. The approach to such resources is one that may require an imaginative vision and an ability to excavate from a tradition's past as well as from beneath the façade of its Eurocentric structures. This reconstitution of the imperative to deconstruct Eurocentrism also points to a less rigidly delineated view of the scholar's own positionality with respect to multiple traditions of thought. It allows us to conceive of scholars as straddling the intersection of boundaries between these traditions, as simultaneously cultivating the perspective of insider/outsider to each one at different points. Eventually, they may bring to bear these perspectives on the tasks of dislocation and relocation without being "trapped" in any one set of disciplinary practices, or attaching to any of them in any fixed or final sense.

THE EUROCENTRISM TRAP

I begin by examining the assumption that Eurocentrism is an inevitable "trap" for our scholar. I use Eurocentrism very broadly to mean a view that sees knowledge as emerging primarily from the EuroAmerican West. Eurocentrism also frames all other ways of knowing and being according to its presumptions, locating subjectivity and agency to know in the West. It treats other ways of life and other standards of knowing as objects to be studied, rather than as sources of knowledge. It is not only a set of institutional structures but also a posture or an attitude toward knowledge— a posture that is often implicit rather than explicit, and one that almost anyone trained within its boundaries cannot avoid imbibing. Indeed, Eurocentrism's very appearance in the academy—along with the strident critiques it has generated— suggest not a well-defined phenomenon, but rather an apparition with too many limbs and forms to be easily destroyed.[2]

Already well-known are the critiques that emerged from postcolonial and subaltern theorists such as Edward Said and Gayatri Spivak, who have catalogued how the rules and structures of Western knowledge production colonized the worlds and minds of non-Western peoples.[3] As late as 2001, theorists of Eurocentrism were struggling with the question of how one might be responsive to colonized people's own perspectives on the phenomenon of Eurocentrism. The reenvisioning of non-Western peoples as subjects and non-Western civilizations as sources of studying human experience were still something to be pondered.[4] And, the "discursive price of admission" for having one's voice heard in venues where such deconstruction is conducted continues to be participation in West-centered discourses and in West-centric language.[5] It seems, as Immanuel Wallerstein reminds us, that the project of criticizing or reframing Eurocentric premises is itself haunted by the danger of replicating its assumptions. It is tempting to suggest therefore that Eurocentrism is an inevitable trap for anyone who wants to *think about* or *do* political theory in the West, and the solution lies in withdrawing entirely from such a disciplinary framework and relocating oneself within another discipline.

But any immersion in a non-Western tradition will immediately reveal how problematic it is to assume that other disciplinary structures are presumably sanitized from or not infiltrated by this Eurocentrism. The questions and preoccupations of non-Western traditions are in many cases formed in opposition to, in dialogue with, and already permeated by Western ones. But the problem goes even further to what Syed Farid Alatas has called "academic" imperialism or dependency: a systemic relationship of dependence and derivativeness that makes it, in Dipesh Chakrabarty's words, "impossible to *think* . . . without invoking certain categories and concepts, genealogies of which go deep into the intellectual and even theological traditions of Europe."[6] Chakrabarty acknowledges the difficulty of "cleansing" the consciousness of formerly colonized peoples from European theoretical frameworks. Categories or words borrowed from Europe have "found new homes in" the everyday lives and practices of ordinary Indians, without the problem of "Europe" ever being consciously named or discussed.[7] Even in the social science departments of many Asian universities, Alatas claims, Westcentric assumptions, practices and institutional structures perpetuate the hegemony of Eurocentric categories. Models, methodologies and research priorities are said to originate in the West, and there is a general neglect of local literary and philosophical traditions, as well as an often uncritical adoption or mimesis of Western social science models.[8] The selection of topics and the prioritization of research agendas take their cues from Western social science establishments, leading to a general dependence on ideas generated in Western universities, books and scientific journals.[9]

How would one reframe the categories of Western political inquiry imbibed from the vantage point of immersion in otherness, if self-dislocation only ends up teaching us that the methods, preoccupations and categories of other traditions are shot through with Eurocentrism? Is Eurocentrism so pervasive that the whole project of a non-Eurocentric political theory is defeated before it can even begin? But it will soon transpire that such a view holds much evidence to the contrary. Area studies scholars, anthropologists and others well grounded in immersive self-dislocation in other scholarly communities will claim that it is equally absurd to suggest that non-Western civilizations have no existing traditions of thriving independent scholarship. It is implausible to suggest that exceptions may not exist to the hegemony of Westcentric categories and practices, or that the scholarly discourses of other traditions are not often driven by their own unique preoccupations and conducted through methods of inquiry that are self-sufficient, autonomous and distinctive to each tradition.

Alatas chronicles the richness of many communities of scholarship in Asian nations. Leigh Jenco has written about the highly autonomous and self-sufficient tradition of studying Chinese political thought in East Asian scholarly communities.[10] Debates among Islamic scholars about Islamic legal theory and Koranic interpretation have been internal to the concerns and categories of Islam over centuries. Issues of Koranic hermeneutics, struggles over *ijtihad* (or independent interpretation), the exegesis of ideas about political authority and organization from the Koran and the *hadith*, all pertain to preoccupations and debates that have remained almost untouched by non-Islamic concerns and interventions. Comparative political theory literature increasingly suggests that the imperative to destabilize Eurocentrism requires complete immersion in the self-sufficient, autonomous modes of inquiry of foreign epistemic communities and discourses.[11]

However, thinking more carefully about the relationship between the dislocation of Eurocentrism and a cosmopolitan political thought requires a problematization of this seemingly clear-cut approach. I turn to Indian intellectual history, scholarly debates and public discourse to cast critical light on the seemingly unambiguous argument that immersion in otherness is the obvious antidote to Eurocentrism. The case of political practice and scholarly discourses in India stands in stark contrast to the relatively straightforward experience of its counterparts in the words of Arab-Islamic or Chinese-speaking East Asian scholarship.

In the case of Arab-Islamic political thought, we are easily able to delineate those concerns, methods and modes of inquiry that are internal to the tradition. In contrast to the Indian case, debates about the meaning of specific Koranic injunctions and passages have always occurred with reference to categories that are fully internal to Islam's own preoccupations. So too with the ways in which problems are framed and responses theorized. Debates about the meaning of Koranic injunctions and passages are fully alive and relevant to the lives and practices of both Muslim believers and scholars of Islamic intellectual history. They are also relevant to contemporary scholarly exchange among Islamic scholars on topics such as the nature of political rule and authority, the status of women, or the terms of political exchange between Muslims and non-Muslims.[12] Similarly, among scholars in communities preoccupied with the Chinese tradition of political thought (in East Asian countries such as Singapore, Hong Kong and Taiwan), the internal legacies and of Chinese civilization and political thought are alive and well.

If this is true, then the scholar seeking sources of destabilizing discourses may face the relatively straightforward task of immersing herself in the autonomous and independent discourses readily available within these traditions. But the Indian case problematizes this seemingly intuitive approach, for it is a tradition in which the ability to negate Eurocentrism is neither straightforward nor simply realized by the immersion in otherness. Eurocentrism here is not a self-contained and well-defined problem for which the solution lies in escaping its structure and finding oneself located in an utterly "other" scholarly structure. The symptoms of Eurocentrism are so pervasive that the goal of sanitizing scholarship from any sign of it simply by remaining immersed in a non-Western tradition of thought will soon throw up limitations.

The examples I draw upon will demonstrate that there are limited sites of scholarly discourse that are entirely "free" of Eurocentrism's hegemony. Moreover, the recovery of these sites and scholarly discourses is a complex matter: simply turning one's back on one's Eurocentric disciplinary home hardly constitutes a comprehensive solution to the problem. The game of "when have we gone far enough in disavowing, decentering, dislocating, challenging, expunging this Eurocentrism?" is a self-defeating one. Instead, we need to avoid the presumptions that it is possible to distinguish easily between those sites of indigenous discourse that are "unpolluted" by Western influence, and those that are not, and that such sites are clearly available to be accessed and discovered by anyone who seeks to do so.

The question of destabilizing or deconstructing Eurocentrism thus requires reframing as a matter of excavation and imagination, rather than simply identifying available models of resistance. In many postcolonial nations with long histories of imperial experience, such resistances often lie buried underneath existing discourses, lost in history, or often sidelined by mainstream social and political discourses. Recovering sites of non-Eurocentric discourse in such societies will often be a matter of rediscovery and revivification rather than of simple discovery—often an act of imagination rather than identification of existing discourses.

The Indian examples demonstrate how a cosmopolitan political theorist can also work *within* the parameters of Eurocentric pervasiveness that often define non-Western discourses. The theorist may do so by remaining vigilant to sources of resistance that often appear between the cracks, and reviving long forgotten or often neglected historical and experiential resources. The task is to unearth the destabilizing possibilities underlying contemporary discourses still seemingly permeated by Eurocentric preoccupations. The project of recovery may often be one of *digging beneath* or *looking through* the apparent structures of Eurocentric permeation to identify sites of resistance that are often seen only if we look through certain kinds of eyes with creative vision.

To that end, our project is recentered in order to ask more meaningful and relevant questions about the task at hand. First, can we speak meaningfully about the uniqueness, autonomy or self-sufficiency of political theory discourse within any given tradition, and if so, how may we interrogate the categories of uniqueness and autonomy in that tradition? To what extent are concepts, categories and methods emerging from that tradition existentially, historically and intellectually alive, and how may we distinguish between these? Finally, what are the political questions and dilemmas that preoccupy scholars in these communities of discourse, and what can we learn by centering their preoccupations about their own problems? Asking—and answering—these questions will provide our scholar with a more sophisticated set of tools to destabilize the self-referential and parochial modes of political inquiry in Western political theory.

IDENTIFYING SITES OF RESISTANCE: AUTONOMY, UNIQUENESS, SELF-SUFFICIENCY

Our scholar's first important task in identifying sites of resistance is to determine what precisely constitutes "non-Eurocentric" discourse. To what extent can such non-Eurocentrism be identified with the uniqueness, indigeneity, autonomy or self-sufficiency that characterize a tradition's conceptual resources and methods of inquiry? This in turn requires one to interrogate critically the categories indigeneity, autonomy, or uniqueness. Alatas claims that an "autonomous" tradition of inquiry is one that "independently raises problems, creates concepts and creatively applies methodologies without being intellectually dominated by another tradition . . . [and] raises its own problems and develops concepts and methods that are appropriate to the treatment of its problems."[13]

But these claims point immediately to the problematic nature of how to identify a self-sufficient or distinctive political argument that is internal to a tradition's concerns. In the case of the Indian tradition, it is often tempting to assign a primordial uniqueness to the earliest and most metaphysical work of the Hindu tradition, namely the Vedic and Upanishadic texts of 1500 BC to 200 BC. It is often argued that the unique metaphysical claims contained in these earliest texts, along with their subsequent political elaborations in the *dharmashastras* or *smritis* (early Brahmanical works on sacred law), the treatment of political ideas in Kautilya's *Arthashastra*, and in the epics *Mahabharata* and *Ramayana*, constitute a vital, flourishing body of work pertaining to political life in classical India. Hindu thought conceptualized political life, it is argued, in terms of uniquely Vedic concepts such as *dharma*, (variously translated as duty or force of moral order or the law of sacred duties); *danda* (discipline, force, restraint); the pursuit of the four great ends of life, the *purusharthas*; and a mainly monarchical system of *rajadharma* or kingly rule in which the king's main function is to maintain the well-established social order upholding dharma. The dharma of individuals and social groups was elaborated by various *dharmasastras* (such as the *Manusmriti* or *Laws of Manu*), and the failure by individuals to follow their dharma, or by the king to enforce and maintain social order through danda, would lead to *varnasankara* (the confusion of castes or social groups), *arajakata* (lawlessness), or *matsyanyaya* (the law of the sea in which fish eat one another). The overall consequence of the failure of rajadharma is *adharma*— cosmic chaos and disorder in the universe.[14]

But even this highly repeated narrative locating indigenously Indian conceptual and linguistic vocabulary for political theorizing in classical Hindu texts is controversial. Recall Bhikhu Parekh's claim that despite a long tradition of systematic *philosophical* exploration, premodern Hinduism developed no systematic tradition of *political* philosophy.[15] The implication of Parekh's argument need not be to doubt the existence of anything recognizably like political theory in classical Hindu thought, but to interrogate the simple and uncritical location of indigenously Indian theorizing about political life in accepted classical narratives. It quickly becomes clear that the categories of autonomy and indigeneity in the Indian case could easily rely on insider-outsider distinctions that are neither uncontroversially constituted nor clearly demarcated. In fact, the tradition's very pursuit of specifically *political* theorizing may require an investigation into its connection to the colonial experience. Parekh's claim implies that *systematic* theoretical reflection on politics in India may have been further developed in conjunction with and consequent to various colonial experiences—*both* the Muslim and the British. Such reflection may have at least partially been made possible by the categories of Arab-Islamic political thought as well as those of Western modernity. If this is so, it may be necessary to view the very development of theorizing about politics in the Indian context as somewhat interwoven with its relationship to otherness of various kinds. Equating "unique" Indianness unprobematically with Vedic Hindu resources also perhaps necessitates the dangerous otherizing of modes of non-Hindu influence—Buddhist, Islamic, Christian, and many others—along with the assignation of "foreign" or "outsider" status to them.

For instance, India's great traditions of religious pluralism and toleration are often said to be the result of the ecumenicism and pluralism inherent in classical Vedic thought. In contrast to monotheistic or Abrahamic faiths, it exhibits a spiritual humanism in which all individual souls (*atman*) are part of a divine absolute consciousness, and the seemingly disparate creeds and ideologies of humankind are simply different modes of uniting with the same divine consciousness.[16] But such a narrative ignores non-Hindu traditions of precolonial religious accommodation, toleration and interfaith coexistence arising from the influence of Buddhist and Muslim rule in India. Both the Mughal Emperor Akbar (descendant of an Islamo-Turkic-Persian dynasty that ruled much of what is now India for several centuries) and the Buddhist king Asoka instituted modes of rulership and political practice that encouraged the toleration of minority religions. They also actively valued syncretism, religious pluralism and interfaith dialogue, through edicts and support of public debates and discussions.[17] We could not even begin to address the question of an autonomously Indian discourse of religious pluralism without reference to the fascinating mélange of Vedic metaphysical pluralism combined with later Buddhist *and* Islamic political practice.[18]

The lesson here need not be that we cannot speak in any meaningful way about the autonomy or uniqueness of Indian discourses, or presume that such discourses are not what we call political theory. Rather, if we do so, we are required to take account of the vast internal complexity of the categories to which such autonomy or uniqueness are ascribed. It may be possible to distinguish between various subtraditions of thought within India and to investigate the extent to which each one's methods of inquiry and choice of topics are internally self-sufficient. We may explore whether they are either independent of any reliance on methods of inquiry and topics emerging from other civilizational influences, or necessarily interwoven with such influences. To what extent can one delineate clear boundaries between the theoretical subtraditions—Vedic, Islamic, Buddhist, etc.—of the subcontinent? To what extent, as well, can the characteristics of autonomy and distinctiveness in each tradition be linked to the predating of contact with one other, or with Western models of thought?

As an example, the Vedic tradition of hermeneutics clearly draws on concepts that emerge solely from its own internally self-sufficient textual corpus.[19] It refers to texts that are composed or revealed in Sanskrit, to sacred scriptures and commentaries on such scriptures that are easily categorized into a distinctly recognizable grouping of classical texts across a certain timeline. Moreover, the concerns that preoccupy its main strands of interpretation and commentary—the importance of *sakshatkara* (realization) and *anubhava* (experience) over purely scholarly and linguistic textual mastery, the requirements of *dharmic* (righteous) conduct and *rsitva* (sageness)—are self-referential. That is, they refer to concepts and categories of human experience and understanding that are comprehensible in terms internal to this corpus. As such, this can be said to be a distinctly Vedic mode of textual interpretation. It predates both Islamic and Western colonial influence, and provides a language and a set of categories for inquiry that are not permeated by any conceptual or theoretical influences from other civilizations. In such cases, it may be possible to speak meaningfully about a uniquely or distinctly Vedic mode of textual interpretation. Asking rich and complicated questions about the qualities of "uniqueness" or "self-sufficiency," reminds us to treat these criteria in sophisticated ways. It allows us to problematize them when necessary and thus remain highly sensitive to the variety and genealogical complexity of "indigenous" or "autonomous" discourses.

RECOVERY, REVIVIFICATION AND REIMAGINATION

This now leads us to the second task. We now require a distinction between those concepts, categories and preoccupations that are existentially alive within any given tradition, those that are historically alive, and those that are intellectually alive. By existentially alive, we refer to those concepts or categories that serve as guiding precepts and framing questions for everyday practices and life-worlds in a tradition. Meanwhile, those concepts and categories that serve as sources of theory building for contemporary scholarly discourse can be said to be intellectually alive, and those that serve as objects of historical scholarship may be historically alive. In the Indian tradition, as we have seen, many classical Hindu concepts such as dharma are existentially alive in a modern sense. That is, they continue to serve as important sources of meaning and belief guiding everyday practice in communities. And, we have also seen that they are historically alive, as an important source of classical or historical scholarship. Volumes have been written in multiple languages by both Indian and

Western scholars about the meaning, historical importance, and exegetical status of terms such as dharma.[20]

But, crucially, concepts like dharma have, through most of colonial and postcolonial Indian history, been mostly ignored as a source for contemporary problem framing or theorizing about politics. Thus they have not quite been *intellectually* alive in the postcolonial societies whose historical and existential reality they constitute. Chakrabarty writes that the "so-called European intellectual tradition is the only one alive in the social science departments of most, if not all, modern universities."[21] By this he means that the intellectual heritage of the West continues to be thought of as "alive" and "belonging to" their own time and all places by those in the non-Western world. Meanwile, they neither treat their own traditions as intellectually alive in any similar sense, nor use them as resources for contemporary critical thought. Reliance on or creative engagement with India's own premodern intellectual tradition within contemporary theorizing has been a relatively recent phenomenon. This does not mean that Indian thinkers and their ideas have not been analyzed at length, or that no attention has been paid to the richness of Indian theoretical resources. Rather, it means that contemporary analysis has not frequently drawn upon the resources of India's own classical or precolonial past in order to theorize about Indian political problems. The resources of India's premodern past are seen mostly as repositories of historical knowledge about (and perhaps, a consequent pride in) one's own intellectual tradition. But few have viewed them as sources of concept formation and theory building. That is, they may be seen as *objects* of scholarship, rather than as *sources* of conceptual and theoretical innovation.[22] In contrast, many of the historical resources of Western political thought, both premodern and modern—including concepts such as democracy, the social contract, the preoccupations of liberal individualism, Marxist ideas of class and revolution—are thought to be contemporary theoretical resources for *all*, as well as objects of scholarship in India and in other postcolonial contexts.[23]

Here, too, Gandhi is instructive as an exemplar of the ability to unearth a uniquely Indian theorizing about politics through excavation and revivification. Gandhi remains creatively engaged with India's premodern intellectual resources in order to forge a political discourse specific to Indian problems in modern political times. He is one of the few figures in modern Indian history—along with Tagore, Tilak, Aurobindo, Ambedkar—to attempt the operation of bringing *intellectual* life to premodern Indian concepts and categories. These were already alive in a *historical* and *existential* sense, but he updated and reinterpreted classical material in order to make it suitable for what Anthony Parel calls a "recognizably Indian" way of thinking about modern politics.[24] He was, as Bhikhu Parekh claims, "one of the first non-Western thinkers of the modern age to develop a political theory grounded in the unique experiences and articulated in terms of the indigenous philosophical vocabulary of his country."[25] Political thinking in modern colonial India relied heavily on the egalitarian, individualist or humanist traditions of the West, and even when opposing colonial rule, many nationalist-era Indian thinkers did so through the lens of liberal-humanist or Marxist assumptions. They displayed what Sudipta Kaviraj has called a "quintessentially heteronomous" mode of thought and a "peculiar insidious dependence" on Western categories.[26] Gandhi and a few of his nationalist-era contemporaries updated the relevance of classical, premodern or precolonial Indian resources for the problems of India's modern political experience.

As we have seen, Gandhi's unique reinterpretation of dharma recasts the concept in terms of a duty toward specifically nonviolent action in all realms of life. Taking the assumptions of Vedic metaphysics and epistemology, Gandhi constructed a theory of political action that not only drew on these ancient resources, it situated their relevance for contemporary problems of moral and political action. He revivified the classical concept of dharma and recast the dharma of nonviolence as a response to the problems of contemporary politics, and of a political world governed by specifically Hindu metaphysical assumptions. The attempts of Gandhi, Tagore and others to bring contemporary intellectual life to classical Indian thought had until recently been relegated to the heap of Indian intellectual history. While many scholars were content to conduct detailed exegetical analyses of Gandhi's thought, these endeavors remained mostly at the level of historical and analytical scholarship. In some cases, Gandhi's thought can be said to be existentially alive among communities of neo-Gandhians, in Gandhian ashrams such as Sevagram, or in political communities such as the neo-Gandhian alternative science and environmental movements. Meanwhile, Tagore's thought is clearly existentially alive at Santiniketan, the university he founded, where his spiritual humanism and internationalism are clearly evidenced in the pedagogical and intellectual structures of the institution. But little contemporary theorizing and public discourse *within* India *about* modern Indian politics had chosen to follow Gandhi or Tagore's lead by casting the problems of Indian political experience in terms that are distinctive to its own premodern, precolonial intellectual history. It relied instead on terminologies, frames and preoccupations of mostly Western discourses. Even postcolonial and subaltern discourses, which focused mainly on the problems and experiences of South Asian subalterns, tended to do so through theories emerging mainly from the West. Only recently have contemporary Indian intellectuals taken up the task of framing the problems of modern Indian political experience according to its own precolonial concepts and categories.[27]

The lesson from Gandhi's creativity is that we need not concern ourselves simply with recovering pieces of "unpolluted" theorizing prior to Western influence, or writing off the project of political theory as a product of Eurocentrism if no such evidence is available. Instead, we might think carefully, as Gandhi and Tagore have done, about how classical Indian texts asked certain questions and addressed certain problems. We may recognize the very different tools and preoccupations with which early Indian thought proceeded, and follow Gandhi and Tagore in calling upon classical resources in novel ways. We may bring premodern resources to *intellectual* life by excavating and reconstructing their relevance to problems of contemporary political experience.

QUESTIONS AND PREOCCUPATIONS: THE INDIAN CASE OF SECULARISM

This leads us to the third task for our scholar, namely that of investigating the emergence of new questions and preoccupations in non-Western scholarly communities. Such questions may present fertile ground for theoretical exploration stemming from the uniqueness of postcolonial or non-Western political experience. One example would be the Indian political experience of multireligious secularism combined with state intervention in religious practice.[28] Rather than conforming strictly to the Westcentric model of church-state separation, secularism in India was defined not as equal distance from or neutrality toward all religions, but "equal respect" for all religions. It often manifested as equal tolerance toward, intervention in— and sometimes embrace of—all the myriad forms of public and private expressions of faith. Meanwhile, the state's intervention in the majority religion (Hinduism) through the legal abolition of untouchability coexists uneasily with its reluctance to intervene in the gender-biased legal practices of Islam, a minority religion. This raises new questions about the role of the postcolonial democratic state with respect to social engineering through intervention in religious belief and practice. The theorization of these experiences in a deeply religious *and* multireligious society like India presents the potential to rethink Westcentric preoccupation with secularism understood only in terms of tolerance and religious neutrality.

Recent Indian theorizing about these questions, rather than rehearsing West-centered concerns about the integration of religious minorities into a liberal framework, focuses on the different possible understandings and applications of terms such as secularism or religious tolerance. They trace the evolution of these terms as they seeped into Indian political vocabulary and experience, or examine their conceptual equivalents in vernacular languages and in premodern historical experience. Recently a number of Indian political theorists have engaged in scholarly debates about the unique nature of the secularist project in India: whether a uniquely

Indian brand of secularism can coexist with state interventions in religious practice; whether modern Indian statist secularism, with its emphasis on religious interventions, is the most appropriate fulfillment of the secularist ideal; and what, if any, premodern existential modes of interfaith toleration might serve as alternatives. A turn toward the particularities of these debates will reveal that the challenge to Eurocentrism may arrive not necessarily from discourses that are "independent" of Eurocentric categories and premises, but from displacing the centrality of Eurocentric preoccupations with the generation of new ones that are unique to the political experience of a non-Western society. The generation of such questions often requires a synthetic mode of thinking that both consumes and subverts the *specifically modern* categories of Western thinking and its preoccupations. It centers political questions about secularism and tolerance on the resources available in precolonial political experience and vernacular discourses, while acknowledging and *working within* the inevitable presence of modern liberal democratic impulses as a result of the colonial experience. I turn now to the specifics of these debates.

For most Western theorists, secularism means the strict disestablishment of religion from state, or the strict exclusion of religion from all state affairs for the sake of promoting the religious liberty and equal citizenship of all individuals. Indian secularism, in contrast, not only departs from the Western model, Rajeev Bhargava argues that it provides an alternative model, a new way to reconceptualize the very notion of secularism itself. Indian secularism challenges the Westcentric conceptual and normative structure of secularism, particularly the notion that religious freedom and liberty requires the state to be detached from any official religious affiliation.[29] The distinctiveness of the Indian experience of secularism can best be understood, Bhargava claims, by placing it within its appropriate socio-cultural-historical context and drawing attention to four distinctive features of this context. First, the extraordinary religious diversity within India generates intractable value conflicts. Second, the primacy of religious practice over belief results in a valorization of community identifications and thus intercommunal conflict. Third, the preponderance of religiously sanctioned illiberal and inegalitarian practices such as the caste system and untouchability in Hinduism necessarily calls upon enormous institutional power for reform. Fourth, the doctrinally eclectic nature of India's majority religion—Hinduism—along with its lack of an organized central authoritative institution requires effective reform to come from an external source, namely the state, rather than from within.[30] Thus, the Indian Constitution, even as it implies the strict separation of state and religion, explicitly recognizes the rights of religious minorities, commits the state to give aid to educational institutions established and administered by religious communities, and permits religious education in institutions partially funded by the state.

More significantly, from its very inception, the Indian Constitution required the state to intervene in religious affairs by abolishing untouchability in Hinduism and by making the enforcement of any disability arising out of it an offence punishable by law. It thus legally enshrined a robust attack on Hinduism's caste system and enjoined the state to interfere in the affairs of one particular religion. Bhargava argues that rather than embodying a repudiation of secularism or a deviation from it, the Indian case makes the argument for a reconceiving of the very notion of secularism itself as contextually variable. This notion of secularism requires particularistic, contextual moral reasoning and an accommodation of multiple, often conflicting values internal to secularism.[31] Rather than requiring the state to maintain a strict distance and equal neutrality from all religions, Bhargava argues that the Indian case teaches us that secularism can be redefined as a "principled" distance. In contrast to doctrines of strict separation and mutual exclusion, "principled" distance refers to a doctrine through which the state can reserve the right to intervene in and engage with specific religions and religious practices, depending on social and historical context, and on the promotion of certain values constitutive of secularism (however these are defined). In the promotion of values constitutive of secularism (such as equality and freedom of belief) some religions, relative to others, may require more interference from the state. If equality is to be protected, for instance, it may be required of the state that it interferes in caste-ridden Hinduism much more than, say Islam or Christianity. The state can neither strictly exclude considerations emanating from religion nor keep strict neutrality with respect to religion. It cannot antecedently decide that it will always refrain from interfering in religions or that it will interfere in each equally. It may not relate to every religion in society in exactly the same way, or intervene in each religion to the same degree or in the same manner. Indeed, such an argument assumes that the values constitutive of secularism will be plural and often conflict with one another. Thus, Indian secularism must of necessity be a multivalued doctrine, dictating in advance no unique outcome favorable to the protection of any one value.

Meanwhile, theorists such as Ashis Nandy allege that the statist model of secularism in India is itself responsible for much interreligious strife, because of its attempt to exorcize religion from public life. Secularism, Nandy claims, is linked to an unnecessary emphasis on modernization and rationality, to a desacralization and erasure of religion from public life, to a neglect of religious community, and to a misplaced valorizing of modern statist intervention. Rather than undermining primordial religious loyalties and consigning them to the realm of the private, Nandy recommends drawing on traditional, precolonial modes of interreligious coexistence for maintaining a vibrant political culture in a multireligious polity. The heavily statist and interventionist model of Indian secularism—motivated by liberal assumptions such as rationalism, desacralization and scientific progress—is responsible for exacerbating interreligious conflict in India. It undermines primordial loyalties and premodern commitments in the effort to preserve values that are consonant with liberalism. Thus, religious violence in contemporary India is a result and a symptom of modernization, for it has something to do with the urban-industrial vision of life and with the political processes that these visions let loose. In contrast, Nandy claims that the hope for a tolerant and egalitarian society can only come from *within* traditional religious models, not *despite* them, and not through statist intervention in them.[32]

Rather than valuing secularism as a principle or a policy goal, Nandy suggests that we turn toward alternative models of religiously motivated toleration and mutual respect. Indian theorists and policymakers should value the *outcomes* of toleration, interfaith respect and dialogue, excavating the presecular and premodern origins of such tolerance, and recentering the nation's core commitments on the practices of tolerance emerging from within various faiths. "Traditional ways of life have, over centuries, developed internal principles of tolerance," Nandy reminds us, and these principles must play a part in contemporary Indian politics.[33] A return to the oft-cited edicts of the Buddhist Emperor Asoka, he emphasizes, must recognize that his exhortations to interfaith cooperation and toleration came from *within* Buddhist beliefs, not from a commitment to secularism understood as state neutrality from religion. Similarly so for the deep interfaith tolerance promoted by the Mughal emperor Akbar, which came from his commitment to Islam and a concomitant reading of Islamic doctrine and practice. Of course, the ultimate exemplar of such religiously motivated tolerance, in Nandy's view, is Gandhi, whose idea of religious tolerance came from his antisecularism and his unconditional rejection of modernity. Recasting orthodoxy within Hinduism as precisely the *Vedic* doctrine of pluralism of metaphysical belief, Gandhi cast himself as a premodern pluralist whose metaphysical pluralism was the result of his *sanatana* or orthodox Hinduism.

Nor should the possibilities for interfaith tolerance emerge solely from the doctrines of mainstream religious beliefs: rather they can emerge from the everyday practices and "little traditions" of local community life with its premodern or primordial modes of being. Contrary to modern beliefs, such premodern beliefs are multilayered and open-ended rather than inflexible, retrograde or parochial. Left alone, Nandy argues, traditional community structures have more effective civilizational resources than the institutions of the modern state to resolve disputes and tolerate differences. Nandy does not explore at length how a comprehensive political-theoretic model of interfaith respect and tolerance might be crafted from India's premodern religious resources. But he leaves the discussion rich with possibilities for imaginative excavation and recentering of theoretical priorities. Turning to non-statist precolonial practical and existential modes of interfaith tolerance, Nandy suggests, would have more theoretical force as a model for a uniquely multireligious society like India, than would existing modes of secular rationalist liberal discourse.

Like Nandy, Partha Chatterjee critiques the immediate post-independence imperative toward modernity, secularization and rationalization, holding it responsible for the impasse over minority religious rights and conflicts that has resulted in India. However, in a solution that differs from both Nandy's and Bhargava's, Chatterjee calls for a politics that neither seeks a wholesale rejection of the secularist-modernist project, nor seeks to redefine secularism entirely for Indian purposes. Like Bhargava, Chatterjee calls for an explicit recognition of secularism as a modern Western discourse transplanted in an Indian context, thus giving rise to specific difficulties of implementation. Yet, Chatterjee also calls for a reconfiguring of the problem of secularism in India on new conceptual grounds that acknowledge its modern genesis. He calls for an alternative discourse beyond the traditional liberal-democratic-secular-modernist one, recognizing its theoretical poverty for problems specific to the Indian context and rejecting simplistic dichotomies such as Western/non-Western and modern/premodern.[34] And, unlike either Bhargava or Nandy, Chatterjee's solution seeks neither to disavow nor embrace the Indian state's right to intervene in religion. Instead, Chatterjee calls for a recognition of the historically given reality of the intricate involvement of the Indian state in the affairs of religious institutions, and he proposes a criterion by which state involvement in the domain of religion can be justified as legitimate and fair. This criterion would require that those citizens who are members of minority religious groups and who demand toleration and noninterference from the state for the group's beliefs, should also demand that their group publicly seek and obtain from its members consent for its practices insofar as those practices have regulatory power over the lives of members. They should thus both resist the normalizing attempt of the modernist state to define, classify and fix the identity of minorities on their behalf, but also demand that the regulative powers *within* the religious community be established on a more internally representative basis. The validity of the practices of the religious group can be discussed and judged only in its own forums, but they must satisfy the same criteria of publicity and representativeness that members of the group demand of all public institutions. Nonintervention in the affairs of a religious community, Chatterjee suggests, should be predicated on internal representativeness and democratic structures *within* religious groups and their institutions, and the hegemonizing and homogenizing power of the modernist state can be resisted by the devolution of authority to religious communities, if those communities can demonstrate democracy and representativeness internally.

Thus, Bhargava defends the secularist ideal in principle, calling for its revision in the Indian context which has a history of systematic statist intervention in religion for the preservation of certain values. Nandy and others claim that the secularist liberal ideal must be rejected altogether in favor of precolonial, noninterventionist dialogical models of coexistence. Chatterjee, meanwhile, seeks a theoretical relocation of the terms of discourse on conceptual ground that is specifically Indian *and* modern, both recognizing the genealogical force of modernist-secular discourse in shaping the immediate post-independence imperatives of the Indian state, yet seeking to recenter the discussion outside and beyond the territory of modernist-secular dilemmas.

More broadly, however, the unique Indian experience of religious pluralism raises questions about the legal-constitutional structures of postcolonial nations grappling with the burdens of righting the wrongs of deeply inegalitarian practices within various religious communities. Historically, British rule in India had tried to remain neutral on disputes over religion. Thus, while it enacted uniform codes of civil and criminal law, personal law (involving matters such as marriage, property and inheritance) continued to be governed by the respective religious laws as recognized and interpreted by the courts. At the establishment of the independent Indian nation, this policy of ostensible legal noninterference in religious law was continued by the framers of the Indian Constitution, who decided to permit religious systems of "personal law" to continue governing matters such as marriage, property and inheritance, while setting forth a uniform system of civil and criminal law for all citizens.

Simultaneously, the Indian Constitution codified sweeping reforms of Hindu religious practice, outlawing untouchability in the caste system and thus enshrining in the Constitution the state's legitimate right to intervene in the personal legal code of the majority religion. Thus, in the arena of personal law, Muslims could be governed by *sharia* law untouched and unreformed by the Indian state, as could other minorities by their respective legal codes. This dual legal system was seen as a way for the Indian state to protect the religious and cultural identity of its minorities. In contemporary Indian politics however, debates about the lack of a uniform legal code of personal law for all Indians irrespective of religion (known as the Uniform Civil Code) have taken on even further urgency. In 1978, the Indian Supreme Court ruled in favor of a Muslim woman named Shah Bano who applied for economic restitution under civil law following her divorce. The court granted Shah Bano monthly alimony and recommended that the state do away with the deeply gender-biased Muslim personal legal code. The reigning government, in response to an outcry from Muslim religious authorities, later overturned the Supreme Court's decision in 1986. It introduced a law explicitly stating that the maintenance of divorced women would be a matter strictly internal to and governed by the sharia norms of the Islamic community. The Indian state's reluctance to interfere in the affairs of the minority Islamic community—even though intervention in Hindu religious practice is enshrined in the constitution—has subsequently been decried from all sides as a measure of the state's deeply inegalitarian intervention in religious communities' affairs. Hinduism, the Hindu right-wing cries, is singled out for social reform through state intervention, while minorities are left free to follow their own religion's legal codes in matters of personal law, no matter how retrograde, inegalitarian and contrary to the principles enshrined in the Indian Constitution.[35] Feminists, meanwhile, decried the valorization of minority religious freedom over the imperative to correct deep gender-based imbalances in religious laws.[36] Secular liberals insist that a Uniform Civil Code superseding and nullifying the various systems of personal law be created and applied, thereby adhering to the principle that equal citizens in a democracy be treated equally by being governed by the same legal code in all legal matters, regardless of religious belief.[37]

I mention these debates not in order to provide any comprehensive analysis of them. Nor do I suggest that the positions described here are anywhere near complete in their representation of the complexity of these issues. My treatment of these matters is quite preliminary, and it is a measure of the steadily increasing richness of India's scholarly discourses that a wide array of voices have provided commentary on these matters.[38] I make reference to these debates because they offer a novel set of open-ended questions and preoccupations that depart from the well-rehearsed concerns of Western political thought. These debates on the precise relationship of the state to religious communities in India, and indeed of religious communities to one another, emerge from experiences that are unique among multireligious democracies. They imply a recentering not only of the nation's political priorities, but also an attendant recentering of theoretical preoccupations on an entirely different set of questions than those that have long preoccupied scholars in the West. In most Western democracies struggling with questions of identity politics and multiculturalism, theoretical preoccupations center on the presumed necessity of accommodating often illiberal beliefs of religious and/or immigrant minorities in the presumed modern liberal framework of tolerance. Debates center around the integration of religious communities into this existing framework, and modes of accommodation that allow for communitarian affiliations to coexist within the basic framework of the modern liberal secular state.[39] Questions are asked about how the liberal state may tolerate the intolerant, what the liberal state's obligations are to its individualist commitments as well as its to its more communitarian citizens, and how, if at all, these conflicting commitments may be reconciled.

The debates emerging from India's political experience suggest not necessarily new answers to old questions, but a new set of questions with which to grapple. They relate not to the narrow Westcentric focus on the accommodation or integration of cultural or religious minorities within an overall liberal democratic framework that values individual liberty, but rather to a different set of questions pertaining to a different kind of political experience. How best can a deeply multireligious polity—constituted from communities of extraordinarily strong religious affiliations that most often trump individualist self-identifications—best manage its religious diversity? Should its approach be state-centric, society-centric, or religion-centric? Can such a polity affirm the value of secularism, and if so, how? Or must it either reject secularism in favor of an ethic of tolerance, or redefine secularism entirely, in order to cope with the unique contextual factors that define its situation? Must it negate entirely secularism as an overall political and theoretical goal? And if so, should it rely instead on existential, practical and socioreligious models of religious pluralism and interfaith coexistence, rather than theoretical ones? Is the commitment to tolerance best achieved outside the framework of modern liberal secularism, and if so, how?

Meanwhile, debates over the establishment of a uniform civil code provide a new center of theoretical questioning concerning whether and how the postcolonial state might bear the burden of corrective social reform using its legal structures and resources. Does the imperative to intervene in one highly inegalitarian religious practice—namely, untouchability in Hinduism—imply a commitment to egalitarian individualism and a concomitant need to intervene in other minority religions in order to correct gender-based imbalances? Are statist legal measures such as a uniform civil legal code appropriate or effective, given the extent to which the Indian state seems to be committed not specifically to religious neutrality (as most Western liberal democracies are), but to the active promotion and flourishing of religious identity? To what extent can such a postcolonial state balance its commitment to equality with its commitment to the flourishing of religious diversity?

Notice, then, that the questions of secularism and affirmative action themselves are only made possible only through colonial history and contact with modern liberalism. The discourses I describe need not be considered strictly indigenous or autonomous, for they clearly center to some extent on questions defined by Western categories of secularism and religious liberty. Nor does the uniqueness of non-Western political experience elaborated here necessarily entail a rejection of modernity, for Indian theorists are deeply divided on the question of which premodern modes of religious accommodation and dialogue—if any—provide relevant resources for contemporary theorizing in India. Moreover, many of the major voices in these debates are trained in Westcentric modes of theorizing, if not literally educated in the West. They are thus conversant with—and inclined to make use of—the language of political-theoretic discourse familiar in the West. The lesson here is that in many postcolonial nations, contemporary discourses about politics may continue to be dominated by Western linguistic and conceptual apparatuses. They are neither entirely free of modern Western presumptions (precisely because the political experiences of these nations have been inextricably intertwined with modern impulses), nor entirely rooted in their own premodern civilizational resources. But this need not be problematic, for the narrow concentration on assessing which local discourses are permeated (or not) by Eurocentric assumptions dilutes the focus of our scholar's energies. Rather, what matters here is the precise shape that these questions have taken in contemporary Indian debates.

The debates described here teach us that *even* when the parameters of a discourse are defined by Western conceptual frameworks, the particularity of non-Western political debates can throw up preoccupations that are unique to each nation's experience. They can sidestep the primary concerns of Westcentric theorizing and in some cases, reconceive what counts as an important political question. Our scholar can look beyond what seems like the pervasive intervention of Westcentrism, excavating underneath it the imaginative possibility of a uniquely Indian reframing of questions about religious coexistence and toleration. These debates can be read as sites for potential theoretical recentering because they represent the nascent, inventive reconstruction of political possibilities. This unearthing of possibilities can then focus on modes of political practice that either lie dormant in the premodern, presecular and prerational resources of a tradition (as Nandy might suggest); or seek a fusion of premodern modes of communal authority with modern democratic practice (as Chatterjee suggests); or redefine entirely the conceptual, normative and practical dimensions of a modern idea like secularism in response to the Indian context (as Bhargava suggests). In immersing oneself in the preoccupations emerging from these debates, our scholar learns that the destabilizing of Eurocentric presumptions can occur by attending to the novelty of critical interrogations that emerge from within a political experience unique to a particular postcolonial history, even when this experience seems linked to modern Western imperatives and impulses.

CONCLUSION: RESOURCES FOR DESTABILIZING EUROCENTRISM IN A COSMOPOLITAN POLITICAL THOUGHT

In what sense might the Indian case be considered a resource for the cosmopolitan political theorist grappling with the imperative to dislocate Eurocentrism through an immersion in otherness, even while acknowledging its pervasiveness? Addressing the three questions described earlier constitutes the prerequisite for historically excluded "others" to discipline our own inquiries, for the possibility of "fundamental transformations in knowledge-production"[40] and replacement rather than simply dislocation of the terms of theoretical discourse. The terms of political inquiry emerging from other traditions can be viewed as more than "additional voices" designed merely to shed light on the variety of available modes of inquiry. Instead, they can be viewed as viable disciplinary alternatives offering compelling frameworks to refigure existing Western disciplinary practices and displace the terms of existing Westcentric debates altogether.[41] The processes described here can eventually allow our scholar to generate new questions and new modes of framing political inquiry, which draw upon the resources, concerns and preoccupations of another tradition. In this way, Western political inquiry can constitute the target of an intellectual intervention from the perspective of its other. Such an intervention not only reveals the self-referentiality and provinciality of its frameworks, but also provides new approaches and frameworks. The potential outcomes of such recentering are radically subversive and transgressive, for they point to the possibility of supplanting (rather than merely supplementing) dominant streams of political-theoretic discourse.[42]

The Indian case also demonstrates that such questions, in order to destabilize or to reframe, need not emerge from the "pure" domain of one tradition over another. Reframing Eurocentric political inquiry through the interventions of non-Western traditions does not necessarily—and perhaps cannot—mean generating theoretical frameworks that are isolated from or independent of Western influences. Nor can it mean disseminating modes of inquiry that are cleansed, sanitized or decontaminated from Western ones. Rather, it requires a keen eye for the destabilizing possibilities inherent *within* the categories and frameworks already influenced by Eurocentric presumptions, a sensitivity to material that is marginalized or ignored as a theoretical possibility. But the recovery and excavation of such possibilities does not seek to leave "pristine" or "untransformed" the non-Western concepts and ideas encountered. The recovery attempt is itself implicated in a transformative process that transgresses notions of cultural purity. The very project of turning to these resources *from* a contemporary perspective *for* the purpose of contemporary debates has already implicated them in a transformative dialogue that causes them to lose their "pristine" nature.[43] The move toward seeking replacements for Westcentric modes of inquiry in otherness is transgressive and transformative, not only for the Westcentric disciplinary home, but especially for those others who would constitute its challengers and competitors.

Reconceiving the dilemma of Eurocentrism in this way reminds us that destabilizing Western knowledge production also involves grappling with the complexities of multiple positionalities at different times and in different ways. A cosmopolitan political thought stands in a complicated and fruitful relationship to the scholar's location at the intersection of disciplinary traditions and her role as both participant and commentator in multiple traditions. No doubt the questions and frames of inquiry that destabilize Westcentric presumptions must emerge from our scholar's internal positionality in the categories, terminologies, and preoccupations of another tradition. But to suggest that these moments of self-dislocation cannot occur except through disavowing one's "insider" status in the West is to suggest that one can only be an insider to one tradition at a time. It suggests the impossibility of multiple positionalities, of highly self-critical and self-reflexive engagements with multiple traditions, and of the ability to straddle boundaries. It is not simply that becoming an insider in another tradition allows us to bring the insights of that tradition to bear on ours. Rather, it can give us the wherewithal to both inform and reform our own tradition beyond recognition, to displace the very provinciality of its categories and to subvert its preoccupations from the vantage point of another intellectual world.

Once located at this positionality, we do not speak as Westerners "bringing back" a few select imports; rather, we can speak as insiders to another tradition, and are able to look back at the Western one with a combination of our own insider status in both—indeed perhaps in multiple—traditions. Moving beyond the continual indulging of Westcentric themes and concerns requires seeing the vantage points of "insider" and "outsider" not as clearly-demarcated, but as mutually implicated and interconstitutive. The destabilizing questions asked, the new preoccupations put forth, the reframing of political inquiry itself, emerge not because we bring back fresh insights, like travelers who want to bring home exotic foods and spices to plant, use and consume. Instead, they occur from the simultaneous capacity for multiple insider perspectives. One is neither "trapped" in the methods and practices of the Eurocentric home, nor is one forced to choose between such rigid entrapment and its other, equally rigid, alternative: to remain immersed in another tradition of inquiry, with no possibility of bringing its dislocating force to bear on the Eurocentric home.

For this reason, the approach to cosmopolitanism I advocate does not follow the all-inclusive "multiculturalist" model that includes a series of voices along with the Western canon, thereby inoculating Western knowledge from the charge of parochialism. Nor does it seek to ignore the subjectivity and agency of foreign others by turning their discourses into objects of analysis, "bringing" their exotic insights back to be dissected and analyzed on home turf. Rather, it seeks to change how political theorists trained and located in the Westcentric disciplinary home can formulate their engagement with non-Western categories. It seeks to show that by dislocating and relocating the West-centered self in numerous ways an important shift can occur in challenging Eurocentric modes of knowledge. I do not claim that the processes involved are themselves free of the very same pitfalls that appear in Eurocentric analyses and approaches. Nor do I claim that they can provide a complete or pure alternative to other Eurocentric models. Rather, I show that the vantage point of immersion provides no easily identifiable loci of non-Eurocentric thinking. Our scholar may find that her own Westcentric presumptions are perfectly familiar on other turfs, and that her inhabiting of its insider perspective does not necessarily require a simple disavowal of such presumptions. It requires instead a serious understanding of the ways in which such Westcentric presumptions are operational within the non-Western society she is immersed in, as well as an ability to interrogate, excavate and revivify intellectual resources in that tradition. Finally, it requires an ability to place oneself at the intersection of civilizational concerns, and bring these resources to bear in novel and creative ways that displace the centrality of Western experience. The task of a cosmopolitan scholar of political thought therefore is the necessary swing of the pendulum between the polarities of self-dislocation into otherness and relocation into one's disciplinary home.

CONCLUSION: TOWARD A POST-EUROCENTRIC

PARADIGM IN A COSMOPOLITAN POLITICAL THOUGHT

COSMOPOLITANISM: A POST-EUROCENTRIC
PARADIGM OF COEVAL ENGAGEMENT

WHAT "POST-EUROCENTRIC" POSSIBILITIES for political inquiry are generated by the cosmopolitan vision suggested in the previous chapters? In chapter 5, I elaborated on the following critical view often put forth by proponents of area studies methodology: any disciplinary intervention that targets Western audiences, disciplines and concerns is itself an indication of Eurocentric preoccupation, especially if it conducts its investigations in Western languages and publishes in English for the Western academy. The project of a cosmopolitan political thought continues to be Eurocentric if its investigations are conducted for Western scholars' edification, and indeed, even within the auspices of the discipline we call political theory. On such a view, engaging with otherness only becomes interesting as an instrument for the Eurocentric world's self-reflexive learning. Future political inquiry, it is suggested, should therefore remain centered on the disciplinary worlds of the "others." It should be disciplined by their preoccupations and methods of inquiry rather than seeking to reenter Westcentric debates.

But this position, despite its attentiveness to the predominance of Eurocentric motives, ends up reinforcing the Enlightenment's most dichotomous understanding of self-other relations. Self-hood is, of course, as notoriously slippery a concept as there is, and to speak about the location of selves is almost inevitably to call upon conceptions of self-hood that are specific to a particular culture. This critique, however, seems to invoke a binary construction of the self, in which it is assumed that "we" and "they" must be utterly separate categories. It assumes that such categories are defined by a radical unfamiliarity in which violence is done when "we" try to bring "their" knowledge back into our world. Moreover, this binary construction of self-hood suggests that self, too, must be tied strongly to one particular kind of location and attached to one set of cultural or disciplinary presumptions. It precludes the possibility of multiply located selves and the possibility of a subjectivity that can be refracted through the lens of these multiple locations and sets of presumptions.

A cosmopolitan political thought seeks to interrogate and eventually move beyond the binary categories that lie at the heart of such critiques. It holds to a more coeval idea of the relationship between multiple selves and multiple others, variously located in multiple relations with one another, and thus to a more fluid set of possibilities for political inquiry. In its dislocations and relocations, the self is neither entirely attached solely to one tradition, nor entirely an outsider to any. It views the world neither from a "God's eye-perspective," nor from the perspective of deep immersion in any one tradition. Subjectivity is thus not only multiplied, it is refracted and diffused.

Such an understanding of the self and its possibilities for location, rather than reinforcing the schisms implicit in the structure of Enlightenment understandings of self-hood, ruptures these understandings. It also underscores an important fact that is emphasized by many subaltern and postcolonial theorists, but often overlooked by political theorists: namely, that the "self/other" relations that underlie encounters of civilizational alterity are rarely simple or monolithically constructed. The West-centered "self" is neither singularly understood nor located entirely "inside" the presumptions of one particular tradition. It often already has a relationship to the very thing it seeks to investigate. Navigating its encounter with civilizational alterity requires, at different times, separation from and immersion in otherness. The motivations of complete self-understanding and complete other-understanding are frequently intertwined, and it is no easy task to separate these, or to emphasize one motivation to the exclusion of the other.

A reification of "otherness" as always radically separate and distinct from "us" leaves no room to awaken and give voice to what Homi Bhabha calls the multiple unrecognized othernesses within.[1] A cosmopolitan political theory can displace Eurocentric hegemonies and privileges, without falling prey to a discourse that sees immersion in radical otherness and self-reflection as necessarily mutually exclusive. It need not subscribe to the dichotomous notion of Westcentric "selves" and radically alien "others." In this way, the authority of the Eurocentric center is destabilized through an ongoing decentering of the Enlightenment's specific ways of constructing self-hood. It is destabilized through a series of fluid and ever shifting locations of a "self," that places itself in a multiplicity of relationships to various traditions.

Phenomenologists and other continental thinkers have of course resisted the specificities of Enlightenment "selves" that continue to predominate in Western political thought. Following their lead, so too have feminist theorists,[2] postmodernists, and poststructuralists, speaking of the "decentered" subject for whom there is no essence other than what is constructed discursively or socially.[3] Political theorists interested in studies of civilizational alterity, however, have all too easily capitulated to the predominance of Enlightenment understandings of self-hood and subjectivity, even when they are motivated by the legitimate desire to counter Westcentric disciplinary practices. This is especially true if they see permanent immersion in radical otherness as the only possible means of displacing Westcentric predominance.

But another kind of objector might ask: does the continued focus on the Eurocentrism of the disciplinary "home" reinscribe the hegemony of the center? The postcolonial scholar Bart Moore-Gilbert reminds us that the consistent emphasis on destabilizing the dominant suggests that "[postcolonial] resistance depends upon the continuing authority of the dominant for its operation and consequently risks reconstituting that dominant."[4] As Derrida cautions, oppositional or confrontational modes of decentering the center can simultaneously recenter it.[5] How does a cosmopolitan political thought avoid the charge of a reverse essentializing, in which the continuing authority of the "center" could be reinforced by "peripheral" postcolonial, minoritarian formations defining themselves solely in resistance to the center? What future paradigms of cultural formation and exchange among non-Eurocentric modes of thought can be envisioned as alternatives to this reconstitution of Eurocentrism's dominance?

A cosmopolitan understanding of political theory may require not simply resistance to the hegemony of Eurocentrism, but rather a blueprint of post-Eurocentric paradigms of exchange. A cosmopolitan political thought requires modes of interchange for a theoretical world where the center is no longer the center, once Eurocentrism has been displaced. Postcolonial formations of various kinds—cultural, gender, class, religious, ethnic and so on—rather than competing with one another or uniting in opposing the center, can be coeval partners, along with Western thought, in such exchange. A post-Eurocentric cosmopolitan political thought will eventually involve webs of plural and coeval engagement of, say, Confucian with Vedic, Buddhist with African, or Japanese with Latin American thinkers, texts and themes. The engagement between a thinker from the Indian *dalit* tradition and one from the Japanese Shinto Buddhist tradition will remain as relevant to the task of political theorizing as is the engagement between Gandhian nonviolence and Western liberalism. Just as Indian modes of secularism become possible resources for European and/or American politics, Islamic models of feminist autonomy and agency could turn into a resource for gender issues among East Asian feminists. Conceptual aspects of African tribal models of leadership and collective organization could be woven into models for the political problems of other postcolonial societies, and so on. But such a paradigm of post-Eurocentric exchange between and among formerly "postcolonial" or "minoritarian" discourses requires, crucially, that the center no longer be the center. The ongoing destabilization of the dominant is a precursor for such post-Eurocentric paradigms.

The continued emphasis within postcolonial thought on which formations can challenge the hegemony of the center is illuminating, because it suggests that the destabilizing of the center is a gradually strengthening, but far from complete, project.[6] This is nowhere more true than in political theory. While research by comparative political theorists focusing on non-Western thinkers and themes may be proliferating, the continued predominance of EuroAmerican thought is nowhere close to collapse. Attentiveness to non-Western thought is still considered to be a marginal and optional field of interest, while training in the substantive and methodological canons of EuroAmerican political inquiry is thought to be crucial for anyone seeking to enter the discipline. Meanwhile, political science departments that offer (not to mention *require*) courses in non-Western thought are as yet in a small minority. The destabilization of the center, far from being close to completion, has barely begun in full swing. Until the dominant center is destabilized, it will likely continue to intervene in attempts to build coeval webs of engagement. The interchange of, say, Vedic metaphysics with Confucian political thought, may continue to be refracted through the prism of Eurocentric paradigms and presumptions, until the center has been sufficiently destabilized, such that it too is able to take its place in the web of coeval voices and modes of thought.

It may be wise at this point to issue a cautionary note of realism, in the light of recent commentary on the state of the discipline. Timothy Kaufman-Osborn has suggested that even as political theory is characterized by an increasingly productive fragmentation that underscores its internal plurality, the hegemony of liberalism is paradoxically strong enough to domesticate and subsume all those who stray. The subfield has long survived through a *modus vivendi* in which other approaches can at best nibble at the margins of, and at worst, be domesticated by the hegemony of liberalism.[7] Meanwhile, political theorists claim a measure of autonomy and distance from "real world" politics, which ostensibly allows them to serve as its critical and dispassionate moral voice. Yet, thanks to professionalization, there is also a "symbiotic enmeshment" of the discipline and of the contemporary university "within a politicized economy governed chiefly in accordance with the norms of neoliberalism."[8]

On this view, the parochialism of Westcentric political theory is more than simply a result of its substantive focus on certain kinds of texts and its particular methodological commitments. In fact, it is a result of the very terms of disciplinary organization that have been entrenched as a result of historical intradisciplinary turf battles. Under perceived threat from behavioralism and in order to retain its co-equal status with other subfields, political theorists have acquiesced to the reigning formation of subfields—American, IR, Comparative and Theory. As a relic of the Cold War, this disciplinary formation institutionalized the configuration of forces that accompanied the rise of post–World War II nationalism and the ascendancy of the American nation-state, recapitulating the core presuppositions informing American Cold War hegemony. It thus "render[s] unrecognizable or not entirely real political issues that do not fall readily onto the terrain demarcated by these subfields . . . scholarship informed by this structure may remain unwittingly invested in perpetuation of the political world out of which that structure first emerged and in which its categories once proved intelligible."[9] Thus, political theorists are complicitous in preserving a certain structure of the discipline, which allows their own marginal existence to be tolerated. Moreover they are implicated in an unwritten accord that espouses pluralist tolerance while retaining the centrality of liberal norms, institutions and preoccupations. That is, they may write and research all they want about critical race theory, Derrida, or, for that matter, Confucian metaphysics. But in the end the norms that govern their professional—and thus intellectual—lives are the same liberal ones that underwrite the ascendancy of American liberal democracy.

If we take seriously this picture, then we must think carefully about what it means that a cosmopolitan political thought endeavors to be post-Eurocentric. If liberalism's hegemony is so thorough that the terms of entry into the subfield are to stay nibbling at its margins while not upsetting the unspoken consensus that keeps the myth of pluralist tolerance in place, then perhaps the project of disrupting Eurocentric disciplinary presuppositions is far too ambitious. And perhaps it is the very enmeshment in disciplinary structures—universities, journals, associations, aspirations to tenure—which are funded by the neoliberal global order that would make even more remote the possibility of genuine dislocation of Westcentric presumptions.[10]

Instead, why not give real consideration to the possibility of rejecting the Westcentric disciplinary initiative altogether?[11] To this end, we may reexamine the contention that "recentering" the study of political theory on the disciplinary practices of traditions outside the West—that is, their training, institutional incentives, expectations and resources—while orienting one's work to the audiences in these traditions, is the way to controvert foundational propositions about knowledge. It allows us to "[replace] the academic conventions and commitments that originally marked the identity of political theory."[12] Remaining immersed in regional discourses of indigenous intellectual production, much as area studies scholars remain immersed in the geographical regions they study, will offer means of knowledge production that "radically supplant (rather than merely supplement) dominant streams of political-theoretic discourse."[13] This may even imply rejecting political theory as a disciplinary initiative in favor of other ways to organize knowledge.[14]

But how exactly would these radical possibilities for (re)organization of scholarship controvert rather than simply nibble at the margins of Western political theory's—and specifically liberalism's—dominance? This begs the question of whether such initiatives would be any more immune from the reach of the neoliberal global order (or from the unspoken agreements that hold together Western political thought's dominant liberal consensus) simply because they are not located in the West. As I demonstrated in chapter 5, many non-Western disciplinary formations are thoroughly permeated by the presumptions and modes of knowledge production characterized by Westcentric inquiry. Scholarly institutions in non-Western academic worlds may not be as beholden to the structure of the neoliberal global economy, and may thus retain a measure of independence from and critical perspective on political theory's Westcentric assumptions. But one has to ask whether remaining immersed solely in such critical discourses without bringing them into the very worlds of disciplinary organization being critically analyzed has much meaning for the project of destabilization.

The goal of controverting foundational propositions about knowledge suggests that there needs to be an object *toward* which such controverting discourse is directed. To seek to controvert, challenge or replace hegemonic assumptions is to require *uptake* from the very object of one's challenge. It seems unclear what sort of supplanting can occur as long as members of Westcentric disciplinary formations remain sheltered from having to confront those challenges directly, on their own home turf. In such cases, supplanting or controverting assumptions may remain simply an internal conversation among non-Western "others" who share these assumptions—and presumably, have done so for many years.

Scholars aiming toward a cosmopolitan political thought need not remain content to slide peacefully into the pluralistic yet liberally dominated regime of tolerance currently underlining political theory's *modus vivendi*. I suggest instead that they take on a deliberately confrontational and challenging—perhaps even offensive, to use Andrew Rehfeld's terminology[15]—posture toward the Westcentric disciplinary turf. Such a posture explicitly seeks to displace its presumptions, rather than acquiesce to the existing regime and to the presumptions of liberalism's centrality to the project of political theory.[16] Earlier attempts by comparative political theorists have often suffered from precisely this timidity, imagining that the inclusion of non-Western voices into a "niche" of political theory is a sufficient challenge. Indeed, such destabilization requires that scholars from the center are *themselves* actively engaged in the project of destabilizing EuroAmerican propositions about knowledge. It is fitting then, that the cosmopolitan political thought described here has focused on displacing the subjectivities and positionalities of the West-centered scholar. Without such active participation by West-centered scholars, even the attempted cultivation of individual non-Western scholars and scholarly traditions into West-centric discourse would not have much impact. Non-Western scholars and subjects can be politely applauded when they give talks in the West and sent back home to their enclaves. Awareness of the source of Western political theory's parochialism, along with a willingness to transgress its unwritten rules and displace reigning hegemony, is a prerequisite for a post-Eurocentric paradigm of coeval engagement.

POLITICAL THEORY'S "AUTONOMY" FROM POLITICAL PRACTICE

The vision of cosmopolitan theorizing I have put forth here also requires reflection on the relationship between theorizing on the one hand and "real world" political practices and experience on the other. Another way of reflecting on the question is to ask what the relationship is between empirical and theoretical (or "normative") political science, namely the study of the world of actually occurring politics and the study of how things ought to be. On the one hand, as we have seen, political theorists seem to pride themselves on remaining at a sufficient distance from the world of actual political practice, so as to sharpen their critical abilities. Some descriptions of political theory suggest that it is precisely this kind of distance from the exigencies of the "real world" that provides political theory with the capacity for critique. Ben Barber tells us that the real strength of political theorists is that "the prudent among them recognize that nobody has elected them to do anything and that their work demands a certain autonomy from practical politics on which their credibility . . . depends."[17] Ian Shapiro calls it the task of political theory to "[serve] as roving ombudsmen for the truth and the right by stepping back from political science as practiced to see what is wrong with what is currently being done and say something about how it might be improved."[18]

Yet we have also seen that this critical ability is hardly wholly innocent; to suggest that political theorists have secured sufficient distance from the discipline to identify and rectify its wrong turns is, Kaufman-Osborn argues, another version of what Donna Haraway calls the "god trick." Someone whose position is in fact situated and local claims to be nowhere in particular and, for that reason, able to see everywhere (and innocently so).[19] And, even as critiques of positivism have demonstrated the linkages between description, explanation and evaluation, many political theorists continue to represent their own work as deeply "normative" and anti-empirical. They cast their task in terms of a dichotomous view of the normative versus the empirical, de-emphasizing the extent to which their theoretical work is often driven by and implicated with real world politics. Kaufman-Osborn calls for this binary contrast of "normative" with "empirical" to be dropped, given that it is a relic of the "behavioralist war," which no longer has much relevance for political theory.[20] Barber also reminds us that "students of politics . . . must learn how to stand close enough to comprehend what is happening—pure objectivity is neither desirable nor even an option; but not so close as to be consumed by the flames."[21] Meanwhile, Andrew Rehfeld suggests that, if anything, there is too *much* autonomy of political theory from empirical politics: except for some notable exceptions, empiricists and theorists use each other's findings in only the most superficial of ways. There seems to be no real shared purpose as yet between theorists and empirical scholars, he claims; simply a "live-and-let-live-attitude."[22] These recent analyses suggest that political theorists should emphasize, rather than deny, the extent to which their work is embedded in the historical or material realities within which it is conceived and through which it casts its light. They suggest that it is time for political theory to de-emphasize its autonomy from, and recognize more self-consciously its linkages with, the empirical world of political experience.[23]

But many proponents of such a view often seem to forget that the "world" of political experience and practice usually meant in such discourses is the Western liberal democratic world. Although it is a platitude to say the "real world" of political experience is highly variegated and variously constituted, this realization does not easily translate into how theorists use political experience—if at all—as a guide to their theorizing. The "real world experience" they call upon for inspiration in choosing questions and problems is often limited to the common liberal democratic ones. Rarely have Western political theorists taken inspiration from the political practice and experience outside the West. Usually, accounts of non-Western political experience and practice are considered candidates for empirical analysis, both qualitative and quantitative (as in comparative politics), and now, increasingly historical-interpretive analysis (as in some variants of comparative political theory). But rarely do they constitute the sort of "normative" or theoretical inspiration that would characterize the shared purpose between theorists and empirical scholars that Rehfeld describes.[24]

Following Kaufman-Osborn's example, I point to another implicit—and paradoxical—consensus governing this state of affairs. On the one hand, there is an assumption that we study comparative political theory because it will explain something to us about "other" societies and how they go about their moral and political business. Politics in other nations must be predicated on and benefit from each tradition's own normative or theoretical assumptions, just as politics in

Western nations is predicated on assumptions undergirding European and American history, practices and values. In that case, the Confucian origins of Chinese political thought must be appropriate for explaining Chinese political experience, Indian political thought for Indian political experience, and so on.

But in practice, of course, this is only half true: the political structures, institutions and experiences of many non-Western nations are thoroughly infiltrated by various (often hybridized) strands of Westcentric political theory. While actual political practice may display much local color and flavor, the basic institutional structures of many non-Western nations are patterned on Western presumptions about constitutionalism and democratic governance. But accepting the suggestion that political practices in other traditions must be as closely tied to their own theoretical heritage as the Western political practice is to its own allows many political theorists to continue overlooking the uncomfortable fact that non-Western political practices are far more permeated by foreign normative traditions than their own. In turn, this allows them to ignore the possibility of their own Westcentric political inquiry and practices being similarly infused by foreign normative concepts.

Simultaneously, few political theorists seem willing to argue that liberal democratic practice in India should be *replaced* by something more indigenous—say, modes of political experience and practice rooted in Vedic, Buddhist, Jain or South Asian Islamic literatures. Although subaltern and postcolonial scholars writing in and on India are ostensibly committed to a critical position on all Eurocentric views, rarely does this translate into a full-scale interrogation of liberal democratic norms. Similarly, few scholars of Islamic political thought seem to want to argue that models of governance, and practices emerging from this tradition represent a clear and viable normative alternative to Western ones. What appears to undergird this precarious balance is the underlying ambiguity in political science about taking on liberal orthodoxy, combined with the fear of the accusation of relativism. The idea of theory as a "normative" enterprise, Kaufman-Osborn reminds us, got a further boost from the twin specters of relativism and subjectivism. Theorists felt the need to demonstrate that their enterprise was not going to degenerate into a relativist free-for-all, and to show that it would continue to make possible evaluative judgments and commitments.[25]

Thus, the awkward and disconcerting choice that faces many who engage in encounters with the normative alterity of non-Western civilizations is as such: if we believe that all human beings are equal, and if something is thought to be right for us, then shouldn't what is normatively right for Indian or Chinese politics be no different than what is normatively ideal for Westerners? Alternatively, if we acknowledge that other forms of thought might have normative validity for their societies, then they might have some validity for our society. We therefore have to consider the possibility of calling into question the universality—and therefore—validity of our own liberal commitments. This haunts even the most well-intentioned and normatively open-minded political theorists who encounter civilizational otherness: can we approach our study of other traditions sympathetically without committing to full-blown relativism and thus abandoning our "normative" high ground, or questioning liberal commitments (the first of which often seems to be a natural outgrowth of the second)?

This is of course an issue for political theorists in a way that it is not for empirical political scientists. Because of the ongoing wall of separation between "normative" and "empirical" theorizing, scholars of political practice in other civilizations (that is, comparativists) are let off the hook from having to consider the normative implications of the practices they study, since such "normative" work is usually left to the theorists. But the normative implications of these political practices raise too many prickly questions that would reveal precisely how attached West-centered scholars are to the presumptive superiority of their norms and would risk branding all theorists interested in non-Western thought as relativists (a charge that carries far more weight, it would seem, in political science than in other disciplines). The upshot is that as long as projects of studying non-Western thought and political practice remain mostly of historical, interpretive and empirical interest rather than of normative interest or inspiration, as they have thus far, no truly unsettling questions have to be addressed. Political scientists can continue to put off questions like the following: is the West's attachment to liberal democratic political commitments only one among many possibilities, conditioned by its own history? Can specific non-liberal experiences and practices provide useful, provocative and *normatively valuable* alternatives to liberal ones, in specific contexts? That is, as long as political scientists continue to cling to the fiction of an "autonomous" normative theorizing that stands at a critical distance from empirical political practice, this allows them to continue perpetuating another kind of consensus, namely, one that keeps the universality of Westcentric liberal norms from being truly called into question.

EXEMPLARY CHALLENGES: CONFUCIAN VALUES AND VEILING IN ISLAM

Some promising exceptions—and brave attempts to turn away from this consensus—can be found in the works of political theorists working on Chinese political thought and traditions. Daniel Bell has argued that East Asian political practice, often based on the norms of China's Confucian traditions, are not only more appropriate for the East Asian context, but also provide morally legitimate alternatives to Western-style liberal democracy *and* may be defensible for contemporary Western liberal-democratic contexts.[26] Such scholars provide rigorous, sympathetic accounts of Confucian-style political practice, and are willing to argue that it may represent a set of political choices superior to Western-style liberal democracy in certain cases. They also show precisely *which* elements of Westcentric liberalism could productively be disrupted by such interventions. In addition to a study of theoretical modes, such scholarship also focuses on concrete, particular *practices* and institutions, suggesting that such normative challenges are to be understood through the intersection of theory and practice.

Bell and Onuma Yasuaki emphasize that Confucian-style political practice emulates the classical Confucian emphasis on the state's *primary* obligation to securing its citizen's basic material welfare. When material or economic rights conflict with political ones such as liberty or choice, the former are given priority.[27] Thus, despite a general commitment to free-market principles, most of the nations influenced by the Confucian legacy have all significantly curtailed individual property rights. Taiwan and Korea both engaged in massive land redistribution programs after World War II, the Singaporean government has expropriated land for industrial development and public housing, and the Hong Kong government technically owns all land within its territory. Many of these practices, Bell claims, can be traced to imperatives in Confucian texts justifying constraints on land ownership so that the state may maintain a relatively equitable distribution of land and wealth to secure the basic material welfare of all. Meanwhile, the Confucian moral requirement that one should take one's family as an autonomous unit from the rest of society, "flourishing or suffering as a whole,"[28] is manifested in various East Asian legal codes pertaining to inheritance and family law. Filial piety is meant to take precedence over competing moral obligations; thus, productive adults have an obligation to care for old or needy family members, and such duties often trump narrowly defined individual self-interest. The practice of joint family ownership of property legally enshrines this principle of filial duties and obligations. The intergenerational transfer of property through bequest and inheritance is constrained by the need to provide aid for less well-off members of the family, including children and aged parents. Even in contemporary communist China, inheritance laws embody traditional Confucian ideas and enshrine the need for family members to provide for one another: heirs who abandon or mistreat the decedent forfeit their right of inheritance, and decedents are constrained by the requirement to provide for heirs who are elderly, infirmed or underage. In Hong Kong, it is mandatory for part of an inheritance to be used to support disabled members of the family, even if they have been explicitly left out of the deceased's will.[29] In Singapore, parents above age sixty can appeal to a tribunal to claim maintenance from their children.[30] In contrast to liberal democratic societies with their regimes of individual-centered property rights, East Asian governments use different combinations of legal sanctions and financial incentives to facilitate the right of needy family members to a share in family property and maintenance. Social welfare responsibilities lie first with the family, then with the local community, and finally, with the state as the provider of last resort.[31]

Another compelling example with the potential to disrupt liberal commitments is provided by a discussion of veiling among women in the Muslim world. Historically speaking, the very politicization of veiling came about as a result of Western colonial discourse. Nineteenth-century British imperialists viewed the veil as the ultimate symbol of Eastern backwardness, and colonial measures against veiling were asserted in the name of women's rights. This "feminism," however, emerged as part of the development of a colonial narrative that emphasized the dominance of West over East,[32] often giving an account of Islamic oppression of women based on misperceptions, or vague and inaccurate understanding of Muslim societies.[33] Even as the Victorian male establishment devised theories to contest, deride and reject the claims of European feminism, they captured its language and redirected it in the service of colonialism. The idea that "Other men in colonized societies beyond the borders of the civilized West oppressed women was to be used in the rhetoric of colonialism to render morally justifiable the project of undermining or eradicating the cultures of colonized peoples."[34] As the feminist agenda for Muslim women was set by colonial Europeans, native Arab elites too quickly internalized this Orientalist view of themselves.[35] The campaign against the veil was thus neither initiated by women themselves, nor in the name of women's choice; rather, it was part of elite colonial men's attempts to ensure state control over the individuals of a nation.[36] Lost in all of this were the choices, experiences or voices of actual women, which rarely appeared in any of these early discourses, whether colonial or anticolonial.

In this way, the history of Western colonial attempts to "liberate" Muslim women simply replaced one form of social control for another. It reinscribed women's bodies as symbols of the assumed superiority of Western modes of thought, where once they were symbols of patriarchy.[37] In a manner that has become typical of the Arab narrative of resistance to colonialism, Leila Ahmed tells us, both proponents and opponents of veiling have often appropriated the terms of debate first set in place by colonial discourse, even when their objective is to argue against them. Discussions of women in Islam continued either to reenact the Western narrative of Islam as oppressor, or conversely, to insist on the necessity of preserving Muslim culture as a sign of resistance to imperialism.[38] Until recently, more contemporary writings about veiling have remained for the most part tied to this dichotomy, centered on arguments about Islamic oppression of women and the Western liberal or democratic ability to either liberate these women or to tolerate this illiberal practice.

Even as contemporary Western feminism has been arguing for a number of years about sensitivity to cultural difference, veiling is most often interpreted by many contemporary Western liberals and feminists[39] as a patriarchal imposition that seeks to mark women as invisible, to control their sexuality, and to limit their agency and autonomy. Given that much religious belief is thought to be hostile to liberal and/ or feminist normative commitments,[40] it is often argued by such scholars that Islam, like any patriarchal religion, subordinates women. The veil, feminist scholar Fatima Mernissi tells us, "can be interpreted as a symbol revealing a collective fantasy of the Muslim community; to make women disappear, to eliminate them from communal life, to relegate them to an easily controllable terrain, the home, to prevent them from moving about, and to highlight their illegal position on male territory by means of a mask."[41] Even voluntary veiling is sometimes treated as a kind of false consciousness, without any possibility of critical perspective on one's own situation.[42] Among political theorists concerned with defending or problematizing liberal commitments, debates over the veil are often subsumed under debates about how far multicultural liberal societies should go in order to accommodate non-liberal practices.[43] Treatments of veiling in political theory are organized mostly around questions emerging from the normative value of liberal commitments to ideas like freedom and equality.[44]

But more recent analyses of veiling situate themselves in the contexts in which veiling occurs. They emerge from different disciplinary formations and borrow from a variety of methodological viewpoints—anthropology, feminist studies, cultural-ethnic studies and Middle East studies. Such analyses reveal that veiling, rather than being treated as an abstract, homogenized normative commitment, is to be seen through the fractured lens of a multiplicity of motivations and meanings. Chandra Talpade Mohanty famously reminds us that Westcentric feminist writings can "discursively colonize the material and historical heterogeneities of the lives of women in the third world, thereby producing/re-presenting a composite, singular 'Third World Woman,'" an arbitrarily constructed image that carries "the authorizing signature of Western humanist discourse."[45] Western feminist scholarship, inscribed as it often is within the West's monopoly of scientific, economic, legal and sociological discourses, "sets up its own authorial subjects as the implicit referent," that is, the "yardstick by which to encode and represent cultural Others."[46] As a result, it often relies on the assumption of women as an already constituted, coherent group with identical interests and desires, bound together by the "sameness" of their "oppression."[47] Third World women are thus encoded as powerless, exploited, sexually constrained, domesticated, tradition bound, and therefore victimized.[48] The explanatory potential of gender difference as the origin of oppression gains an unquestioned privileged position, and all revolutionary struggles are locked into binary structures of power and powerlessness, exploiters and victims.[49] The specificity of meanings and practices that vary according to cultural and ideological context are often ignored, as are contradictory or subversive aspects of a particular practice or institution. Marginal or resistant modes of experience are erased.[50] The universalizing, homogenizing narrative of veiling set in place by the terms of colonial discourse (and often repeated in contemporary discourse) sees all veiled women as oppressed, domesticated and rendered invisible. In contrast, a disaggregated, pluralistic, fragmented understanding of veiling is made possible when the issue is approached contextually, through the lens of the experiences and practices of particular groups of veiled women in particular contexts.

Fortunately, such disaggregated, contextualized and experiential analyses have increasingly become the norm rather than the exception in more recent scholarship about veiling.[51] Examining the actual *practices* of veiling, in a manner that begins from and takes into account the experiences of veiled women themselves, demonstrates that voluntary veiling can be seen as a form of resistance to Westcentric notions of freedom and equality. It can constitute a challenge to the Westcentric emphasis on complete equality of bodily comportment and visibility in the public sphere as the appropriate remedy for the problem of gender inequality. There is no doubt that in Islamic contexts—as in many Western ones—women continue to be subject to patriarchal structures that oppress, marginalize and mark them as inferior.[52] But the experience of voluntary veiling, when read through a diversity of contextual and historical lenses, can serve as a practice- oriented challenge to the normative value of certain liberal commitments.

We learn from these accounts that the purposes and motivations behind voluntary veiling are highly pluralized and can scarcely be reduced to any singular explanation: marking one's own pride and membership in a community of faith;[53] symbolizing resistance to Westernization and the purported return to an "authentic" practice of Islam free of Western influences;[54] as a form of revolutionary or political protest;[55] honoring custom;[56] marking one's social status;[57] gaining access to employment in the public sphere;[58] protecting oneself from sexual harassment in the public sphere by symbolically declaring oneself pure or modest.[59] In a study of Bedouin Arab cultures, Lila Abu-Lughod shows that veiling and seclusion are often seen by women as a source of pride and honor, signifying that they do not need the company of men and declaring their independence.[60] The veil serves as a statement that the wearer is intent on preserving herself as separate from others, emotionally and psychologically as well as physically; it is a tangible marker of separateness and independence. It marks not only modesty, but also a kind of autonomy in which the wearer declares herself free of the "'natural' needs and passions."[61] In a context where autonomy is defined by the ability to transcend desire, and honor is equated with the ability to deny one's sexuality, the veil signifies independence, as well as modesty and honorable conduct. Arlene MacLeod, in a study of contemporary Egyptian women in Cairo, also finds that most women viewed the veil favorably and took to it by choice.[62] Here again, taking the veil was seen as a marker of agency. For Egyptian women, "individual agency" was to locate themselves in a community of women and in cultural membership with other Muslims. The veil allowed women entry into the working world, protecting them from sexual harassment and visibly demanding respect from men by attesting to their adherence to Islam. Veiling also set women off as a unique group, creating strong feelings of gender identity, binding women together into a social, economic and emotional community,[63] and affording a sense of personal space and privacy from the intrusions of the male gaze that was not otherwise available.[64] In these and other analyses, Muslim women not only participate voluntarily in the practice of veiling, they often claim it as a mark of resistance, agency and empowerment, whether it pertains to cultural membership, political protest, religious identification or other motivating assumptions.[65]

What emerges from a variety of otherwise disparate contexts is that veiling is seen both as a protest against and as a solution to the sexualization and objectification of women, whether Western or Islamic. An Islamic educational institution says regarding the veil:

> [Men and women] will then be evaluated for intelligence and skills instead of looks and sexuality . . . "*We want to stop men from treating us like sex objects, as they have always done. We want them to ignore our appearance and to be attentive to our personalities and mind. We want them to take us seriously and treat us as equals and not just chase us around for our bodies and physical looks.*" A Muslim woman who covers her head is making a statement about her identity . . . Many Muslim women who cover are filled with dignity and self-esteem . . . [they] do not want [their] sexuality to enter into interactions with men in the smallest degree.[66]

Many Muslim women believe, then, that the veil is a way to *secure* a kind of personal space, confidence and self-esteem in a world that objectifies women, by allowing them control over the visibility of their own bodies in the public sphere.[67] Understood in such terms, the veil protects women from the sexualizing gaze, not only of men in particular, but of an entire social structure including public images and media portrayals, which often cast women as sexual objects. It subverts control over such a gaze, symbolically denying men the power to cast their sexual gaze upon women as they like. In fact, in such a view, not only women, but men too are liberated from a framework of gender relations that often encourages both sexes to view one another predominantly in terms of their physical attributes or sexual desirability. Many veiled women express the belief that a public sphere where sexuality is tightly controlled, rather than given free and full expression, is a more healthy one for the purposes of gender equality, and thus more comfortable for many of them.[68] Indeed many of them expressed a desire for freedom construed as freedom *from* the male, public sexualized gaze, rather than the freedom *to* express their personhood or sexual agency through autonomy of dress more commonly found in Westcentric thought.[69]

In many contexts of gender imbalance, veiling emphasizes the belief that the expression of sexuality can be an impediment to the full recognition of personhood. Public spaces where sexual tension potentially intervenes can *inhibit* the full exercise of personhood. This is not a claim that Westcentric liberals might argue with. But Western liberalism's response is to mark out spaces for free sexual expression in the private sphere, while correcting the underlying patriarchal imbalance in the public sphere that might afford the freedom of sexual choice and expression to one gender but not the other. More recent versions of the Western liberal ideal take as given the notion that autonomy of sexual choice and free expression of sexuality are integral to personhood fully defined, and that both genders must aspire equally to such choice of self-expression. But the politics of Muslim veiling might offer a different and non-liberal kind of solution to this notion. It may suggest that in certain contexts, the potential for sexualized interaction must deliberately be minimized, in order for persons to see, recognize and interact with one another as equal human beings.[70] Resisting capitalism's emphasis on the body and materiality, along with its objectification and commodification of bodies, veiling allows them to control their public self-presentation and visibility. As a result, rather than the dehumanization or invisibility of the "non-person" that Western critics claim is the result of the veil, many veiled women claim that they feel *more* humanized when veiled.[71]

Many have argued that veiling serves to absolve men of the responsibility for controlling their behavior. Even when seen as an act of resistance, Nancy Hirschmann reminds us, veiling still operates within normative parameters that were not created by women. Thus, women who veil are still conforming to an externally imposed patriarchal standard. But, crucially, this may be no different from Western women: just like Muslim women, Western women too do not take part in "constructing the framework within which decisions about dress take place, but rather are forced to respond in conflicting directions to frameworks constructed by men."[72] Western feminists have been most vocal about the ways in which Western women subject themselves to standards of dress, physical beauty and body image that are patriarchally imposed—standards that often reduce women to objects of sexual pleasure and undermine the nonphysical aspects of their being.[73]

The issue, then, is not simply whether voluntary veiling is in fact a statement of choice and autonomy (which some may claim it is).[74] Rather, I want to ask what happens when we shift the terrain of debate away from Westcentric liberal feminism, and its focus on the full expression of one's sexual agency and autonomy for both women and men.[75] What happens when sexual agency and autonomy cease to be seen as central pillars of human life?[76] I argue that most political-theoretic analyses of veiling, when seen through the lens of a liberal framework and organized around the primacy of values like autonomy, choice, sexual agency or equality, miss something important. An experiential, historicized and practice-oriented account of the multiple meanings and manifestations of veiling can shift altogether our ideas of what counts as an important question by asking precisely what is considered normatively valuable in these non-liberal worldviews and frameworks.

What if, rather than desiring sexual control and agency as a mark of equality, some women desire a complete de-sexualization of the self in certain contexts? In the context of veiling in Muslim worlds, these interrogations can question the centrality of sexual agency and expression to the concept of full personhood. They provide an alternative, non-liberal account of ways in which resistance can be offered to gender imbalance. We can acknowledge as pervasive the continuing fact of patriarchy, as well as the continuing presence of the sexualizing male gaze as an ongoing fact of gender relations. But the practice of veiling asserts that the resistance to the sexualizing gaze in such contexts comes through deliberately rejecting one's own potential sexuality in certain public contexts, and through the removal of oneself as a potentially sexual being in such contexts. Resistance to the over-sexualization of patriarchy, rather than requiring an assertion of sexual agency, in fact gravitates toward the opposite. In a manner that is reminiscent of Gandhi's *brahmacharya* discussed in chapter 2, it expresses the idea that empowerment arrives from shedding or negating one's role as a potential sexual being rather than embracing it.

Until political theorists (as opposed to anthropologists, Middle East studies or East Asian studies scholars) start routinely producing such scholarship, it will be relatively easy to keep in place the consensus that inhibits any serious critical interventions into the normativity of Westcentric liberal commitments. Such scholarship can productively unsettle this consensus by suggesting that a symbiotic relationship between political experience and political theorizing can occur across cultural, geographic, civilizational and national boundaries. That is, just as non-Western *thought* can serve as a destabilizing inspiration to Western political theorists, so can actual political *practice* and experience from other traditions serve as inspiration to normative and theoretical work occurring in the West. We need to consider the relationship between normative and empirical work in a new sense: as potentially attached to, embedded in and inspired by a *variety of* possibilities of political experience. Cosmopolitanism in political theory is intertwined with the contentious but important project of unhooking political theory from its traditional position of ostensible detachment from political experience and reality, while expanding the set of political experiences that can serve as normative inspiration for political theorists.

A COSMOPOLITAN POLITICAL THEORY AND THE NORMATIVE/EVALUATIVE ENTERPRISE

What can be said about the normative or evaluative enterprise in a cosmopolitan political thought? Does the commitment to the centrality—in *methodological* terms—of destabilizing Eurocentrism, and specifically its liberal variant, involve a substantive *normative* rejection of liberal norms such as autonomy? And, does it therefore involve a rejection of critical evaluation about the content of non-EuroAmerican thought due to an embrace of relativism? Precisely what sort of normative inquiries across cultures are made possible—or foreclosed—by a cosmopolitan political thought?

It should be evident that the cosmopolitan imperative to challenge the predominance of liberal norms need not imply a commitment to the repeal of all parts of the liberal project. A cosmopolitan political thought does not seek to prejudge the outcome of every normative contemplation by suggesting that the liberal commitment would be a mistake in every such case. Rather, it seeks to avoid the *presumptive* authority of liberal or Eurocentric commitments in every case. Moreover, such ethical reflection does not seek to assess the validity of entire doctrines or traditions of thought, or to definitively resolve questions in ways that are systematic or final. A cosmopolitan political thought need not require that "our" commitments or beliefs on some given topic are to be assessed in contrast to "theirs" with a view to settling the which values and commitments are more appropriate. Rather, the challenges and dislocations I advocate are open to constant renegotiation and evolution. As the sources and contexts from which political theorizing takes its cue become even more plural, and the set of normative ideas it grapples with are derived from a multiplicity of cultural contexts, political theorists do need to accept that the project of finding eternal truths and the possibility of entirely objective knowledge about the human good become even more remote.

Yet, this should not imply that a cosmopolitan political thought can therefore have *nothing* meaningful to say about the human good. The task of political philosophy, Isaiah Berlin suggests, can only be pursued in a pluralist world; that is, only in a world of normative conflict where ends collide do questions regarding the human good have any meaning at all.[77] If anything, the cosmopolitan interventions I suggest should further animate and galvanize the normative motivations of political theory. That is, they give us even more kinds of normative questions to investigate, while furthering the productive multiplication of possibilities as to *how* and *why* such questions might be investigated. In this sense, the relationship of a cosmopolitan political theory to existing disciplinary practices of normative inquiry becomes one of further pluralization. It pluralizes the contexts within which and the ways through which we ask questions about various kinds of human good. And, as Berlin reminds us, these are precisely the conditions for political theory's flourishing.

The cosmopolitan intervention I envision presumes of course that there cannot be a singular monolithic set of answers that provide objective knowledge about the human good. Moreover, it is a productive task of political theorists to disaggregate and further multiply the modes of asking questions about the matter. Indeed, such fracture has long been under way; political theory as it is currently practiced is nothing if not highly fragmented in its search for answers to questions about normative value. As Stephen White reminds us, Berlin's famous pinpointing of the crisis of the death of political theory was followed not by a reemergence of "grand theory" in the fashion of Locke and Hobbes.[78] Instead it led to a deeper fragmentation, a confrontation with pluralism, and a further move away from meta-narratives. As the challenges of feminism, multiculturalism, environmentalism, critical race theory, and other competing discourses arose, political theory was left with "more paradoxes than platitudes," that is, more puzzling problems than grand solutions, a greater diversity of approaches to such problems than grand theories that resolved them. The predominance of liberalism, then, is not to be replaced in a cosmopolitan political thought by the predominance of some other narrative or school of thought from any tradition. Rather, it reveals the genuine fragmentation of possibilities regarding the normative enterprise, along with the genuine participation of non-liberal and non-Western modes of thought in this enterprise.

Nor should the fragmentation of the normative enterprise suggest a squeamishness to make critical judgments about ideas from other civilizations. After all, to consider any way of life immune from normative critique is, in Charles Taylor's words, an act of deep condescension, if it does not hold those practices to the same eligibility for normative critique as our own Western presumptions.[79] But if we have rejected the presumptive universality of liberal norms, what constitute good standards by which to evaluate any set of ideas or norms that one encounters and to argue for one set over another? Moreover, as suggested in chapters 3 and 4, the perspective of immersion and adherence contained in an existential hermeneutic locates the scholar *within* the perspective of an insider to the tradition. It suggests that alterity is best understood from within the systems of meaning that construct its ways of life. But this perspective of self-dislocation and immersion also suggests a paradox for the normative enterprise: can the primacy of self-dislocation as the predominant mode of understanding otherness move the scholar from complete immersion in a way of life to ethical reflection upon the values and norms embedded within it? In other words, can normative judgment of a culture's ideas or practices emerge from a deeply situated internal positionality that *already* takes as true the standards of reason giving, judgment and criticism internal to that culture?

Indeed, it can. Insiders to a tradition are often as critical as outsiders, and the warrant for normative critique requires no necessary repositioning as outsider, or subscribing to external norms of judgment. Critiques and evaluations of a tradition's texts and ideas by its insiders often occur precisely on the terms and standards internal to a culture. Critiques of the hierarchical intolerance in Vedic Hinduism produced by Gandhi, Bankim Chandra Chatterjee, Dayananda Saraswati and Aurobindo Ghose were all internal. That is, they claimed that the *Brahmanic* hierarchy of caste violated the principle of oneness central to the Vedic tradition itself, that untouchability had no scriptural basis in Hinduism's most authoritative texts, and that the caste system was a perversion of classical Hinduism understood in a particular way.[80] Thus, an evaluative judgment about the practice of caste need not dismiss certain Vedic texts because they contain hierarchical, illiberal premises about caste and gender that are at odds with liberal Westcentric norms of egalitarianism and autonomy. Rather, it may do so precisely by subscribing to the very values internal to the Vedic or Hindu tradition, arguing, as Gandhi, Kabir, Mirabai or Bankim might do.

Two kinds of objections arise to this view. The first asks: Does not such a view commit us to some version of relativism? The answer here is that political theorists *do* need to be less timid about owning up to some version of relativism as the natural accompaniment to the cosmopolitan political thought I have identified. This need not imply a coarse relativism where we deny the possibility of objective grounds upon which to obtain any knowledge about the good because all knowledge arises from relations of domination, or settled conventions. Rather, we might adhere to a more sophisticated kind of relativism in which we are suspicious of any clear identification and specification of the notion of a human good. We may therefore hold a Gandhian commitment to the plurality, fluidity and obscurity of the idea of the good. Gandhi asserts that any one individual's grasp of knowledge about the moral world is necessarily incomplete, and the totality of Truth remains elusive to any individual person or set of people, due to its internal complexity, fluidity and plurality.[81] The path toward Truth is ridden with difficulty, and the constant possibility of errors in understanding. Gandhi famously distinguishes between what he calls Absolute Truth—the totality of the good that remains obscure and elusive—and "relative truth." Relative truth refers to particular claims and components of moral projects in specific contexts and human lives, which usually contain some fragment of

Absolute Truth. And, precisely because the totality of the human good is so difficult to know, the good remains a project for particular understanding and action in specific contexts of moral action and moral knowledge. Absolute Truth is so multifaceted that it cannot adequately be captured by any one mind or manifested entirely in any given human life. Thus, relative truths are appropriate—though provisional and contingent—guides to moral action, for they are all that most humans have access to in any given instance. The ethicist Samuel Fleischacker similarly claims: "The good is mysterious not because it is nonempirical, but because it is essentially a project for action, hence something that remains incomplete as long as there remains action to be taken . . . It is elusive, but ever more distinctly visible the more action we take."[82] Thus, knowledge about the good only emerges in particular contexts of action and knowledge, and answers to questions about the good can often vary or conflict, depending on the particularities of each context. This ontology has a long, sophisticated and culturally varied pedigree. Value pluralists and ethicists in the Western tradition, as well as metaphysical views emerging from the Hindu tradition, elaborate on this ontology in different ways.[83] This more sophisticated version of relativism constitutes the appropriate ontological commitment for the cosmopolitan scholar of political thought.

The second objector asks: Surely, not all practices can be critiqued through internal criticism? Surely at some point we will require evaluative critiques of a tradition that need to draw upon standards of reason giving that are *not* internal to that tradition? Indeed, as Fleischacker reminds us, there will be rare moments when an idea or a practice or a norm cannot be critiqued in the culture's own terms, because that culture simply contains no internal norm that we can recognize as respect for humanity.[84] But in a cosmopolitan political thought, such critiques, rather than emerging purely from an external—and ostensibly transcultural—vantage point, instead acknowledge the local color and "tribal" nature of the arguments being used. In the end, multiply located scholars, through their repeated self-dislocations and relocations, are uniquely positioned to provide ethical reflections and critiques that do not simply claim to be the result of universalizable reason and morality, but rather recognize the particularity of the external norms being relied upon. This tribalist appeal to our own local moral traditions is a more solid basis for normative intervention. It is, in Fleischacker's words "both a more human and more easily backed-away-from approach than setting ourselves up as the avenging angels for the principles of universal morality . . . emphasizing the local color in our visions for humanity rather than being embarrassed about it."[85]

Finally, in what ways has this analysis clarified, deepened, or reconfigured the concept of cosmopolitanism? On the view I have elaborated, cosmopolitanism in political thought *is* ongoing displacement by scholars who are located, at different times, in different relations of insidership and outsidership to the Westcentric tradition. It is continuing destabilization; it is continuing confrontations with the hegemony of liberalism's normative *and* structural hegemony. It is the (perhaps long and arduous) work of building coeval and post-Eurocentric possibilities of engagement through repeated self-dislocation and relocation. Cosmopolitanism, rather than being attached to a particular set of normative or institutional assumptions, becomes an ongoing set of practices by scholars themselves. It is a series of methodological interventions involving the *disciplined* carrying out of dislocative and relocative practices, which leads to a shift in *disciplinary* self-understanding. According to the current *status quo* in political theory, new, competing counter-formations that challenge liberalism's hegemony are easily integrated into a constellation of minoritarian satellite discourses, while liberal norms remain both substantively and structurally unthreatened. A cosmopolitan political thought moves toward a disciplinary practice in which liberalism and other Westcentric modes of thought take their place in a series of plural and coeval engagements of thinkers and texts from all traditions, moving through and past the dichotomies that ground these encounters. It is from this possibility that we can begin to envision a political theory *beyond* Eurocentrism, that is, after the presumptions of Eurocentrism's primacy have been challenged and disestablished.

Notes

CHAPTER 1

1. See, for instance, Martha Nussbaum, *For Love of Country* (Boston: Beacon Press, 2002); Kwame Anthony Appiah, *Cosmopolitanism: Ethics in a World of Strangers* (New York: Norton, 2007); Kok-Chor Tan, *Justice Without Borders: Cosmopolitanism, Nationalism, Patriotism* (Cambridge: Cambridge University Press, 2004); Gillian Brock and Henry Brighouse, *The Political Philosophy of Cosmopolitanism* (Cambridge: Cambridge University Press, 2004).

2. Bruce Robbins, "Introduction Part I: Actually Existing Cosmopolitanism" in Bruce Robbins and Pheng Cheah, eds., *Cosmopolitics: Thinking and Feeling Beyond the Nation* (Minneapolis: University of Minnesota Press, 1998), p. 1.

3. See Timothy V. Kaufman-Osborn, "Political Theory as Profession and as Subfield?" *Political Research Quarterly* 63 (3), 2010, p. 657.

4. Long before political theorists had even thought of turning beyond the West, philosophers had inaugurated a subdiscipline called "comparative philosophy," in which the philosophical underpinnings of non-Western traditions were vigorously examined and debated. Its intellectual antecedents reached back to the progress of comparative mythology, comparative religions and comparative linguistics in nineteenth-century Europe. The first East-West philosophers conference was held in 1939, and the journal *Philosophy East and West*, exploring non-Western philosophical traditions, was established in 1951. See Gerald James Larson "Introduction: The 'Age-Old Distinction Between the Same and the Other,'" in Gerald James Larson and Elliott Deutsch, eds., *Interpreting Across Boundaries, New Essays in Comparative Philosophy* (Princeton, NJ: Princeton University Press, 1988), p. 5; Eric Sharpe, *Comparative Religion: A History* (London: Duckworth, 1975); and Wilhelm Halbfass, "India and the Comparative Method," *Philosophy East and West* 35 (1), 1985.

5. For various descriptions of the project of comparative political theory, see Roxanne L. Euben, *Enemy in the Mirror: Islamic Fundamentalism and the Limits of Modern Rationalism: A Work of Comparative Political Theory* (Princeton, NJ: Princeton University Press, 1999); Roxanne L. Euben, *Journeys to the Other Shore: Muslim and Western Travellers in Search of Knowledge* (Princeton, NJ: Princeton University Press, 2006); Anthony J. Parel and Ronald C. Keith, eds., *Comparative Political Philosophy: Studies Under the Upas Tree* (New Delhi: Sage Publications, 1992); Fred Dallmayr, ed. *Border Crossings: Toward a Comparative Political Theory* (Lanham, MD: Lexington Books, 1999); Leigh Jenco, "What Does Heaven Ever Say?: A Methods-Centered Approach to Cross-Cultural Engagement," *American Political Science Review* 101 (4), November 2007; Andrew March, "What Is Comparative Political Theory?" *Review of Politics*, 71 (4), Fall 2009. See also *Review of Politics*, 59 (3), Summer 1997, symposium titled Non-Western Political Thought.

6. Fred Dallmayr, "Beyond Monologue: For a Comparative Political Theory," *Perspectives on Politics* 2 (2), 2004, p. 253.

7. Fred Dallmayr, *Beyond Orientalism: Essays on Cross-Cultural Encounter* (Albany, NY: SUNY Press, 1996).

8. Raimundo Panikkar, "What Is Comparative Philosophy Comparing?" in Gerald James Larson and Elliott Deutsch, eds., *Interpreting Across Boundaries: New Essays in Comparative Philosophy* (Princeton, NJ: Princeton University Press, 1988), p. 127.

9. Ibid., p.128.

10. Ibid., pp. 132–33.

11. The predominance within CPT of Gadamerian dialogical hermeneutics via Panikkar's essay can scarcely be understated. See Michaelle Browers, *Democracy and Civil Society in Arab Political Thought: Transcultural Possibilities* (Syracuse, NY: Syracuse University Press, 2006), pp. 213–14; and Jenco "What Does Heaven Ever Say," pp. 742–45, both of which identify dialogical hermeneutics as the predominant mode of cross-cultural theorizing. See also Cary J. Nederman, "Varieties of Dialogue: Dialogical Models of Intercultural Communication in Medieval Inter-religious Writings," in Takashi Shogimen and Cary Nederman, eds., *Western Political Thought in Dialogue with Asia* (Lanham, MD: Lexington Press, 2009), p. 45.

12. Euben, *Enemy in the Mirror*, p. 16.

13. Fred Dallmayr, *Dialogue Among Civilizations: Some Exemplary Voices* (New York: Palgrave Macmillan, 2002).

14. See, for instance, Daniel Bell, *East Meets West: Human Rights and Democracy in East Asia* (Princeton, NJ: Princeton University Press, 2000); Mohammed Khatami, "Islam, Iran, and the Dialogue of Civilizations," in Neve Gordon, ed., *From the Margins of Globalization: Critical Perspectives on Human Rights* (Lanham, MD: Lexington, 2004); Fred Dallmayr and Abbas Manochehri, *Civilizational Dialogue and Political Thought: Tehran Papers* (Lanham, MD: Lexington, 2007); Bhikhu Parekh, "Non-Ethnocentric Universalism," in Tim Dunne and Nicholas J. Wheeler, eds., *Human Rights in Global Politics* (Cambridge: Cambridge University Press, 1999) and Bhikhu Parekh, *Rethinking Multiculturalism: Cultural Diversity and Political Theory* (Cambridge, MA: Harvard University Press, 2000). Relatedly, Michaelle Browers points to the concept of "parallelism" in early CPT studies like Parel and Keith, *Comparative Political Philosophy*. The writings of (early) CPT, she claims, "tend to treat non-Western works as 'parallel developments' in the history of political thought . . . tend[ing] to give the impression that the traditions compared developed independently of each other." Browers, *Democracy and Civil Society in Arab Political Thought*, p. 212. See also Parel and Keith, *Comparative Political Philosophy*, p. 7.

15. Brett Bowden, "The Ebb and Flow of Peoples, Ideas and Innovations in the River of Inter-civilizational Relations: Toward a Global History of Political Thought" and Antony Black, "Toward a Global History of Political Thought," both in Shogimen and Nederman, eds., *Western Political Thought*, pp.37, 88–94.

16. See also Azizah Y. al-Hibri, "Islamic Constitutionalism and the Concept of Democracy," in Dallmayr, ed., *Border Crossings*; M. A. Muqtedar Khan, ed., *Islamic Democratic Discourse: Theory, Debates and Philosophical Perspectives* (Lanham, MD: Lexington Books, 2006); Bell, *East Meets West*; Brooke A. Ackerly, "Is Liberalism the Only Way Toward Democracy? Confucianism and Democracy," *Political Theory* 33 (4), 2005.

17. See Stephen Angle, *Human Rights and Chinese Thought: A Cross-Cultural Inquiry* (Cambridge: Cambridge University Press, 2002), and *Sagehood: The Contemporary Significance of Neo-Confucian Philosophy* (New York: Oxford University Press, 2009); Roger Ames, *The Art of Rulership: A Study in Ancient Chinese Political Thought* (Honolulu: University of Hawaii Press, 1983).

18. Francis Oakley, *Kingship: The Politics of Enchantment* (Oxford, UK: Blackwell, 2006); Antony Black, *The West and Islam: Religion and Politics in World History* (Oxford: Oxford University Press, 2008), and *The History of Islamic Political Thought: From the Prophet to the Present* (New York: Routledge, 2001).

19. Andrew March calls these the "epistemic," "global-democratic" "critical-transformative," "explanatory-interpretative" and "rehabilitative" motivations for the establishment of a comparative political theory. See March, "What Is Comparative Political Theory?"

20. See Dallmayr, "Beyond Monologue": "Moving from the habitually familiar toward the unfamiliar will help to restore the sense of 'wondering' (*thaumazein*) that the ancients extolled as pivotal to philosophizing," p. 254. See also Dallmayr, "Comparative Political Theory: What Is It Good For?" in Shogimen and Nederman, eds., *Western Political Thought*, p. 5; Antony Black, "Toward a Global History of Political Thought," in Shogimen and Nederman, eds., *Western Political Thought*, pp. 26, 36–37: "It is possible that we ourselves today may learn something from other cultures.... The general assumption is that ... the West is today uniquely equipped to teach others and cannot learn from them."

21. See Dallmayr, "Beyond Monologue": "In contrast to hegemonic and imperialist modes of theorizing, the term [comparative political theory] implies that one segment of the world's population cannot monopolize the language or idiom of the emerging 'village,' or global civil society," p. 249. See also Roxanne Euben, "Contingent Borders, Syncretic Perspectives: Globalization, Political Theory, and Islamizing Knowledge," *International Studies Review* 4 (1), 2002, p. 26.

22. Antony Black, "Toward a Global History of Political Thought," in Shogimen and Nederman, eds., *Western Political Thought*, pp. 29–30: "knowledge of non-Western political traditions is necessary for political science, and for the practical purposes of policy-making ... We need to understand the history of these traditions in order to understand their present predicaments." Black also characterizes this as a necessary prerequisite for self-reflective learning: "The study of non-Western cultures is necessary on *scientific* grounds for the study of Western culture itself. ... One cannot claim adequate knowledge of why Western political thought developed the way it did, nor of what were its distinguishing characteristics, without looking at what kinds of political thought there were elsewhere, where these differed, and why the end results have been so different," p. 27. Ackerly claims that such explorations will "inspire our curiosity about the vibrant theoretical discussions about democracy taking place in Chinese," in "Is Liberalism the Only Way Toward Democracy?" p. 548. Euben asserts that "interpretive accounts not only make fundamentalist ideas

intelligible but also contribute to current social science explanations of the increasing power of Islamic fundamentalism by making them causally adequate," *Enemy in the Mirror*, p. 156.

23. Dallmayr in "Beyond Monologue" calls comparative political theory "a mode of theorizing that takes seriously the ongoing process of globalization, a mode which entails, among other things the growing proximity and interpretation of cultures," p. 249.

24. Parel, *Comparative Political Philosophy*, p. 12. This genre continues to draw its inspiration from literature in comparative philosophy, much of which continues to be focused, for instance, on topics such as comparing "Socrates' Euthyphro and Confucius' Analects," or "the theories of Zhu Xi and Ronald Dworkin." See, for instance, Tim Murphy, "Confucianizing Socrates and Socratizing Confucius: On Comparing *Analects* 13:18 and the *Euthyphro*," *Philosophy East and West* 60 (2), April 2010; and A. P. Martinich and Yang Xiao, "Ideal Interpretation: The Theories of Zhu Xi and Ronald Dworkin," *Philosophy East and West* 60 (1), January 2010.

25. Stephen Angle, *Sagehood*; Peter Zarrow "Chinese Conceptions of the State during the Late Qing Dynasty," in Shogimen and Nederman, eds., *Western Political Thought*, pp. 235–60; Anthony Parel, "Gandhi and the Emergence of the Modern Indian Political Canon," *Review of Politics* 70 (1), 2008; Antony Black, *The History of Islamic Political Thought: From the Prophet to the Present* (New York: Routledge, 2001); Leigh K. Jenco, *Making the Political: Founding and Action in the Political Theory of Zhang Shizhao* (Cambridge: Cambridge University Press, 2010).

26. Good examples of problem-driven yet exegetically rigorous scholarship are Andrew March, *Islam and Liberal Citizenship: The Search for an Overlapping Consensus* (New York: Oxford University Press, 2009) and "Theocrats Living Under Secular Law: An External Engagement with Islamic Legal Theory," *Journal of Political Philosophy* 19 (1), 2011.

27. See Francis Oakley, *Kingship*; and Stuart Gray, "A Historical-Comparative Approach to Indian Political Thought: Locating and Examining Domesticated Differences," *History of Political Thought* 31 (3), 2010.

28. Antony Black, "Toward a Global History of Political Thought," in Shogimen and Nederman, eds., *Western Political Thought*, and *The West and Islam*.

29. Michaelle Browers, "Islam and Political *Sinn*: The Hermeneutics of Contemporary Islamic Reformists," in Michaelle Browers and Charles Kurzman, eds., *An Islamic Reformation?* (Lanham, MD: Lexington, 2004). See also Jenco, "What Does Heaven Ever Say?" and March, "Theocrats Living Under Secular Law" and "Are Secularism and Neutrality Attractive to Religious Minorities? Islamic Discussions of Western Secularism in the 'Jurisprudence of Muslim Minorities (*Fiqh Al-Aqalliyyat*) Discourse,'" *Cardozo Law Review* 30 (6), 2009.

30. In *Democracy and Civil Society in Arab Political Thought*, Browers undertakes a deep and situated discourse analysis, focusing specifically on the concepts of "democracy" and "civil society" in the Arab world, both of which have entered the discourse of Arab intellectuals and activists. She analyzes the history of these concepts in Arab and Islamic political thought, the more recent emergence of a discourse on civil society, transformations as a result of Arab interventions into international discussions, and what this tells us about the status of ideological and conceptual conflicts in the region.

31. In "Indian Secularism: An Alternative, Trans-cultural Ideal," in V.R. Mehta and Thomas Pantham, *Political Ideas in Modern India: Thematic Explorations* (New Delhi: Sage Publications, 2006), Rajeev Bhargava makes the argument that Indian secularism provides a new way to reconceptualize the very notion of secularism itself, challenging the Westcentric conceptual and normative liberal-democratic structure of secularism, particularly the notion that religious freedom and

liberty requires the state to be detached from any official religious affiliation. In "The Conceptual Vocabularies of Secularism and Minority Rights in India," *Journal of Political Ideologies* 7 (2), 2002, Rochana Bajpai challenges this contrast between Western and Indian "models" of secularism. Bajpai also examines public parliamentary debates on group-preference quotas and celebrated legal cases in order to examine the status of minority rights discourse in India. See "Redefining Equality: Social Justice in the Mandal Debate, 1990," in Mehta and Pantham, eds., *Political Ideas in Modern India*. See also Rajeev Bhargava, *The Promise of India's Secular Democracy* (Delhi: Oxford University Press, 2010) and *Politics and Ethics of the Indian Constitution* (Delhi: Oxford University Press, 2008).

32. Farah Godrej, "Nonviolence and Gandhi's Truth: A Method for Moral and Political Arbitration," *Review of Politics* 68 (2), 2006; Jenco, "What Does Heaven Ever Say?"

33. Andrew March, "What Is Comparative Political Theory?" *Review of Politics* 71 (4), Fall 2009; Farah Godrej, "Response to 'What Is Comparative Political Theory?'" *Review of Politics* 71 (4), Fall 2009; Farah Godrej, "Towards a Cosmopolitan Political Thought: The Hermeneutics of Interpreting the 'Other'" *Polity* 41, 2009; Megan Thomas, "Orientalism and Comparative Political Theory," *Review of Politics* 72 (4), Fall 2010; Leigh Jenco "Re-Centering Political Theory: The Promise of Mobile Locality," *Cultural Critique* 79, Fall 2011.

34. Dallmayr, *Beyond Orientalism*. See also Steve F. Schneck, ed., *Letting Be: Fred Dallmayr's Cosmopolitical Vision* (Notre Dame, IN: University of Notre Dame Press, 2006).

35. Dallmayr, *Dialogue Among Civilizations*, p. 26

36. Dallmayr, *Achieving Our World: Toward a Global and Plural Democracy* (Lanham, MD: Rowman and Littlefield, 2001), p. xi.

37. Euben, *Journeys to the Other Shore*, p. 186

38. Fred Dallmayr, "Cosmopolitanism: Moral and Political" *Political Theory*, 31 (3), p. 438: "To be properly cosmopolitan, this civic culture needs to be as inclusive as possible, that is, to embrace not only people similar to 'us,' but precisely those who are different or 'other,'—potentially even those who are now categorized (rashly) as 'enemies.'" See also Roxanne Euben, "Journeys to 'the Other Shore,'" *Political Theory* (28) 3, June 2000, p. 405.

39. Remarkable exceptions are Jenco, "What Does Heaven Ever Say?" and March, "What Is Comparative Political Theory?"

40. In keeping with Breckenridge et al.'s contention that cosmopolitanism "is a project whose conceptual and pragmatic character is as yet unspecified . . . it awaits detailed description at the hands of scholarship. We are not yet exactly certain what it is [for it] is awaiting realization" I speak therefore of cosmopolitanisms rather than cosmopolitanism in the singular. See Carol Breckenridge, Sheldon Pollock, Homi K. Bhabha, and Dipesh Chakrabarty, eds., *Cosmpolitanism* (Durham, NC: Duke University Press, 2002), p.1.

41. Martha Nussbaum, "Kant and Stoic Cosmopolitanism," *Journal of Political Philosophy* 5 (1), 1997, p. 7.

42. See Immanuel Kant, "Perpetual Peace: A Philosophical Sketch" in Hans Reiss, ed., *Kant: Political Writings* (Cambridge: Cambridge University Press, 1991) and Nussbaum, "Kant and Stoic Cosmopolitanism," pp. 12–18.

43. See Simon Caney, *Justice Beyond Borders: A Global Political Theory* (New York: Oxford University Press, 2006); Kok-Chor Tan, *Toleration, Diversity and Global Justice* (Philadelphia: Pennsylvania State University Press, 2000); Brian Barry, "Humanity and Justice in Global Perspective," in Robert E. Goodin and Philip Petit, eds., *Contemporary Political Philosophy: An Anthology* (Malden, MA: Blackwell Publishers, 1997).

44. Garrett Wallace Brown, "Kantian Cosmopolitan Law and the Idea of a Cosmopolitan Constitution," *History of Political Thought*, 27 (3), 2006; and "Theory and Practice: Moving Cosmopolitan Legal Theory to Legal Practice," *Legal Studies*, 28, (3), 2008. See also Allen Buchanan, *Justice, Legitimacy, and Self-Determination: Moral Foundations for International Law* (Oxford: Oxford University Press, 2004).

45. Thomas Pogge, *World Poverty and Human Rights: Cosmopolitan Responsibilities and Reforms* (Cambridge, UK: Polity Press, 2002).

46. David Held, *Democracy and the Global Order: From the Modern State to Cosmopolitan Governance* (Stanford, CA: Stanford University Press, 1995).

47. Kok-Chor Tan, *Justice Without Borders*; Jeremy Waldron, "What Is Cosmopolitan?" in *Journal of Political Philosophy* 8 (2), 2000; Jürgen Habermas, "Kant's Idea of Perpetual Peace, With the Benefit of Two Hundred Years Hindsight," in James Bohman and Matthias Lutz-Bachmann, eds., *Perpetual Peace: Essays on Kant's Cosmopolitan Ideal* (Cambridge, MA: MIT Press, 1997); Habermas, *The Postnational Constellation: Political Essays* (Cambridge: Polity, 2001); Habermas, *The Inclusion of the Other: Studies in Political Theory* (Cambridge, MA: MIT Press, 1998); Joshua Cohen, ed., *For Love of Country* (Boston: Beacon Press, 2002); Kwame Anthony Appiah, *Cosmopolitanism: Ethics in a World of Strangers* (Norton, 2007).

48. Cosmopolitanism as a set of moral commitments that justifies the sorts of institutions we may impose on individuals is to be distinguished from cosmopolitanism as a specific set of global institutions and organization representing a world state. See Charles Beitz, *Political Theory and International Relations* (Princeton, NJ: Princeton University Press, 1999), p. 287. Meanwhile, cosmopolitanism as a claim about the irrelevance of cultural membership for personal identity formation and autonomy is to be distinguished from cosmopolitanism as a claim about the irrelevance of boundaries for the scope of justice. See Samuel Scheffler, *Boundaries and Allegiances: Problems of Justice and Responsibility in Liberal Thought* (Oxford: Oxford University Press, 2001), pp. 112–13.

49. For the most obvious examples, see Held, *Democracy and the Global Order*, p. 227; Caney, *Justice Beyond Borders*, p. 4; Tan, *Justice Without Borders*, p. 40; Nussbaum, "Kant and Stoic Cosmopolitanism"; and Waldron, "What Is Cosmopolitan?"

50. Nussbaum does refer to Tagore, but paints his cosmopolitanism as comporting conveniently with Kant and the Stoics, leaving unaddressed the question of Tagore's alterity. Simon Caney similarly makes an all-too-brief allusion to Mo Tzu, claiming that he defends "recognizably cosmopolitan ideals." But the question of what these ideals are, and how, if at all, they may challenge Western understandings of cosmopolitanism remains unaddressed.

51. Robbins, "Introduction Part I: Actually Existing Cosmopolitanism," p. 2.

52. Ibid., p. 2.

53. Ibid., p. 2.

54. Paul Rabinow, "Representations Are Social Facts," in James Clifford and George E. Marcus eds., *Writing Culture: The Poetics and Politics of Ethnography* (Berkeley: University of California Press, 1986), 258.

55. Arjun Appadurai, "Global Ethnoscapes: Notes and Queries for a Transnational Anthropology," in Richard G. Fox, ed., *Recapturing Anthropology: Working in the Present* (Santa Fe, NM: School of American Research Press, 1991), p. 92.

56. Sheldon Pollock, "Cosmopolitan and Vernacular in History," *Public Culture* 12 (3), 2000, p. 601.

57. Ibid., p. 602.

58. Ibid., p. 604.

59. Ibid., p. 606.

60. Pheng Cheah, "Introduction Part II: The Cosmopolitical—Today" in Robbins and Cheah, eds., *Cosmopolitics: Thinking and Feeling Beyond the Nation*, p. 22.

61. Norbert Elias, "The Retreat of Sociologists into the Present," in Volker Meja, Dieter Misgeld, and Nico Stehr, eds., *Modern German Sociology* (New York: Columbia University Press, 1987), pp. 150–72.

62. Pollock, "Cosmopolitan and Vernacular in History," p. 595.

63. See, for instance, Bonnie Honig, *Democracy and the Foreigner* (Princeton, NJ: Princeton University Press, 2001); Michael Sandel, *Democracy's Discontent: America in Search of a Public Philosophy* (Cambridge, MA: Harvard University Press: 1996), pp. 342–43; Seyla Benhabib, *Another Cosmopolitanism* (New York: Oxford University Press, 2006); Waldron, "What Is Cosmopolitan?"; Euben, *Journeys to the Other Shore*; Pratap Mehta, "Cosmpolitanism and the Circle of Reason," *Political Theory* 8 (25), 2000.

64. Euben, *Journeys To the Other Shore*, p. 5.

65. Dipesh Chakrabarty, *Provincializing Europe: Postcolonial Thought and Historical Difference* (Princeton, NJ: Princeton University Press, 2000), pp. 29, 43; Gyan Prakash, "Subaltern Studies as Postcolonial Criticism," *American Historical Review* 99 (5) 1994, p. 1475, n. 1.

66. See Syed Farid Alatas, *Alternative Discourses in Asian Social Science: Responses to Eurocentrism* (New Delhi: Sage Publications, 2006), Rajani Kannepalli Kanth, *Against Eurocentrism: A Transcendent Critique of Modernist Science, Society and Morals* (New York: Palgrave Macmillan, 2005), Samir Amin, *Eurocentrism*, trans. Russell Moore (New York: Monthly Review Press, 1989).

67. Leigh Jenco, "Re-Centering Political Theory: The Promise of Mobile Locality," *Cultural Critique* 79, Fall 2011, pp. 8–9.

68. As a remarkable exception, see Jenco, "What Does Heaven Ever Say?" See also Daniel A. Bell, *Beyond Liberal Democracy: Political Thinking for an East Asian Context* (Princeton, NJ: Princeton University Press, 2006); Daniel A. Bell and Hahm Chaibong, eds., *Confucianism for a Modern World* (Cambridge/New York: Cambridge University Press, 2003); Daniel A. Bell, Kanishka Jayasuriya and David M. Jones, eds., *Towards Illiberal Democracy in Pacific Asia* (New York: St. Martin's Press, 1995).

69. A promising exception is available in Leigh Jenco, "Re-Centering Political Theory."

70. See Andrew March, "What Is Comparative Political Theory?" p. 565

71. Pollock, "Cosmopolitan and Vernacular in History," p. 593.

72. Ibid., p. 625.

73. Indeed, such a continuous and process-oriented vision cannot but acknowledge its intellectual debt to the philosophical posture and attitude elaborated briefly by Raimundo Panikkar in his famous article, "What Is Comparative Philosophy Comparing?" Panikkar's article serves, however, as the tentative and preliminary sketch for a vision that I hope will be more fully and rigorously articulated here.

74. Herodotus, *The Histories*, trans. George Rawlinson (New York: Alfred A. Knopf, 1997), 1.30

75. Euben, *Journeys to the Other Shore*, p. 22

76. Ronald Beiner, ed., *Hannah Arendt: Lectures on Kant's Political Philosophy* (Chicago: University of Chicago Press, 1982), pp. 42–43.

77. Euben, *Journeys to the Other Shore*, p. 86.

78. See Scott L. Malcomson, "The Varieties of Cosmopolitan Experience," in Robbins and Cheah, eds., *Cosmopolitics: Thinking and Feeling Beyond the Nation*, p. 33: "Alexander and Diogenes were both, in their ways, extreme cosmopolitans . . . Cosmopolitans, most of them influenced by Stoicism, took their universal citizenship as a license either to withdraw from the world or to master it . . . Those who did not [withdraw] tended to use their citizenship toward one of two purposes: to study the world or to control it . . . whereas Diogenes had withdrawn from the world, Alexander was bent on subjugating it."

79. March, "What Is Comparative Political Theory?" p. 533.

80. John Gunnell, *The Descent of Political Theory: The Genealogy of an American Vocation* (Chicago: University of Chicago Press, 1993), p. 268.

81. Kaufman-Osborn, "Political Theory as Profession and as Subfield?" p. 657

82. Ibid., pp. 663–66.

CHAPTER 2

1. See, for instance, Roxanne Euben, *Enemy in the Mirror*; Anthony J. Parel, "Gandhi and the Emergence of the Modern Indian Political Canon," *Review of Politics* 70 (2008); Russell Arben Fox, "Confucianism and Communitarianism in a Liberal Democratic World," in Fred Dallmayr, ed., *Border Crossings: Toward a Comparative Political Theory* (Lanham, MD: Lexington Books, 1999); Anthony J. Parel and Ronald C. Keith, eds., *Comparative Political Philosophy: Studies Under the Upas Tree* (Lanham, MD: Lexington Books, 1992); Margaret Kohn and Keally McBride, *Political Theories of Decolonization: Postcolonialism and the Problem of Foundation* (New York: Oxford University Press, 2011).

2. Some exceptions arise to this. Leigh Jenco, "What Can Heaven Ever Say?" is a rare work of comparative scholarship that both justifies the choice of and exegetes certain lesser-known Chinese political thinkers. In "What Is Comparative Political Theory?" Andrew March addresses at length the question of what makes certain non-Western thinkers fodder for political inquiry and not others.

3. Parekh, "Some Reflections on the Hindu Tradition of Political Thought," in Thomas Pantham and Kenneth L. Deutsch, eds., *Political Thought in Modern India* (New Delhi: Sage Publications, 1986), pp. 17–31.

4. Leo Strauss, *What Is Political Philosophy?* (Glencoe, IL: The Free Press, 1959), *City of Man* (Chicago: University of Chicago Press, 1977), and *Natural Right and History* (Chicago: University of Chicago Press, 1953).

5. John Passmore, "Philosophy" in Paul Edwards, ed., *The Encyclopedia of Philosophy*, Vol. 6 (New York: Macmillan, 1967), pp. 217–18, cited in Stephen G. Salkever and Michael Nylan, "Comparative Political Philosophy and Liberal Education: 'Looking for Friends in History,'" *PS: Political Science and Politics* 27 (2), June 1994, p. 240.

6. Salkever and Nylan, "Comparative Political Philosophy and Liberal Education," p. 239.

7. See Anthony J. Parel, "The Comparative Study of Political Philosophy," in Parel and Keith, eds., *Comparative Political Philosophy*, pp. 11–12.

8. See Hajime Nakamura, *Parallel Developments: A Comparative History of Ideas* (Tokyo: Kodansha Press, 1975).

9. "It follows that such a study is nothing other than the process, first of identifying the 'equivalences,' and second, of understanding their significance." Anthony J. Parel, "The Comparative Study of Political Philosophy," p. 12.

10. Roxanne Euben, *Enemy in the Mirror*.

11. Ibid., p. 93.

12. Browers, *Democracy and Civil Society in Arab Political Thought*, p. 213.

13. Leigh Jenco points us to this dilemma when she reminds us that the "dialogical" approach to much comparative work in political theory assumes a frame of inquiry in which the cross-cultural encounter is pictured as a "conversation" among Western investigators and non-Western others, in which speech and language are privileged as counterpoints to the violence of Western hegemony. This privileging, however, raises all kinds of problems: language is often not a neutral carrier of meaning, speech may not be a universal or universally transparent form of communication, its relationship to violence may not be simply one of countering or overcoming it, privileging the substance of utterances may come at the expense of forms of nonverbal expression and discourse which may be rendered silent, and texts and personalities not directly amenable to conversation are given no chance to dissent to its imposition. Ultimately, Jenco points out, "the theorist who initially staged the dialogue may change her own opinions as a result of the engagement, but the frame of inquiry she imposes remains always the same." Jenco, "What Does Heaven Ever Say?" pp. 743–45

14. Joseph Chan, "Is There a Confucian Perspective on Social Justice?" in Takashi Shogimen and Cary Nederman, eds., *Western Political Thought in Dialogue with Asia* (Lanham, MD: Lexington Press, 2009), p. 265.

15. Ibid., p. 269.

16. Azizah Y. al-Hibri, "Islamic Constitutionalism and the Concept of Democracy," in Dallmayr, ed., *Border Crossings*, p. 62.

17. Timothy V. Kaufman-Osborn, "Political Theory as Profession and as Subfield?" *Political Research Quarterly*, 63 (3), 2010, p. 657.

18. Along with Ackerly, the following are good examples of work that explicitly situates the investigations of thinkers and ideas within the context of the preoccupations and frameworks internal to a particular tradition: Anthony Parel, *Gandhi's Political Philosophy and the Quest for Harmony* (Cambridge: Cambridge University Press, 2006); and Bhikhu Parekh, *Gandhi's Political Philosophy: A Critical Examination* (Notre Dame, IN: University of Notre Dame Press, 1989).

19. I would point here to Leigh Jenco's work on Chinese political thought and Andrew March's work on Islamic political thought. See also Stuart Gray, "A Historical-Comparative Approach to Indian Political Thought: Locating and Examining Domesticated Differences," *History of Political Thought* 31 (3), 2010, pp. 383–90.

20. See, for instance, Fred R. Dallmayr, "Preface," in Fred R. Dallmayr, ed., *Comparative Political Theory: An Introduction* (New York: Palgrave Macmillan, 2010), p. xi; Parel, "Gandhi and the Emergence of the Modern Indian Political Canon" and "The Comparative Study of Political Philosophy"; Elliot Deutsch, "Knowledge and the Tradition Text in Indian Philosophy," in Gerald James Larson and Elliott Deutsch, eds., *Interpreting Across Boundaries: New Essays in Comparative Philosophy* (Princeton, NJ: Princeton University Press, 1988).

21. In such a view, for instance, both Gandhi and Tagore, otherwise very different, are said to write in a tradition that is directly and distinctly influenced by the Vedas; otherwise diverse thinkers such as Al-Farabi, Ibn Khaldun and Sayyid Qutb by the Koran; and Mencius and a whole host of other Chinese thinkers by Confucius and so on. Not all comparative political theorists tend to conduct their investigations in such terms, nor do they explicitly articulate such presumptions, but the language of traditionally bounded canonicity is widely available, and even when

comparative scholars do not directly address entire "traditions" as objects of inquiry, it seems almost unavoidable for them to make reference to the importance of a tradition as a backdrop for a particular thinker or text they are addressing.

22. No discussion of Indian political thought could be complete without an exploration of the tremendous influence of Islam, yet many scholars are easily misled into identifying Indian political thought with thinkers influenced mainly by the elite, brahminical, Vedic texts of Hinduism. See U.N. Ghoshal, *A History of Indian Political Ideas* (Oxford: Oxford University Press, 1959); Bhikhu Parekh, "Some Reflections on the Hindu Tradition of Political Thought," in Thomas Pantham and Kenneth Deutsch, eds., *Political Thought in Modern India* (New Delhi: Sage Publications, 1986), Amritava Banerjee, "Political Thinking in Ancient India: A Brief Outline," in Harihar Bhattacharya and Abhijit Ghosh, eds., *Indian Political Thought and Movement: New Interpretations and Emerging Issues* (Kolkata: K.P. Bagchi & Co., 2007). Similarly for the long and ancient tradition of exchanges between Indian and Chinese scholars: most analyses of the Chinese tradition neglect to mention the influence of Buddhism from India in its development. See Stephen Angle, *Sagehood: The Contemporary Significance of Neo-Confucian Philosophy* (New York: Oxford University Press, 2009), p. 6; Philip J. Ivanhoe, *Ethics in the Confucian Tradition: The Thought of Mencius and Wang Yangming* (Indianapolis, IN: Hackett, 2002).

23. Edward Said's arguments about the relationship between colonial power and the epistemic authority to construct self/other "essences" are of course too well-known to rehash here. See Edward Said, *Orientalism* (New York, Vintage Books, 1979).

24. Ronald Inden, *Imagining India* (Cambridge, MA, and Oxford, UK: Blackwell, 1990), p. 4.

25. Lloyd and Susanne Rudolph point out that the "civilizational eye" of many Orientalist scholars—particularly those sympathetic to and eager to immerse themselves within the local tradition they studied and governed—saw the traditions they governed as "large, coherent, cultural wholes defined by great languages and their classic texts." Lloyd I. Rudolph and Susanne Hoeber Rudolph, *Occidentalism and Orientalism: Perspectives on Legal Pluralism* (Ann Arbor: University of Michigan Press, 1997), p. 225. Routinely ignored were diverse local customs defined by oral traditions, what Ashis Nandy has called the "little traditions" of everyday life, folk understandings and practices that departed from the grand literary tradition in multiple ways. See also Ghoshal, *A History of Indian Political Ideas*; Parekh, "Some Reflections on the Hindu Tradition of Political Thought"; Banerjee, "Political Thinking in Ancient India: A Brief Outline."

26. A prime example of such colonial influence in the construction of self-understanding is the influence of Warren Hastings' 1772 regulation which began the process of fixing relatively fluid identity categories into rigid ones with the codification and canonization of legal codes for Hindus and Muslims in then British-ruled India. Based on specific texts of each religion deemed "canonical" by the colonial authorities, personal law in India was gradually transformed, Nivedita Menon tells us, "from being a vast body of texts and locally variegated customs, all of which was constantly interpreted to a rigid, codified body of legal rules." Nivedita Menon, "Nation, Identity, Citizenship: Feminist Critique in Contemporary India," in V. R. Mehta and Thomas Pantham, eds., *Political Ideas in Modern India: Thematic Explorations* (New Delhi: Sage Publications, 2006). This transformation of legal codes in turn affected the identity-boundaries and self-understandings of each religious community, permeating their categories of self and social identification. Until this rigid codification, "Hindu" and "Muslim" were not natural, stable or self-evident categories, but rather a series of fluid, nonexclusive and often overlapping ethnic, communal and territorial identities. It was not until the colonial constructions of these religious

groups that such reified categories seeped into the self-understanding of colonial subjects, solidifying in turn a renewed sense of self and social identification based on these so-called canonical texts. See Rudolph and Rudolph, "Occidentalism and Orientalism," pp. 224–25; and Lloyd I. Rudolph and Susanne Hoeber Rudolph, *The Modernity of Tradition: Political Development in India* (Chicago: University of Chicago Press, 1967), pp. 251–93.

27. The political theorist Meera Nanda is one voice among such discourses emerging from within India, arguing that Buddhism's challenge to the primacy of mystical, transcendental and metaphysical forms of knowledge over the mundane was rooted in Hinduism's own Lokayata and Samkhya schools of philosophy, each with a strong realist, empiricist and anti-metaphysical bent. Not only does Nanda chronicle the existence and influence of these moments within the tradition, she argues keenly for a return to these empiricist, rationalist and materialist commitments in contemporary Indian public discourse and policy. Nanda, *Breaking the Spell of Dharma and Other Essays* (New Delhi: Three Essays, 2002), pp. 87–88. The philosophers of the Lokayata school, who were non-Brahmin and lower-caste, were famous for putting Vedic teachings to a test of practice in everyday life, denying any notion of a spiritual self over and above the material body, and explaining all observed phenomena by natural laws. See Debiprasad Chattopadhyaya, *Lokayata: A Study of Ancient Indian Materialism* (New Delhi: People's Publishing House, 1959). Meanwhile, the Samkhya philosophers, with whom Siddhartha Gautama is said to have studied, held that the regularities and laws of nature were to be understood through evidence of experience in the here and now, rather than in the transcendental realm. See also Nanda, *Prophets Facing Backward: Postmodern Critiques of Science and Hindu Nationalism in India* (New Brunswick, NJ: Rutgers University Press, 2003). Among Western analysts, Martha Nussbaum and Amartya Sen argue, for instance, that despite the undeniable importance of mysticism and nonrationality in Indian intellectual history, it is erroneous to emphasize exclusively the spiritual and nonargumentative nature of Indian thought to the neglect of its urbane, worldly and rationalist traditions. They challenge the standard view that the chief mark of Indian philosophy in general is its concentration on the spiritual, and they claim that this view underemphasizes the influence of materialist, hedonist and rationalist currents in Indian philosophy. They point appropriately to the unrestrained hedonism and atheism of the *Carvaka* school of thought, the importance of worldly sexual pleasures in texts such as the *Kama-sutra*, the development of sampling procedures for personal and business calculations in the Mahabharata, the teaching of practical wisdom and shrewdness in the *Hitopadesa* and *Panchatantra*, and the critical challenges presented to the spiritual thrust of the Vedic period by the empiricism and realism of later schools. Martha C. Nussbaum and Amartya Sen, "Internal Criticism and Indian Rationalist Traditions," in Michael Krausz, ed., *Relativism: Interpretation and Confrontation* (Notre Dame, IN: University of Notre Dame Press, 1989), pp. 302–6. Newer volumes exploring modern postcolonial political thought in India tend also to emphasize the liberal, nonidealist, secularist, materialist or socialist moments in the development of political thinking within modern India, even if these are inevitably fused with and influenced by the legacy of Enlightenment thought. See V. R. Mehta and Thomas Pantham, eds., *Political Ideas in Modern India*; Thomas Pantham and Kenneth Deutsch, eds., *Political Thought in Modern India*; and Harihar Bhattacharya and Abhijit Ghosh, *Indian Political Thought and Movements: New Interpretations and Emerging Issues* (Kolkata: K.P. Bagchi & Company, 2007).

28. In both the Chinese and Islamic traditions, for instance, the notion of a "canon" as an authoritative set of texts does not hold much weight. In the case of the tradition of Islamic thought, it is far more helpful to see it as a tradition with consistent concerns and modes of reasoning,

rather than simply a "canon" of texts and authors. The main mode of thinking about politics in Islam is the legal tradition, also known as the jurist or the juridical tradition. In this tradition, the authority of Islamic law is less about a set of texts or of select authors with individual authority, but rather a history of thinking about things through certain methods and privileging law as the Islamic science par excellence. Modern revivalists such as Sayyid Qutb and al-Mawdudi, despite their modernity and their objections to certain kinds of classical legal scholarship, are still part of the juridical tradition, for they seek to revive the political vision of classical juridical thinkers such as al-Mawardi, al-Ghazali, and Ibn Taymiyya. Even the writings of Sayyid Qutb, who famously decried the provincial and reactionary nature of the Islamic religious scholars, calling for Muslims to go back to the earliest texts, accept almost entirely the presumptions of the classical legal corpus on the specifics of the Islamic political order. Similarly, Leigh Jenco reminds us that method rather than content better characterizes much of what should properly be understood as Confucianism, which is not a philosophy for which Confucius is the official spokesman, but rather a tradition of self-understanding and textual interpretation characterized by participation in certain ways of life and practices. These nuances are thus "obscured when Chinese thought is approached as a series of clear treatises written by philosopher-type figures, who stand in for an entire tradition that spans millennia." Jenco, "What Does Heaven Ever Say?" p. 752.

29. One could scarcely argue, for instance, that there was no meaningful difference between a text such as Kautilya's *Arthasastra*, written clearly in the tradition of Indic Sanskrit texts, and Mencius' neo-Confucian writings, written in the post-Confucian Chinese classical tradition; or that the difference between these texts are not, to some extent, a result of the differences in traditions from which they emerge.

30. For more detailed accounts of this phenomenon across traditions, see S.G.F. Brandon, "Holy Book, Tradition and Ikon" in F. F. Bruce and E. G. Rupp, eds., *Holy Book and Holy Traditions* (Grand Rapids, MI: William B. Eerdmans, 1968), pp. 14–15; also John B. Henderson, *Scripture, Canon, and Commentary: A Comparison of Confucian and Western Exegesis* (Princeton, NJ: Princeton University Press, 1991), p.38.

31. Emperor Wu limited programs of study to the five Confucian classics, and later Han emperors convened conferences in order to discuss and resolve important questions regarding these texts, thereby binding "[this] canon even more closely to the fortunes of the Chinese imperial state." Henderson, *Scripture, Canon, and Commentary*, p. 38. See also Benjamin A. Elman, *From Philosophy to Philology: Intellectual and Social Aspects of Change in Late Imperial China* (Los Angeles: UCLA Asian-Pacific Monograph Series, 2001); and Mark Edward Lewis, *Writing and Authority in Early China* (Albany, NY: SUNY Press, 1999). Equally influential was the effect of the infamous pre-Han Ch'in dynasty (221–206 BC) burning of books, when Ch'in edicts had ordered the destruction of several Confucian texts. The extent to which Confucian writings had actually perished under Ch'in rule is a matter of some debate, but what is undisputed is the political and psychological impact of this event, which left Han-era scholars with the somewhat mythic belief that their tradition had survived only in a defective and fragmented condition, along with a mandate to reassemble a supposedly "lost" classic from bits and pieces of surviving texts. The presumed effect of the Ch'in book burning, Henderson tells us, "increasingly took on the proportions of myth used to justify reconstructions of the canon and its components." Henderson, *Scripture, Canon, and Commentary*, p. 40.

32. The Han historian Pan Ku, for instance, related the books of the canon to the universal moral order signified by the five constant human virtues; later commentators not only correlated

the classics comprehensively with the outer world of ancient history and kingship, but also with the inner world of human qualities. Henderson, *Scripture, Canon, and Commentary*, pp. 46–47.

33. Postcolonial theorists such as Gayatri Spivak have written extensively on the notion of the subaltern "voice" and its recovery. See Gayatri Chakravorty Spivak, "Can the Subaltern Speak?" in Cary Nelson and Lawrence Grossberg, *Marxism and the Interpretation of Culture* (Chicago: University of Illinois Press, 1988).

34. J. Phule, *Collected Works of Mahatma Phule* (Bombay: Government of Maharashtra, 1873); G.P. Deshpande, ed., *Selected Writings of Jotirao Phule* (New Delhi: Leftword Press, 2002); B. R. Ambedkar, *The Buddha and His Dhamma* (Bombay: Siddharth Publications, 1957), *The Untouchables: Who Were They and Why They Became Untouchables* (New Delhi: Amrit Books, 1948), *Annihilation of Caste* (Jalandhar: Bhim Patrika Publications, 1936); Vasant Moon, ed., *Babasaheb Ambedkar Writings and Speeches* (Government of Maharashtra, Department of Education, 1979–98); Periyar, "Matam Een Ozhiyaveendum?" in *Pakuttarivu*, September 9, 1934; "Matakkirukku" in *Pakuttarivu*, January 1, 1939; Velllore Senthamizko, *Periyar in History* (Vellore: Periyar-Gora-Kovoor Atheist Centre, 1987).

35. See Ambedkar, *The Buddha and His Dhamma*, *The Untouchables*, *Annihilation of Caste*. See also Meera Nanda, *Breaking the Spell of Dharma and Other Essays* (New Delhi: Three Essays, 2002), p. 82. Like his predecessors in the Lokayata and Samkhya schools of thought, Ambedkar clearly finds himself in the lineage of those who challenge the predominance of the mystical, transcendental, metaphysical forms of knowledge over the mundane, experientalist and the pragmatic ones. The mystic idealism of Brahmanism in turn "ridiculed, absorbed and in other ways demoted the empirical, experimental understanding of nature as *avidya* or false knowledge" and the eventual history of Indian philosophy is the "grim tale of the victory of Brahmanism" heaping scorn and ridicule upon their experientalist challengers, maintaining the elitism of transcendental knowledge and access to it. Nanda, *Breaking the Spell of Dharma*, pp. 88–89.

36. In addition to the intellectual ferment that Ambedkar's writings created, Nanda claims, "a turn to Buddhism has given the ex-untouchables . . . a new self-confidence and a new culture . . . an explosion of creative expression of new rationalist, humanist themes through song and poetry . . . and above all, a growing sense of self-worth and pride." Nanda, *Breaking the Spell of Dharma*, p. 83.

37. Valerian Rodrigues, "Dalit-Bahujan Discourse in Modern India" in Mehta and Pantham, eds., *Political Ideas in Modern India*, p. 63. Contrary to the traditional narrative, a reinterpretation of the classic text *Ramayana* by Periyar depicts the Dravidian anti-hero Ravana as in fact a benign protagonist against the Aryan invader Rama, who is presented as the far more ignoble of the two. V. Geetha and S. V. Rajadurai, *Towards a Non-Brahmin Millenium: From Iyothee Thass to Periyar* (Calcutta: Samya, 1998), p. 335.

38. Rodrigues, "Dalit-Bahujan Discourse in Modern India" in Mehta and Pantham, eds., pp. 53–54. See also Kanchan Ilaiah, *Why I Am Not a Hindu: A Shudra Critique of Hindutva Philosophy, Culture and Political Economy* (Calcutta: Samya, 1996).

39. For detailed commentary on the practices of scholarship and disciplinary organization in India, see, for instance, Bhikhu Parekh, "The Poverty of Indian Political Theory," *History of Political Thought* 8 (3), Autumn 1992; Rajeev Bhargava "Is There an Indian Political Theory?" in *What Is Political Theory and Why Do We Need It?* (Delhi: Oxford University Press, 2010).

40. K. Jones, *Socio-Religious Reform Movements in British India* (Cambridge: Cambridge University Press, 1994); V. Ramaswamy, *Divinity and Deviance: Women in Virasaivism* (New Delhi: Oxford University Press, 1996).

41. Women-saints such as Mirabai who dedicated themselves at an early age to worship, sub-verted male-oriented norms by avoiding marriage entirely and immersing themselves instead in the single-minded devotional practices of poetic creation and recitation, claiming to be married only to the form of the deity they worshipped. See Rajeev Bhargava, *What Is Political Theory and Why Do We Need It?* (Delhi: Oxford University Press, 2010); P. Mukta, *Upholding a Common Life: The Community of Mirabai* (Delhi: Oxford University Press, 1994); K. Sangari, "Mirabai and the Spiritual Economy of *Bhakti*," *Economic and Political Weekly*, July 7 and 14, 1990. The famous medieval poet-saint Kabir was born into the low-caste weaver community, yet was said to have embraced multiple religions, constantly composing and reciting poetry in which he claimed both Hinduism and Islam as his own. Claiming to be in love with a divine god who was neither Hindu nor Muslim, Kabir lived in a transcendent state, inviting all humankind to do the same by renouncing the specific rituals and beliefs of organized religions, and merging with a transcendent divinity beyond name and form. See G. N. Das, *Love Songs of Kabir* (New Delhi: Abhinav Publications, 1992) and *Mystic Songs of Kabir* (New Delhi: Abhinav Publications, 1996).

42. Jenco, "Recentering Political Theory: The Promise of Mobile Locality."

43. Ibid.

44. Ackerly, "Is Liberalism the Only Way Toward Democracy?" p. 552.

45. For instance, Martha Nussbaum's modern reinterpretation of Aristotle for the purpose of development ethics explicitly relies upon excavating mostly Aristotelian answers to the question: what sorts of capacities are central to the concept of "humanness?" See Martha C. Nussbaum, *Women and Human Development: The Capabilities Approach* (Cambridge: Cambridge University Press, 2000).

46. Angle, *Sagehood*, p. 55.

47. Ibid., p. 54.

48. Ibid., p. 78.

49. Quoted in Angle, *Sagehood*, p. 78.

50. Michaelle Browers, "Islam and Political *Sinn*: The Hermeneutics of Contemporary Islamic Reformists," in Michaelle Browers and Charles Kurzman, eds., *An Islamic Reformation?* (Lanham, MD: Lexington, 2004).

51. Ibid., p. 70.

52. Ibid., p. 56.

53. Browers, "Islam and Political *Sinn*," pp. 60–61.

54. Kaufman-Osborn, "Political Theory as Profession and as Subfield?" p. 668.

55. See Raghavan Iyer, *The Moral and Political Writings of Mahatma Gandhi [MPW]* (Oxford: Clarendon Press, 1986), Vol. III, p. 548: "Is not politics too a part of *dharma*! . . . Politics also re-quires purity of conduct." Also see Vol. I, p. 375: "Political life must be an echo of private life and . . . there cannot be any divorce between the two"; Vol. I, p. 376: "I take part in politics because I feel that there is no department of life which can be divorced from religion"; Vol. I, p. 381: "My politics are not divorced from morality, from spirituality, from religion . . . A man who is trying to discover and follow the will of God cannot possibly leave a single field of life untouched"; Vol. I, p. 391: "For me, every, the tiniest, activity is governed by what I consider to be my religion."

56. Gandhi, Discussion with G. Ramachandran, *Young India*, March 1922.

57. In the yogic branches of Hindu thought, *tapas* literally means the heat of disciplined auster-ity, which burns the impurities between the seeker and truth. See Sri Swami Satchidananda, *The Yogasutras of Patanjali* (Integral Yoga Publications, 1990): "Accepting pain as help for purification,

study and surrender to the Supreme Being constitute yoga in practice," p. 79. This language of self-cleansing and clarifying is prominent in Gandhi's notion of self-suffering. Through this conscious suffering, Gandhi claims, "we realize the greatness . . . of Truth. Our peace of mind increases . . . we understand more clearly the difference between what is everlasting and what is not; we learn to distinguish between what is our duty and what is not. Our pride melts away . . . Our worldly attachments diminish and . . . the evil within us diminishes from day to day." Gandhi, "Letter to Narandas Gandhi," July 28/31, 1930.

58. Through such penance, the seeker "becomes more alert, examines the innermost recesses of his own heart and takes steps to deal with any personal weaknesses he may discover." M. K. Gandhi, *Ashram Observances in Action* (Ahmedabad: Navajivan, 1955). Through conscious suffering, Gandhi claims, "we realize the greatness . . . of Truth. Our peace of mind increases . . . we become braver and more enterprising; we understand more clearly the difference between what is everlasting and what is not; we learn to distinguish between what is our duty and what is not. Our pride melts away . . . Our worldly attachments diminish and . . . the evil within us diminishes from day to day." Gandhi, "Letter to Narandas Gandhi." See also, Iyer, *MPW* Vol. II, pp. 163, 577, 212; Vol. I, p. 508; Vol. III, p. 439. For more detailed treatment of the notion of "self-suffering" in Gandhi's work and its role as a political tool, see also Margaret Chatterjee, *Gandhi's Religious Thought* (Notre Dame, IN: University of Notre Dame Press, 1983), ch. 5.

59. Indeed, Gandhi's lifelong struggle to gain control over his senses and over his sensual desires is nothing if not well-chronicled. For various accounts of Gandhi's asceticism, see Mohandas K. Gandhi, *An Autobiography: The Story of My Experiments with Truth* (Boston: Beacon Press, 1993), Part III chs. vii, viii, ix, Part IV, chs. iv, v, vii, xxiii, xxvii, xxiii, xxix, xxx, xxxi, xxxiv, xxxvi; Bhikhu Parekh, "Sex, Energy and Politics," in *Colonialism, Tradition and Reform: An Analysis of Gandhi's Political Discourse* (New Delhi: Sage Publications, 1989); Lloyd I. Rudolph and Susanne Hoeber Rudolph, *The Modernity of Tradition: Political Development in India* (Chicago: University of Chicago Press, 1967); Joseph S. Alter, *Gandhi's Body: Sex, Diet and the Politics of Nationalism* (Philadelphia: University of Pennsylvania Press, 2000); "Nonviolence, Brahmacharya and Goat's Milk," in Ved Mehta, *Mahatma Gandhi and His Apostles* (New Haven, CT: Yale University Press, 1993).

60. Mohandas K. Gandhi, *The Collected Works of Mahatma Gandhi*, 100 vols. (Delhi: Publication Division, Ministry of Information and Broadcasting, Government of India, 1958–1994), 1: 82–86, 166; 11: 494, 501–10; 12; 79–80, 97. See also Joseph Alter's *Gandhi's Body: Sex, Diet and the Politics of Nationalism.* For instance, Gandhi writes: "I had involuntary discharge twice during the last two weeks. I cannot recall any dream. I never practiced masturbation. One cause of these discharges is of course my physical weakness but I also know that there are impure desires deep down in me. . . . I feel unhappy about this, but I am not nervously afraid." Gandhi, *Collected Works*, 40: 312, as cited in Alter, p. 7.

61. See M. K. Gandhi, *Key to Health* (Ahmedabad: Navajivan Press, 1948); and *Self-Restraint vs. Self-Indulgence* (Ahmedabad: Navajivan Press, 1927).

62. Lloyd I. Rudolph and Susanne Hoeber Rudolph, "Self-Control and Political Potency," in *The Modernity of Tradition: Political Development in India* (Chicago: University of Chicago Press, 1967), p.194 "The king who overcomes attachment, who reigns with mind serene, who achieves that expunging of self-interest, can judge clearly and fairly the interest of others."

63. Ibid., p. 196.

64. Bhikhu Parekh, *Colonialism, Tradition and Reform: An Analysis of Gandhi's Political Discourse* (New Delhi: Sage Publications, 1989), p. 196.

65. Parekh, *Colonialism, Tradition and Reform*, p. 181

66. Alter, p. 6.

67. For instance, Gandhi writes: "I have traveled all over the country and one of the most deplorable things I have noticed is the rickety bodies of young men, though we do physical exercises, we are going to become servants—servants of India, servants of the world." Gandhi, *CW* 32:444, as cited in Alter, p. 16–17.

68. Parekh, *Colonialism, Tradition and Reform*, p. 180.

69. Parel, *Gandhi's Philosophy and the Quest for Harmony*, p. 148.

70. The extent to which this connection between sexual dualism and the violence inherent in political otherizing can be attributed to the Indian tradition is a matter of some debate. See Parekh, pp. 202. See also Parel, pp. 148–49.

71. See, for instance, Lois McNay, "The Foucauldian Body and the Exclusion of Experience," *Hypatia* 6 (3), Autumn 1991; Nancy Fraser, "Unruly Practices: Power, Discourse and Gender," in *Contemporary Social Theory* (Cambridge: Polity Press, 1989); Irene Diamond and Lee Quinby, eds., *Feminism and Foucault: Reflections on Resistance* (Boston: Northeastern University Press, 1988); Judith Butler, *Gender Trouble: Feminism and the Subversion of Identity* (New York: Routledge, 1990) and *Bodies that Matter: On the Discursive Limits of Sex* (New York: Routledge 1995); Susan Bordo, *Unbearable Weight: Feminism, Western Culture and the Body* (Berkeley: University of California Press, 1993).

72. Alter, *Gandhi's Body*, p. 29.

73. Alter, *Gandhi's Body*, pp. 50–51.

74. Kaufman-Osborn, "Political Theory as Profession and as Subfield?" p. 657; Wendy Brown, "At the Edge," *Political Theory* 30(4), 2002, p. 566.

75. See, for instance, Mohandas K. Gandhi, *An Autobiography: The Story of My Experiments with Truth* (Boston: Beacon Press, 1993), p. 68; Anthony Parel, ed., *Gandhi: Hind Swaraj and Other Writings* (Cambridge: Cambridge University Press, 1997), pp. xxxii–xlvii; Bhikhu Parekh, *Colonialism, Tradition and Reform: An Analysis of Gandhi's Political Discourse* (New Delhi: Sage Publications, 1989).

76. See also Godrej, "Towards a Cosmopolitan Political Thought," *Polity*.

CHAPTER 3

1. Fania Oz-Salzberger, "'Lost in Translation' Meets Political Thought: Some Modern Tales of Misreception," Working Paper Series, April 7, 2010 at http://papers.ssrn.com/sol3/papers.cfm?abstract_id=1585891, pp. 22–23.

2. See Margaret Leslie, "In Defense of Anachronism," *Political Studies* 18, 1970, 433–47; Fania Oz-Salzberger, *Translating the Enlightenment: Scottish Civic Discourse in Eighteenth Century Germany* (Oxford: Clarendon Press, 1995), and "The Enlightenment in Translation: Regional and European Aspects," *European Review of History* 13, 2006, 385–409.

3. Gray, "A Historical-Comparative Approach to Indian Political Thought: Locating and Examining Domesticated Differences," *History of Political Thought* 31 (3), 2010, p. 384.

4. Ibid., p. 391.

5. Ibid., p. 396.

6. Irene Bloom, "Biology and Culture in the Mencian View of Human Nature," in Alan Kam-leung Chan, ed., *Mencius: Contexts and Interpretations* (Honolulu: University of Hawai'i Press, 2002), p. 94.

7. Daya Krishna, "Comparative Philosophy: What It Is and What It Ought to Be," in Gerald James Larson and Elliott Deutsch, eds., *Interpreting Across Boundaries: New Essays in Comparative Philosophy* (Princeton, NJ: Princeton University Press, 1988).

8. I owe my use of the term hermeneutic "moments" to Dvora Yanow, whose work emphasizes the notion of a "triple hermeneutic." See Dvora Yanow, "Dear Author, Dear Reader: The Third Hermeneutic in Writing and Reviewing Ethnography," in Ed Shatz, ed., *Political Ethnography: What Immersion Brings to the Study of Power* (Chicago: University of Chicago Press, 2009); as well as Anthony Giddens, *The Constitution of Society* (Berkeley: University of California Press, 1984); and Patrick Thaddeus Jackson, "Making Sense of Making Sense: Configurational Analysis and the Double Hermeneutic," in Dvora Yanow and Peregrine Schwartz-Shea, eds., *Interpretation and Method: Empirical Research Methods and the Interpretive Turn* (Armonk, NY: M E Sharpe, 2006), pp. 264–80. Although I rely on Yanow's conceptual scheme, my "three moments" differ considerably and are geared toward the encounter with non-Western texts.

9. This view can be traced back to two scholars: Friedrich Schleiermacher and Wilhelm Dilthey. Schleiermacher took the first steps toward establishing a "general" hermeneutic methodology, a programmatic understanding of hermeneutics, based on more or less formalized rules. See Friedrich D. E. Schleiermacher, "*The Hermeneutics*: Outline of the 1819 Lectures," in Gayle L. Ormiston and Alan D. Schrift, *The Hermeneutic Tradition: From Ast to Ricoeur* (Albany, NY: SUNY Press, 1990), p. 85. As Schleiermacher sought to make hermeneutics systematically coherent, the discipline was for the first time defined as "the study of understanding itself," emerging from its historical roots in biblical exegesis and classical philology to be understood as the science or art of all understanding. See also Richard Palmer, *Hermeneutics: Interpretation Theory in Shleiermacher, Dilthey, Heidegger and Gadamer* (Evanston, IL: Northwestern University Press, 1969), p. 40. It should be noted that there are important differences between Schleiermacher and Dilthey, see Palmer, p. 99. Often accompanying this view was the notion of objectivity as the one "correct" verbal meaning of a passage or a text, which remains changeless, reproducible and determinate, see Palmer, p. 61. For E. D. Hirsch, unless one recognizes the "glass slipper" of the original verbal meaning intended by the author, there is no way of separating Cinderella from the other girls. E.D. Hirsch, *Validity in Interpretation* (New Haven, CT: Yale University Press, 1967), p. 46. See also Emilio Betti, *Die Hermeneutik als allgemeine Methodik der Geisteswissenschaften (HAMG)* (Tubingen: J.C.B. Mohr [Paul Siebeck], 1962), p. 35. This view holds that hermeneutics is simply about the text as an object of inquiry, held in strict separation from the subject, whose own presumptions only serve to obfuscate rather than add depth to the meaning of the object.

10. Of course, we also need to bring into question the adequacy of Western approaches generally to the cross-cultural hermeneutic encounter. In the conclusion, I will investigate why other Western approaches, such as Straussianism or the Cambridge school, are also inadequate for the purposes of this sort of encounter. Most important, I will argue that they are inappropriate because of the implications about the task and purpose of political theorizing that emerge from their interpretive claims, implications that are ultimately antithetical to the sort of cosmopolitan political thought I will argue for.

11. Both Martin Heidegger (who was deeply influenced by Dilthey) and Hans-Georg Gadamer (a student of Heidegger) sought to emphasize the role that the subjectivity of the interpreter plays in the process of interpretation. See Martin Heidegger, *Being and Time*, John Macquarrie and Edward Robinson, trans. (Oxford, UK: Basil Blackwell, 1973), pp. 78–95, 191–92; Hans-Georg

Gadamer, *Truth and Method* Joel Winsheimer and Donald G. Marshall, trans. (New York: Continuum, 1989), pp. 270, 276, 295.

12. Prejudice, according to Gadamer, is a "judgment that is rendered before all the elements that determine a situation have been finally examined." Gadamer, p. 270. By this he means that rather than understanding ourselves through conscious self-reflection, we understand ourselves through the lenses of the "family, society and state in which we live." See Gadamer, p. 276. See also Gadamer, p. 295: "A person seeking to understand something has a bond to the subject matter . . . and has, or acquires, a connection with the tradition from which the text speaks."

13. See, for instance, Hans Herbert Kögler, *The Power of Dialogue: Critical Hermeneutics after Gadamer and Foucault* (Cambridge, MA: MIT Press, 1996), pp. 144, 127: The other is "tacitly understood, strengthened and judged, but only on the basis of one's own implicit background assumptions, such that the other appears here only as the double of oneself." What gets lost, Kögler reminds us, "is the equally important task of exposing the difference between the other and oneself."

14. See Sarvepalli Radhakrishnan, trans., *The Bhagavadgita* (New Delhi: Harper Collins Publishers India, 1993); Barbara Stoller Miller, trans., *The Bhagavad-Gita: Krishna's Counsel in Time of War* (New York: Columbia University Press, 1986), pp. 2–3; and R.C. Zaehner, ed., *The Bhagavad-Gita* (London: Oxford University Press, 1969), pp. 136–37.

15. See for instance Anthony J. Parel, "The Comparative Study of Political Philosophy," in Anthony J. Parel and Ronald C. Keith, eds., *Comparative Political Philosophy: Studies Under the Upas Tree* (Lanham, MD: Lexington Books, 1992), p. 12.

16. It is, as stated in the *Kathopanisad*: "exceedingly deep, difficult to see, beyond logic . . . it is difficult to be known by [those] who have different views, who follow different faiths, who embrace different interests, who practice differently, and who act differently." *Kathopanisad* 1.21, as cited in Hajime Nakamura, "The Meaning of the Terms 'Philosophy' and 'Religion' in Various Traditions," in Larson and Deutsch, eds., *Interpreting Across Boundaries*, p. 147.

17. M. K. Gandhi, *The Collected Works of Mahatna Gandhi*, 100 vols. (New Delhi: Ministry of Information and Broadcasting, Government of India, 1958–1994), 16: 490–91. See also Bal Gangadhar Tilak, *Srimad Bhagavadgita Rahasya* or *Karma-Yoga-Sastra* (Poona: Tilak Bros., 1935); Anthony Parel, *Gandhi's Philosophy and the Quest for Harmony* (Cambridge: Cambridge University Press, 2006), pp. 26–27, 182–83.

18. M. K. Gandhi, "Anasaktiyoga," in Mahadev Desai, ed., *Anasaktiyoga or the Gospel of Selfless Action: The Gita According to Gandhi* (Ahmedabad: Navajivan Press, 1956), p. 132.

19. This view may not be Gandhian in the strictest sense: Gandhi himself did not self-consciously address the question of hermeneutics, nor did he address the methodological pitfalls of comparative political theory. Nonetheless, I suggest that we may draw on his hermeneutic views in order to grapple with this matter.

20. In fact, we will see later how an implementation of Gandhi's own methodological insights may result in substantive understandings of the *Bhagavad Gita* that contradict his own. I also owe this point to Leigh Jenco, who reminds us that non-Western texts may be sources of methodological as well as substantive insights into political thought, providing not only insights into the nature of the political world, but also ways of reading such insights. See Jenco, "What Does Heaven Ever Say?" p. 742.

21. Gandhi, *Collected Works*, 28: 316, as cited in Parel, *Gandhi's Philosophy and the Quest for Harmony*, p. 106. See also Gandhi, "Anasaktiyoga," pp. 126–27: "It has been my endeavour, as also

that of some companions, to reduce to practice the teaching of the *Gita* as I have understood it . . . The accompanying rendering contains the meaning of the *Gita* message which this little band is trying to enforce in its daily conduct . . . this desire does not mean any disrespect to the other renderings. They have their own place. But I am not aware of the claim made by the translators enforcing the meaning of the *Gita* in their own lives." See also M. K. Gandhi, "The Meaning of the Gita," in Jag Parvesh Chander, ed., *Gita the Mother* (Indian Printing Works, Lahore, 1947), p. 133: "A man who would . . . interpret the scriptures must have the spiritual discipline. He must practice the . . . eternal guides of conduct."

22. Parel, *Gandhi's Philosophy and the Quest for Harmony*, p. 106.

23. Bhikhu Parekh, *Colonialism, Tradition and Reform* (New Delhi: Sage Publications, 1999), pp. 13, 17.

24. The term for "experience" in Indian philosophy is *anubhava* (experience), *darsana* (vision), and *sakshatkar* (realization). The commentarial literature on interpretative strategies within the ancient Vedic tradition is extensive and immensely varied, characterized by complexity and dissent. See, for instance, K. Satchidananda Murty, *Vedic Hermeneutics* (New Delhi: Shri Lal Bahadur Shastri Rashtriya Sanskrit Vidyapeetha, 1993); and P. C. Muraleemadhavan, ed., *Indian Theories of Hermeneutics* (New Delhi: New Bharatiya Book Corporation, 2002). Some strands of interpretation such as the Mimamsa school recall the classical Western view of the text as autonomous "object" of study with a single, irreducible and changeless meaning, emphasizing the importance of purely linguistic and scholarly textual mastery. See Nellickal Muraleedharan, "General Tenets of Hermeneutics," in Muraleemadhavan, ed., *Indian Theories of Hermeneutics*, pp. 198–202. Others, such as Durgacharya, acknowledge the possible multiplicity of textual meanings driven by the individual subjectivities of different readers. Murty, *Vedic Hermeneutics*, p. 30. An important strand of these hermeneutics debates values a praxis-oriented hermeneutic in which the *shastras* or ancient texts were expected to be supplemented by and read in the light of righteous conduct. For instance, Parekh, quoting the *Mahabharata* says: "*Dharmajnahpandito jneyo*: not a learned but a virtuous man is the true *pandit*; and *chaturvedopidurvrittah sa shudratatirichyate*: if he is not of good conduct, a man learned in the four *Vedas* is worse than a *shudra*," *Colonialism, Tradition and Reform*, p. 16. The *Taittiriya Upanishad* claims that teachers should exhort students to study texts by speaking truth and practicing virtue: "Speak the truth. Practise virtue. Neglect not study of the Veda." *Taittirya Upanishad*, I, 11.1, cited in Murty, *Vedic Hermeneutics*, p. 26. The *Nirukta* and the *Taittiriya Aranyaka* claim that *sakshatkara* or realization was the result of the performance of righteous acts (*tapas*) and the subsequent development of sage-like qualities, which bestowed interpretive authority. Those who had the *sakshatkara* (realization) of *dharma* became *rsis* (sages): "to these performing *tapas* the self-manifesting Veda vouchsafed itself, and that made these *rsis*. That is known as the *rsitva* (sageness) of *rsis* (sages)." *Taittiriya Aranyaka* II.9, cited in Murty, *Vedic Hermeneutics*, p. 28.

25. Parekh, *Colonialism, Tradition and Reform*, p. 218. See also Parel, *Gandhi's Philosophy and the Quest for Harmony*, pp. 177–78.

26. "Learning there must be. But religion does not live by it. It lives in the experiences of its saints and seers, in their lives and sayings. When all the most learned commentaries of the scriptures are utterly forgotten, the accumulated experience of the sages and saints will abide and be an inspiration for ages to come." Gandhi, *Collected Works*, 63:153. Meanwhile, as the orthodox textual interpreters of the Hindu scriptural canon made clear their disdain for Gandhi's lack of scholarly, linguistic and exegetical mastery of the texts, Gandhi never sought to deny that "His Sanskrit

was poor, he had not mastered the *shastras*, and he had no interest in undertaking a close study of them." Parekh, p. 22. See also pp. 218–19. Finally, see also Mahadev Desai, "My Submission," in *The Gospel of Selfless Action or The Gita According to Gandhi* (Ahmedabad: Navajivan Publishing House, 1946), pp. 3–4: "Not only was his [Gandhi's] scope limited [in reading the *Gita*], but he disowns all claim to scholarship, and thinks that some of the subjects over which keen controversy has raged have no intimate bearing on the message of the *Gita*."

27. Parekh, *Colonialism, Tradition and Reform*, p. 24. See also p. 218: "I do most emphatically repudiate the claim (if they advance any) of the present *shankaracharya* and *shastris* to give a correct interpretation of the Hindu scriptures." See also Parel, *Gandhi's Philosophy and the Quest for Harmony*, p. 181.

28. Thus the existential hermeneutic also has the advantage of resonating with the methodological insights of many non-Western thinkers. See Jenco, "What Does Heaven Ever Say?": "For both Kang and Wang as well as most Confucian classicists, the extra-textual practices and intense exegetical exercises that characterized their participation in this tradition were necessitated by the very nature of the classical Chinese language in which the texts were written . . . in performing a commentarial exercise, the exegete is in fact forging an identity with the received text that . . . comes to constitute the internalized standard of his moral system," pp. 751–52. In *Journeys to the Other Shore*, Roxanne Euben suggests that the project of CPT see traveling as a means to knowledge of otherness. Euben uncovers the emphasis on *talab al-ilm* (travel in pursuit of knowledge) in Islam, as seen in the travel writings of thinkers such as al-Tahtawi, Ibn Battuta, and Salme. The hermeneutics of travel relies on the authority of autopsy (seeing for oneself), *iyan* (direct observation), and *shahida* (to see with one's own eyes, witness, certify, and confirm). But the sort of existential hermeneutic I outline here parts company with Euben's interlocutors, for it moves beyond the witnessing of spectacles and novelty, to the experience of ways of life from the internal perspective of the adherent.

29. See Jeffery Timm, "Introduction," in Jeffrey R. Timm, ed., *Texts in Context: Traditional Hermeneutics in South Asia* (Albany, NY: SUNY Press, 1992), p. 3.

30. That is, ideas typically represent certain experiences the author (and his intended audience) have had, and they can only be understood well with some appreciation of the experience(s) in question. See, for instance, Eric Voegelin, *The Ecumenic Age*, vol. 4 in *Order and History* (Baton Rouge: Louisiana State University Press, 1974) and "Equivalences of Experience and Symbolization in History," in Ellis Sandoz, ed., *The Collected Works of Eric Voegelin*, vol. 12 (Baton Rouge: Louisiana State University Press, 1989). Martha Nussbaum and Amartya Sen have referred to a "kind of experienced connectedness that would enable [us] to feel and respond to, as well as intellectually apprehend, the values with which [we are] confronted." Martha C. Nussbaum and Amartya Sen, "Internal Criticism and Indian Rationalist Traditions," in Michael Krausz, ed., *Relativism: Interpretation and Confrontation*, (Notre Dame, IN: University of Notre Dame Press, 1989), p. 316.

31. See H. H. Gerth and C. Wright Mills, eds., *From Max Weber: Essays in Sociology* (New York: Oxford University Press, 1946); *Economy and Society: An Outline of Interpretive Sociology* (Berkeley: University of California Press, 1978); Charles Taylor, "Interpretation and the Sciences of Man," in Paul Rabinow and William Sullivan, eds., *Interpretive Social Science: A Reader* (Berkeley: University of California Press, 1979); Richard J. Bernstein, *Beyond Objectivism and Relativism* (Philadelphia: University of Pennsylvania Press, 1983); Fred R. Dallmayr and Thomas A. McCarthy, eds., *Understanding and Social Inquiry* (Notre Dame, IN: University of Notre Dame Press,

1977), Clifford Geertz, "Thick Description: Toward an Interpretive Theory of Culture," in *The Interpretation of Cultures* (New York: Basic Books, 1973), Clifford Geertz, *Local Knowledge: Further Essays in Interpretive Anthropology* (New York: Basic Books, 1983); Peter Winch, "Understanding a Primitive Society," American Philosophical Quarterly I, October 1964.

32. Euben, *Journeys to the Other Shore*, p. 196.

33. Gandhi, "On *Ahimsa*: Reply to Lala Lajpat Rai," *Modern Review*, October 1916.

34. Ibid.

35. For Gandhi's insistence on the relationship *between ahimsa and dharma,* see "Ahimsa or Love," in *Gita the Mother*, pp. 129–30.

36. Community of followers.

37. See Farah Godrej, "Nonviolence and Gandhi's Truth: A Method for Moral and Political Arbitration," *Review of Politics* 68, 2006, pp. 291–94.

38. Anil Mundra, "Mahatma Gandhi's Legacy of Religious Tolerance in India," *Interfaith Voices* radio broadcast, August 30, 2007, www.interfaithradio.org.

39. Marjorie Sykes, trans., *Moved By Love: the Memoirs of Vinoba Bhave* (Wardha, India: Paramdhan Prakashan, 1994).

40. Gandhi, *Gita the Mother*, p. 145. See also pp. 135–36, 144–47, 150–52. See also Gandhi, "Anasaktiyoga," p. 133.

41. Barbara Stoler Miller, trans. *The Bhagavad-Gita: Krishna's Counsel in Time of War* (New York: Columbia University Press, 1986), p. 13.

42. Jenco, "What Does Heaven Ever Say?" pp. 744, 745.

43. Gayatri Chakravorty Spivak, "Can the Subaltern Speak?" in Cary Nelson and Lawrence Grossberg, *Marxism and the Interpretation of Culture* (Chicago: University of Illinois Press, 1988); Edward Said, *Orientalism* (New York: Vintage Books, 1979).

44. Spivak, "Can the Subaltern Speak"; "Subaltern Studies: Deconstructing Historiography," in Ranajit Guha and Gayatri Chakravorty Spivak, eds., *Selected Subaltern Studies* (Delhi: Oxford University Press, 1988); *Outside in the Teaching Machine* (New York: Routledge, 1993).

45. As the critical historian Joan W. Scott observes, the epistemological status of experience is complex, because, rather than being an autonomous sphere that provides explanation for other forces and variables, experience is itself often subject to production and distortion by historical forces and requires explanation as the object of such forces. See Joan W. Scott, "Experience," in Judith Butler and Joan W. Scott, eds., *Feminists Theorize the Political* (New York: Routledge, 1992), and "The Evidence of Experience," *Critical Inquiry* 17, Summer 1991. It should be noted that the existential hermeneutic is complicated in its reliance on two kinds of experience, each of which may be problematic: the experience of the "native exegete," and the experience of the researcher, which is itself implicated in the attempt to reproduce or represent the experience of the "native."

46. James Clifford, "Introduction: Partial Truths" in James Clifford and George E. Marcus, eds., *Writing Culture: The Poetics and Politics of Ethnography* (Berkeley: University of California Press, 1986). The ideology "claiming transparency of representation and immediacy of experience" has crumbled. Clifford "draws attention to the historical predicament of ethnography, the fact that it is always caught up in the invention, not representation, of cultures," p. 599. This awareness, Clifford reminds us, is all the more keen combined with the acknowledgement that such invention is inevitably power-laden and necessarily partial. That is, the investigating subject is significantly involved in the object of critical scrutiny, and the practice of good readings of otherness depends on the self-reflexive awareness of one's own positionality as researcher and an

acknowledgement of the relationship of ethnography to power. See Samer Shehata, "Ethnography, Identity and the Production of Knowledge," in Dvora Yanow and Peregrine Schwartz-Shea, eds., *Interpretation and Method: Empirical Research Methods and the Interpretive Turn* (Armonk, NY: M.E. Sharpe, 2006); Peregrine Shwartz-Shea, "Judging Quality: Evaluate Criteria and Epistemic Communities," in Yanow and Schwartz-Shea, eds., p. 103; Diane Singerman, *Avenues of Participation* (Princeton, NJ: Princeton University Press, 1995); Piya Chatterjee, "Taking Blood: Gender, Race and Imagining Public Anthropology in India," *India Review*, 5 (3–4), July/October 2006.

47. Postcolonial thought reminds us that this analysis should embody "a persistent recognition of heterogeneity" in respect of the cultures of postcolonialism. See Gayatri Chakravorty Spivak, *In Other Worlds: Essays in Cultural Politics* (New York: Routledge, 2006), p. 211. See also Edward Said, *The World, the Text and the Critic* (London: Faber and Faber, 1984), p. 200. For views on how such heterogeneity may be captured in empirical methods, see Schwartz-Shea, "Judging Quality," p. 103: "'Triangulation implies a multidimensionality to the research process . . . methodological discussion of triangulation emphasize this richness by noting not only the extent to which data from multiple sources . . . present possibilities for corroboration, but also that they are likely to bring to light inconsistent and even conflicting findings . . . [compelling] researchers . . . to grapple with, rather than discount, inconsistent findings." See also Martyn Hammersley and Paul Atkinson, *Ethnography: Principles in Practice* (London: Tavistock, 1983).

48. See Meera Nanda, *Breaking the Spell of Dharma and Other Essays* (New Delhi: Three Essays Press, 2002).

49. "The ideologues of Hindu nationalism . . . claimed that the bomb was foretold in . . . the *Bhagwat Gita*, in which God declares himself to be 'the radiance of a thousand suns, the splendor of the Mighty One . . . I have become Death, the destroyer of the worlds.'" Ibid., p. 6.

50. Josiane Viramma and Jean Luc Racine, *Viramma: Life of an Untouchable* (London: Verso, 1997), p. 148, 165–67 as cited in Nanda, *Breaking the Spell of Dharma*, p. 153.

51. See Clifford "Introduction: Partial Truths" in Clifford and Marcus, eds., *Writing Culture*, p. 567.

52. See Dvora Yanow, "Neither Rigorous nor Objective?: Interrogating Criteria for Knowledge Claims in Interpretive Science," in Yanow and Schwarz, eds., *Interpretation and Method*, p. 76.

53. Ibid., p. 79.

54. See Shwartz-Shea, "Judging Quality," in Yanow and Schwarz, eds., *Interpretation and Method*, pp. 103–8.

55. Scott L. Malcolmson, "The Varieties of Cosmopolitan Experience," in Robbins and Cheah, eds., *Cosmopolitics: Thinking and Feeling Beyond the Nation*, p. 238.

56. Certainly, many others have called for engagement with radical alterity and the discomforts it arouses. See Fred Dallmayr, "Cosmopolitanism: Moral and Political" *Political Theory* 31 (3), p. 438: "To be properly cosmopolitan, this civic culture needs to be as inclusive as possible, that is, to embrace not only people similar to 'us,' but precisely those who are different or 'other,'— potentially even those who are now categorized (rashly) as 'enemies.'" See also Roxanne Euben, "Journeys to 'the Other Shore,'" *Political Theory* 28 (3), June 2000, p. 405. My claim, however, is that this engagement with discomfort needs to be both existential and theoretical, and that such engagement in turn has methodological as well as substantive implications.

57. See Jenco, "What Does Heaven Ever Say?" p. 744.

58. Leo Strauss, *What Is Political Philosophy?* (Glencoe, IL: The Free Press, 1959), *City of Man* (Chicago: University of Chicago Press, 1977); *Natural Right and History* (Chicago: University of Chicago Press, 1953).

59. See Quentin Skinner, "Meaning and Understanding in the History of Ideas," *History and Theory* 8, 1969; James Tully, *Meaning and Context: Quentin Skinner and His Critics* (Cambridge: Polity Press, 1988).

60. Andrew Vincent, *The Nature of Political Theory* (Oxford: Oxford University Press, 2004), pp. 41–51; John G. Gunnell, *Political Theory: Tradition and Interpretation* (Cambridge, MA: Winthrop, 1979), pp. 96–126.

61. See, for instance, Saba Mahmood, *Politics of Piety: The Islamic Revival and the Feminist Subject* (Princeton, NJ: Princeton University Press, 2005).

62. Pratap Mehta, "Cosmopolitanism and the Circle of Reason," p. 628. See also Euben, *Journeys to the Other Shore*, pp. 196–197.

63. See Benjamin L. Whorf, *Language, Thought and Reality*, ed. John B. Carroll, (Cambridge, MA: MIT Press, 1956).

64. Henry Rosemont Jr., "Against Relativism," in Larson and Deutsch, eds., *Interpreting Across Boundaries*, p. 44.

65. Ibid., p. 45.

66. Ibid., p. 47.

CHAPTER 4

1. See, for instance, Leigh Jenco, "Re-Centering Political Theory: The Promise of Mobile Locality," *Cultural Critique* 79, Fall 2011. Although Jenco does not explicitly claim that scholars should remain detached from their Eurocentric home disciplines or departments, her emphasis on the ultimate possibility of "dissolving or replacing our own discipline(s)" suggests strongly that the "re-centering" she speaks of should be at least somewhat permanent. See pp. 27, 32, 33.

2. In "What Is Comparative Political Theory?" *Review of Politics* 71 (4), 2009, March explores this possibility. It is not so much that March is committed to this view, but rather, that he draws our attention to its implications.

3. Farah Godrej, "Response to What Is Comparative Political Theory?" *Review of Politics* 71 (4), 2009, pp. 567–82.

4. Jenco, "Re-Centering Political Theory," pp. 7, 15, 16, 29.

5. Roxanne Euben, *Journeys to the Other Shore*, p. 197.

6. Hans-Georg Gadamer, *Truth and Method*, trans. Joel Winsheimer and Donald G. Marshall (New York: Continuum, 1989)., p. 296, and pp. 372–73: "The sense of a text in general reaches far beyond what its author originally intended . . . texts are inexhaustible . . . it is the course of events that brings out new aspects of meaning in historical material"; and p. 290: "The duration of a work's power to speak directly. . . . is fundamentally unlimited." What is fixed in writing, Gadamer claims, "has detached itself from the contingency of its origin and its author and made itself free for new relationships . . . Where are we to draw the line that excludes a reader from being addressed? . . . The idea of the original reader is full of unexamined idealization." p. 395. Margaret Leslie, meanwhile, speaks of a fruitful or defensible anachronism, claiming that historical "truth" of a text is often in conflict with a conceptual richness that often arises out of the reader/interpreter's dialogue with the text, often leading to anachronistic interpretations that may in fact enrich the original work. Margaret Leslie, "In Defense of Anachronism," *Political Studies* 18, 1970, p. 441.

7. Sheldon Wolin addresses the idea of an "intellectual operation" that occurs when a political theory is put to work in circumstances different from those that inspired it. In Wolin's view, this is

exactly what goes on when either Aquinas or Marsilius reinterpret or apply Aristotle to a different era. The same may be said of a Lenin or a Trotsky, with respect to Marx. Wolin, "Paradigms and Political Theories," in Preston King and B. C. Parekh, eds., *Politics and Experience: Essays Presented to Professor Michael Oakeshott on the Occasion of His Retirement* (Cambridge: Cambridge University Press, 1968), p. 142.

8. Laurie L. Patton, ed., *Authority, Anxiety and Canon: Essays in Vedic Interpretation* (Albany, NY: SUNY Press, 1994), 1, 6.

9. Indeed, most interpreters agree that there is not even much consensus on what is meant by the Vedas or the Vedic texts. Depending on what historical period is being discussed, they refer either to the four earliest verses—the *Rg-*, *Sama-*, *Yajur-*and *Atharva-*Vedas—or to an aggregate of early Indian works, including the above mentioned four Vedas, the Brahmanas and the Upanishads. See K. Satchidananda Murty, *Vedic Hermeneutics*, (New Delhi: Motilal Banarsidass, 1993), pp. 1–6; Patton, *Anxiety and Canon*, p. 1.

10. Murty, *Vedic Hermeneutics,* pp. 9–11. See also Ram Gopal, *The History and Principles of Vedic Interpretation* (New Delhi: Concept Publishing Company, 1983), p.14.

11. Murty, *Vedic Hermeneutics*, p. 30.

12. Yaska cited ibid., p. 29.

13. Durgacharya on the *Nirukta* II.8, cited in Murty, *Vedic Hermeneutics*, p. 67, ff. 30.

14. For a detailed discussion of Gandhi's interpretive disagreements with orthodox Hindu scholars, see Bhikhu Parekh, *Colonialism, Tradition and Reform* (New Delhi: Sage Publications, 1999), pp. 13, 16–17, 22–24, 218–19.

15. Ibid., p. 24, 218.

16. Anthony Parel, *Gandhi's Philosophy and the Quest for Harmony* (Cambridge: Cambridge University Press, 2006), pp. 26–27, 182–83. See also Bal Gangadhar Tilak, *Srimad Bhagavadgita Rahasya* or *Karma-Yoga-Sastra* (Poona: Tilak Bros., 1935).

17. Sri Aurobindo, *Essays on the Gita* (Twin Lakes, WI: Lotus Press, 1995); and Parel, *Gandhi's Philosophy and the Quest for Harmony*, pp. 44, 182–83.

18. For views on "authenticity" and "objectivity" in textual interpretation, see, among others, E. D. Hirsch, *Validity in Interpretation* (New Haven, CT: Yale University Press, 1967); and Emilio Betti, *Die Hermeneutik als allgemeine Methodik der Geisteswissenschaften (HAMG)* (Tubingen: J.C.B. Mohr [Paul Siebeck], 1962). Hirsch and Betti understood objectivity as the one "correct" verbal meaning of a passage or a text, which remains changeless, reproducible and determinate. Hermeneutics, in their view, has the task of "setting forth norms by which the determinate, changeless and self-identical meaning can be understood." Richard Palmer, *Hermeneutics: Interpretation Theory in Schleiermacher, Dilthey, Heidegger and Gadamer* (Evanston, IL: Northwestern University Press, 1969), p. 61, For E. D. Hirsch, unless one recognizes the "glass slipper" of the original verbal meaning intended by the author, there is no way of separating Cinderella from the other girls. Hirsch, *Validity in Interpretation*, p. 46.

19. Andrew March, "What Is Comparative Political Theory?" pp. 531–66.

20. Jane I. Smith, *Islam in America* (New York: Columbia University Press, 1999).

21. Srinivas Aravamudan, *Guru English: South Asian Religion in a Cosmopolitan Language* (Princeton, NJ: Princeton University Press, 2005).

22. "What may appear as truth to one person will often appear as untruth to another." See Letter to Narandas Gandhi, in Iyer, *MPW* Vol. II, p. 163. Manfred Steger reminds us that Gandhi's views on the possibility of perfection are notoriously ambiguous: while "to say that perfection

is not attainable on this earth is to deny God," he also simultaneously held that "not one of us is perfect ... [or] able to realize the whole of our spiritual ambition," *MPW* Vol. II, pp. 36–37; and that "only a rare person will succeed completely," *MPW* Vol. II, p. 158. See also Manfred Steger, *Gandhi's Dilemma: Nonviolent Principles and Nationalist Power* (New York: St. Martin's Press, 2000), p. 116.

23. On the relationship between truth and politics in Gandhi, see Partha Chatterjee, "The Moment of Manoeuvre: Gandhi and the Critique of Civil Society," in *Nationalist Thought and the Colonial World: A Derivative Discourse?* (London: Zed for the United Nations University, 1986); Dennis Dalton, *Mahatma Gandhi: Nonviolent Power in Action* (New York: Columbia University Press, 1993), chs. 2–4.

24. M. K. Gandhi, *Speeches and Writings of Mahatma Gandhi*, 4th ed. (Madras: Natesan, 1934), p. 506.

25. See, for instance, Bhikhu Parekh, *Gandhi's Political Philosophy*, and Raghavan Iyer, *The Moral and Political Thought of Mahatma Gandhi*.

26. See Sarvepalli Radhakrishnan, trans., *The Bhagavadgita* (New Delhi: HarperCollins Publishers India, 1993); Barbara Stoller Miller, trans., *The Bhagavad-Gita: Krishna's Counsel in Time of War* (New York: Columbia University Press, 1986), pp. 2–3; and R.C. Zaehner, ed., *The Bhagavad-Gita* (London and New York: Oxford University Press, 1969), pp. 136–37.

27. For Gandhi's insistence on the relationship between ahimsa and dharma, see "Ahimsa or Love," in *Gita the Mother*, pp. 129–30.

28. It is worth noting here that Gandhi seemed not to make much distinction between the spiritual and the moral or ethical, although each of these realms seemed synonymous with truth-seeking: "I use the adjective moral," he claims, "as synonymous with spiritual." Gandhi, *Harijan*, January 1942. Religion, Gandhi claimed, "means a belief in ordered moral government of the universe," Iyer, *MPW* Vol. I, p. 391, thus indicating that for him, the imperatives of ethics and spiritual seeking were linked, if not identical. This view of the "political" stems in turn from Gandhi's general objection to the compartmentalization of human life into separable, distinct realms of action. "Politics, economic progress, etc. are not unconnected matters ... they are all rooted in religion." Gandhi, "Draft constitution of the Satyagraha Ashram, Ahmedabad," in Iyer, *MPW* Vol. II, p. 517; "We needlessly divide life into water-tight compartments." Gandhi, "Letter to Horace Alexander," in Iyer, *MPW* Vol. II, p. 619. "I do not divide different activities—political, social, religious, economical—into water-tight compartments. I look upon them all as one indivisible whole each running into the rest and affected by the rest." Gandhi, "Letter to Dr. Norman Leys," in Iyer, *MPW* Vol. I, p. 408.

29. While this is by no means the only way to think about the Gandhian view of politics, it has been suggested that Gandhi's view of the role and nature of political life was determined by (or, at the very least, in accordance with) the traditional Hindu theory of the four *purusharthas*, in which the pursuit of *kama* (pleasure) and *artha* (power) were to be informed by, and take place in accordance with *dharma* (the imperative of ethical conduct) and *moksha* (spiritual liberation, or the quest for the ultimate meaning in human existence). There has been some debate as to whether the relationship between these four forces was to be hierarchical (i.e., *moksha* being the privileged force that provides the guidance for the other three realms of life) or interactional (i.e., each force being given its particular place, with all four complementing one another). On Gandhi and the *purusharthas*, see Anthony Parel, *Gandhi's Philosophy and the Quest for Harmony*. See also K. J. Shah "*Purushartha* and Gandhi," in Ramashray Roy, ed., *Gandhi and the Present Global Crisis*

(Shimla: Indian Insitute of Advanced Study, 1996); and P. V. Kane, *History of Dharmasastra*, Vol. V, part 2 (Poona: Bhandarkar Oriental Research Institute, 1977), pp. 1620–623.

30. See Iyer, *MPW* Vol. III, p. 548: "Is not politics too a part of *dharma*! . . . Politics also requires purity of conduct." Also see Vol. I, p. 375: "Political life must be an echo of private life and . . . there cannot be any divorce between the two"; Vol. I, p. 376: "I take part in politics because I feel that there is no department of life which can be divorced from religion"; Vol. I, p. 381: "My politics are not divorced from morality, from spirituality, from religion. . . . A man who is trying to discover and follow the will of God cannot possibly leave a single field of life untouched"; Vol. I, p. 391: "For me, every, the tiniest, activity is governed by what I consider to be my religion."

31. Iyer, *MPW* Vol. II, p. 321.

32. Ibid., 302–3.

33. "Non-violence to be a creed has to be all-pervasive. I cannot be non-violent about one activity of mine and violent about others. That would be a policy, not a life-force." Iyer, *MPW* Vol. II, p. 321. But he also claims: "To expect a whole mass of men and women to obey that law [of *ahimsa*] all at once is not to know its working . . . the limited measure of its application can be realized in respect of masses of people within a short time." Iyer, *MPW* Vol. II, pp. 302.

34. I make this argument, in different ways, in both "Nonviolence and Gandhi's Truth: A Method for Moral and Political Arbitration," *Review of Politics* 68 (2), 2006; as well as "Gandhi's Civic Ahimsa: A Standard for Public Justification in Multicultural Democracies," *International Journal of Gandhi Studies* 1, 2011, pp. 75–106. Gandhi's views on this are quite inconsistent. On the one hand, his metaphysical posture commits him to rejecting any separation of public/private, politics/religion, moral/civic. Accordingly, in many instances, he disavows any moves toward a "lesser" form of ahimsa that would lower moral and political standards in order to make it more accessible. He considers this a tainted mode of political action that does not live up to the fullest expression of ahimsa. Yet, Gandhi occasionally wavers: Raghavan Iyer cites various instances in which Gandhi acknowledges that the standard of ahimsa may need to be adjusted for certain situations, that ahimsa as policy was the "next best thing" to ahimsa as creed, and that ahimsa often demands compromises. See Iyer, *The Moral and Political Thought of Mahatma Gandhi*, p. 196–204.

35. Joan Bondurant undertakes a similar exercise when she attempts to lay out the appropriate criteria or steps that define a campaign of *satyagraha*, or what she defines as a "movement growing out of grievances against an established political order," *Conquest of Violence: The Gandhian Philosophy of Conflict* (Princeton, NJ: Princeton University Press, 1988), p. 40. She outlines the steps chronologically as negotiation and arbitration, preparation for direct action, agitation, issuing of an ultimatum, boycott/strikes, noncooperation, civil disobedience, and usurping the government.

36. See Godrej, "Nonviolence and Gandhi's Truth," pp. 301–5.

37. Bondurant, p. 196. Bondurant is also careful to point out why this sort of political action is not based on, and is in fact qualitatively different from, compromise. The satyagrahi, Bondurant says, "is never prepared to yield any position which he holds to be the truth. He is, however, prepared . . . to be persuaded by his opponent that the opponent's position is . . . the more nearly true position . . . When persuasion has been effected . . . there is no sacrificing of position." Bondurant, p. 197.

38. For a more detailed description of the sorts of nonviolent actions that are included within the umbrella of satyagraha, including the fundamental rules and code of discipline governing nonviolent action, see Bondurant, pp. 36–41.

39. Iyer, *MPW* Vol. III, p. 41.

40. For more on the difference between Gandhi's Absolute and relative truth, see Godrej, "Nonviolence and Gandhi's Truth."

41. On the idea of reasongiving in constitutional democracies, see John Rawls, "The Idea of Public Reason Revisited," in Samuel Freeman, ed., *John Rawls: Collected Papers* (Cambridge, MA: Harvard University Press, 1999), pp. 573–615.

42. For a detailed discussion of these issues, see my "Nonviolence and Gandhi's Truth," as well as "Gandhi's Civic *Ahimsa*."

43. Leigh Jenco, "The Past Is Not a Foreign Country: Culture-Centered versus History-Centered Interpretation," paper presented at the proceedings of the 2008 American Political Science Association.

44. Leigh Jenco, "How Meaning Moves: Tan Sitong on Borrowing Across Cultures," *Philosophy East and West* 62 (2), April 2012, pp. 12–13.

45. Ibid., pp. 14, 18.

46. Ibid., pp. 20, 23, 27.

47. Ibid., p. 25.

48. Ibid., pp. 22–23.

49. Ibid., p. 23.

50. Ibid., p. 26.

51. Gayatri Chakraborty Spivak, "Can the Subaltern Speak?" in Cary Nelson and Lawrence Grossberg, eds., *Marxism and the Interpretation of Culture* (Chicago: University of Illinois Press, 1988).

52. In *Orientalism*, Said describes a mode of hermeneutic authority and proprietorship that is established through and stems from an imbalance of power, so that disparities in power are used to establish interpretive authority and ownership. See Edward W. Said, *Orientalism* (New York: Vintage Books, 1994).

53. See Bart Moore-Gilbert, *Postcolonial Theory: Contexts, Practices, Politics* (London and New York: Verso Press, 1997), ch. 5; and Peter Childs and Patrick Williams, *An Introduction to Postcolonial Theory* (London: Prentice Hall, 1997), ch. 6.

54. For a detailed exposition of this challenge, see Andrew March, "What Is Comparative Political Theory?" and Godrej, "Response to What Is Comparative Political Theory?"

55. See Godrej, "Response to What Is Comparative Political Theory?"

56. For more details on the origins of the caste system, Vedic philosophy, and other classical Hindu texts, see U. N. Ghoshal, *A History of Indian Political Ideas*, (Oxford: Oxford University Press, 1959); Sarvepalli Radhakrishnan and Charles A. Moore, eds., *A Sourcebook in Indian Philosophy* (Princeton, NJ: Princeton University Press, 1957); and John B. Chethimattam, *Patterns of Indian Thought: Indian Religions and Philosophies* (Maryknoll, NY: Orbis Books, 1971).

57. Godrej "Nonviolence and Gandhi's Truth."

58. On Gandhi's interpretations of the *Gita*, see Parel, *Gandhi's Philosophy and the Quest for Harmony*; M. K. Gandhi, "Anasaktiyoga," in Mahadev Desai, ed., *Anasaktiyoga or the Gospel of Selfless Action: the Gita According to Gandhi* (Ahmedabad: Navajivan Press, 1956); M. K. Gandhi, "The Meaning of the Gita," in Jag Parvesh Chander, ed., *Gita the Mother* (Lahore: Indian Printing Works, 1947.)

59. March, "What Is Comparative Political Theory?" p. 546.

CHAPTER 5

1. Leigh Jenco remarks that the same critical stance that seeks to undermine the certainty of Europeanized categories often returns the political theorist to the very audience and discourse whose terms originally prompted the critique. Although addressing Eurocentrism on one level, it reconstitutes it on another: the analysis chastens Europeanized categories only insofar as it continues to inhabit them. "Re-Centering Political Theory," p. 5.

2. Immanuel Wallerstein calls it a "hydra-headed monster" with many avatars, a dragon which cannot be slaughtered swiftly. Wallerstein, "Eurocentrism and Its Avatars: The Dilemmas of Social Science," *New Left Review*, 226, 1997.

3. Edward Said, *Culture and Imperialism* (New York: Random House, 1994); Gayatri Spivak, *Outside In the Teaching Machine* (London: Routledge, 1993) and *In Other Worlds: Essays in Cultural Politics* (London: Methuen, 1987); Rajani Kanth, *Against Eurocentrism* (New York: Palgrave Macmillan, 2005).

4. John Mowitt, "In the Wake of Eurocentrism: An Introduction," *Cultural Critique* 47, Winter 2001.

5. Mowitt, p. 9.

6. Dipesh Chakrabarty, *Provincializing Europe: Postcolonial Thought and Historical Difference* (Princeton, NJ: Princeton University Press, 2000), p. 4.

7. Ibid., p. ix.

8. Syed Farid Alatas, *Alternative Discourses in Asian Social Science: Responses to Eurocentrism* (New Delhi: Sage Publications, 2006).

9. Ibid., p. 14.

10. See Jenco, "Re-Centering Political Theory," and "What Does Heaven Ever Say? A Methods-Centered Approach to Cross-Cultural Engagement," *American Political Science Review* 101 (4), 2007.

11. See Jenco, "Re-Centering Political Theory."

12. See Andrew March, "Islamic Legal Theory, Secularism and Religious Pluralism: Is Modern Religious Freedom Sufficient for the *Shari'a* 'Purpose [*Maqsid*]' of 'Preserving Religion [*Hifz Al-Din*]?'" (August 14, 2009). *Islamic Law and Law of the Muslim World* Paper No. 09–78. Available at SSRN: http://ssrn.com/abstract=1452895http://ssrn.com/abstract=1452895. See also Michaelle Browers, "Islam and Political *Sinn*: The Hermeneutics of Contemporary Islamic Reformists," in Michaelle Browers and Charles Kurzman, eds., *An Islamic Reformation?* (Lanham, MD: Lexington, 2004).

13. Alatas, *Alternative Discourses in Asian Social Science*, p. 112.

14. There is some general consensus on this broad narrative, and on its conceptual and linguistic structure, among various well-known commentators on Indian political thought. See, for instance, A.S. Altekar, *State and Government in Ancient India* (New Delhi: Motilal Banarsidass, 1958); U.N. Ghoshal, *A History of Indian Political Ideas* (Oxford: Oxford University Press, 1959); K.P. Jayaswal, *Hindu Polity: A Constitutional History of India in Hindu Times* (Bangalore: Chaukhamba Sanskrit Pratishthan Oriental Publishers, 1967); N.N. Law, *Aspects of Ancient Indian Polity* (Bombay: Gyan Publishing House, 1960); Beni Prasad, *Theory of Government in Ancient India* (Allahabad: The Indian Press, 1958); R.S. Sharma, *Aspects of Political Ideas and Institutions in Ancient India* (Delhi: Motilal Banarsidass, 1968); J. Spellman, *Political Theory in Ancient India: A Study of Kingship from the Earliest Times to Circa A.D. 300* (Oxford: Oxford University Press,

1964); Anthony Parel, "Gandhi and the Emergence of the Modern Indian Political Canon," *The Review of Politics* 70 (2008); Bhikhu Parekh, "Some Reflections on the Hindu Tradition of Political Thought," in Thomas Pantham and Kenneth Deutsch, eds., *Political Thought in Modern India* (New Delhi: Sage Publications, 1986); Amritava Banerjee, "Political Thinking in Ancient India: A Brief Outline," in Harihar Bhattacharya and Abhijit Ghosh, eds., *Indian Political Thought and Movement: New Interpretations and Emerging Issues* (Kolkata: K.P. Bagchi & Co., 2007).

15. Parekh, "Some Reflections on the Hindu Tradition of Political Thought," p. 29.

16. Sarvepalli Radhakrishnan and Charles Moore, eds., *A Sourcebook in Indian Philosophy* (Princeton, NJ: Princeton University Press, 1957); V.P. Varma, *Philosophical Humanism and Contemporary India* (New Delhi: Motilal Banarsidass, 1986); Anil Baran Ray, "Indian Upanishadic Thought" in Bhattacharya and Ghosh, eds., *Indian Political Thought*.

17. See, for instance, Irfan Habib, ed., *Akbar and His India* (Delhi and New York: Oxford University Press, 1997); Vincent A. Smith, *Asoka: The Buddhist Emperor of India* (Oxford: Clarendon Press, 1909).

18. Nor should this lesson negate the very real distinction between the internal otherness cleaving the Indian context, and its confrontation with the power-laden otherness of Eurocentric discourse and practice. Any acknowledgment of the internal multiplicity of uniqueness and autonomy must be balanced with a real concern for how the power of Westcentric scholarly models have historically obscured and occluded traces of independent, distinctively non-Western ways of thinking about politics. Some may insist that all configurations of power are to be seen on par, and the experience of the otherness of Islamic influence in India may in the end be no different from its experience of British colonization, but Edward Said has reminded us that the Westcentric colonial project possessed an unparalleled ability to erase the epistemic authority of premodern non-Western knowledges of all kind, and to reestablish epistemic authority along its own configurations. We may tread with care, then, when we seek to equate the influence of internal non-Western otherness in the Indian context to the vastly different Eurocentrism that arose as a result of the colonial experience.

19. See K. Satchidananda Murty, *Vedic Hermeneutics* (New Delhi: Motilal Banarsidass, 1993); Ram Gopal, *The History and Principles of Vedic Interpretation* (New Delhi: Concept Publishing Company, 1983); P.C. Muraleemadhavan, ed., *Indian Theories of Hermeneutics* (New Delhi: New Bharatiya Book Corporation, 2002).

20. Arvind Sharma, *Modern Hindu Thought: An Introduction* (New Delhi: Oxford University Press, 2005); Anthony Parel, *Gandhi's Philosophy and the Quest for Harmony* (Cambridge: Cambridge University Press, 2006); V. Kane, *History of Dharmasastra*, vol. V, part 2, 2nd ed. (Poona: The Bhandarkar Institute, 1977).

21. Chakrabarty, *Provincializing Europe*, p. 5.

22. See Alatas, "Introduction," in Bhattacharya and Ghosh, eds., *Alternative Discourses in Asian Social Science*, p. xii; Anthony Parel, "Gandhi and the Emergence of the Modern Indian Political Canon"; Bhikhu Parekh, "The Poverty of Indian Political Theory," *History of Political Thought*, 8 (3) Autumn 1992.

23. See, for instance, Rajeev Bhargava, "Is There an Indian Political Theory?" in *What Is Political Theory and Why Do We Need It?* (Delhi: Oxford University Press, 2010).

24. See Anthony Parel, "Gandhi and the Emergence of the Modern Indian Political Canon."

25. Bhikhu Parekh, "Introduction," in *Gandhi's Political Philosophy: A Critical Examination* (Notre Dame, IN: University of Notre Dame Press, 1989), p. 3. Indeed, it must be said that Parel

and Parekh's terminology like "recognizably" or "uniquely" Indian should perhaps modified to read "uniquely" or "recognizably" Vedic or Sanskritic. Despite his well-known ecumenism in practical political matters, Gandhi's intellectual efforts at revivification of tradition focused mainly on Hindu Vedic texts.

26. Sudipta Kaviraj, "The Heteronomous Radicalism of M. N. Roy," in Pantham and Deutsch, eds., *Political Thought in Modern India*, p. 235.

27. See, for instance, Amit Basole, "Whose Knowledge Counts? Reinterpreting Gandhi for the Information Age," *International Journal of Gandhi Studies* 2, 2012; Jyotirmay Bhattacharya, "Rabindranath Tagore: Towards an Indian Perspective of Secularism and Communalism"; and Keshab Choudhuri, "'Development 'Discourse:' Projecting Gandhian Ideas," both in Bhattacharya and Ghosh, eds., *Alternative Discourses in Asian Social Science*.

28. Until relatively recently, Bhikhu Parekh (among others) lamented the paucity of theoretical initiative in addressing the most obviously unique of Indian political experiences. See Parekh, "The Poverty of Indian Political Theory." However, in the last fifteen or so years, many Indian political theorists have turned toward a treatment of such topics.

29. Rajeev Bhargava, "Indian Secularism: An Alternative, Trans-cultural Ideal," in V.R. Mehta and Thomas Pantham, *Political Ideas in Modern India: Thematic Explorations* (New Delhi: Sage Publications, 2006). See also Bhargava, *The Promise of India's Secular Democracy* (Delhi: Oxford University Press, 2010).

30. Bhargava, "Indian Secularism," p. 296.

31. Bhargava, "Indian Secularism," pp. 299–300.

32. Ashis Nandy, "The Politics of Secularism and the Recovery of Religious Tolerance," *Alternatives* 13 (2), 1988. See also Nandy, "The Twilight of Certitude: Secularism, Hindu Nationalism and other Masks of Deculturation," *Alternatives* 22 (2), 1997.

33. Nandy, "The Politics of Secularism and the Recovery of Religious Tolerance," p. 188.

34. Partha Chatterjee, "Secularism and Tolerance," *Economic and Political Weekly*, July 9, 1994, and "Religious Minorities and the Secular State: Reflections on an Indian Impasse" *Public Culture* 8, 1995.

35. Ruth Vanita, "The Special Marriage Act: Not Special Enough," *Manushi* 58, 1990; Agnes Flavia, "Hindu Men, Monogamy and the Uniform Civil Code," *Economic and Political Weekly*, May 14, 1994.

36. See Radha Kumar, *The History of Doing* (New Delhi: Kali for Women, 1993); Archana Parasher, *Women and Family Law Reform in India* (New Delhi: Sage Press, 1992); Nivedita Menon, "Women and Citizenship," in Partha Chatterjee, ed., *Wages of Freedom* (New Delhi: Oxford University Press, 1998), and Menon, *Gender and Politics in India* (New Delhi: Oxford University Press, 1999); Agnes Flavia, "Redefining the Agenda of the Women's Movement within a Secular Framework," in Urvashi Butalia and Tanika Sarkar, eds., *Women and the Hindu Right* (New Delhi: Kali for Women, 1995).

37. Geetanjali Gangoli, *The Law on Trial: The Debate on the Uniform Civil Code* (Bombay: Akshara Women's Resource Center, 1996). See also Rajeev Bhargava, *Politics and Ethics of the Indian Constitution* (Delhi: Oxford University Press, 2008).

38. See Rochana Bajpai, "The Conceptual Vocabularies of Secularism and Minority Rights in India," *Journal of Political Ideologies* 7 (2), 2002, pp. 179–97; T.N. Madan, *Modern Myths, Locked Minds: Secularism and Fundamentalism in India* (Delhi: Oxford University Press, 1997); Thomas Pantham, "Indian Secularism and Its Critics: Some Reflections," *The Review of Politics* 59 (1997),

523–40; Rajeev Bhargava, ed., *Secularism and Its Critics* (Delhi: Oxford University Press, 1998); Sumit Ganguly, "The Crisis of Indian Secularism," *Journal of Democracy* 14, 2003, 11–25; Aditya Nigam, *The Insurrection of Little Selves: The Crisis of Secular-Nationalism in India* (New Delhi: Oxford University Press, 2006); Anuradha Dingwaney Needham and Rajeswari Sunder Rajan, eds., *The Crisis of Secularism in India* (Durham: NC: Duke University Press, 2007); S.N. Balagangadhara and Jakob De Roover, "The Secular State and Religious Conflict: Liberal Neutrality and the Indian Case of Pluralism," *Journal of Political Philosophy* 15, 2007, 67–92; Badrinath Rao, "The Variant Meanings of Secularism in India: Notes Toward Conceptual Clarifications," *Journal of Church and State* 48, 2006, 47–81; Ashis Nandy, "An Anti-Secularist Manifesto," *Seminar* 314, 1985, 14–24; Neera Chandhoke, *Beyond Secularism: The Rights of Religious Minorities* (Delhi: Oxford University Press, 1999); M. M. Sankhdher, ed., *Secularism in India: Dilemmas and Challenges* (New Delhi: Deep and Deep, 1995); André Beteille, "Secularism and Intellectuals," *Economic and Political Weekly* 29, 1994, 559–66; Gurpreet Mahajan, "Secularism as Religious Non-Discrimination: The Universal and the Particular in the Indian Context," *India Review* 1, 2002, 33–51; Shefali Jha, "Secularism in the Constituent Assembly Debates, 1946–1950," *Economic and Political Weekly* 37, 2002, 3175–80; Javeed Alam, "Tradition in India Under Interpretive Stress: Interrogating Its Claims," *Thesis Eleven* 39, 1994, pp. 19–38.

39. See, among others John Rawls, *Political Liberalism* (New York: Columbia University Press, 1993); Amy Gutmann, *Multiculturalism and the Politics of Recognition* (Princeton, NJ: Princeton University Press, 1992); Michael Walzer, *On Toleration* (New Haven, CT: Yale University Press, 1997); Brian Barry, *Culture and Equality* (Cambridge, MA: Harvard University Press, 2001); Bhikhu Parekh, *Rethinking Multiculturalism: Cultural Diversity and Political Theory* (Cambridge, MA: Harvard University Press, 2000); Will Kymlicka, *Multicultural Citizenship* (New York: Oxford University Press, 1995); Charles Taylor, "The Politics of Recognition," in Amy Gutmann, ed., *Multiculturalism: Examining the Politics of Recognition* (Princeton, NJ: Princeton University Press, 1994).

40. Jenco, "Re-Centering Political Theory," p. 6.

41. Ibid., pp. 7, 16, 17.

42. Ibid., p. 7, 25.

43. I am indebted to Sor-Hoon Tan for extensive clarification of this point.

CONCLUSION

1. See Homi Bhabha, *The Location of Culture* (London: Routledge, 1993).

2. See Diana Meyers, "Intersectional Identity and the Authentic Self? Opposites Attract," in Catriona Mackenzie and Natalie Stoljar, eds., *Relational Autonomy: Feminist Perspectives on Autonomy, Agency and the Self* (New York: Oxford University Press, 2000); Marilyn Friedman, "Autonomy and Social Relationships: Rethinking the Feminist Critique" in Diana Teitjens Meyers, ed., *Feminists Rethink the Self* (Boulder, CO: Westview Press, 1997); Maria Lugones, "Purity, Impurity and Separation," *Signs,* Winter 1994.

3. Michel Foucault, *Discipline and Punish: The Birth of the Prison*, trans. Alan Sheridan (New York: Vintage, 1995); Jacques Derrida, *Writing and Difference*, trans. Alan Bass (Chicago: University of Chicago Press, 1978).

4. Bart Moore-Gilbert, *Postcolonial Theory: Contexts, Practices and Politics* (London and New York: Verso Press, 1997), p. 138.

5. Jacques Derrida, *Of Grammatology*, trans. Gayatri Spivak (Baltimore, MD: Johns Hopkins University Press, 1976) p. 302.

6. One dilemma that continues to arise in all major postcolonial analyses is the dilemma between respect for difference and the desire to stress points of connection to make common cause among postcolonial cultures. On the one hand, Homi Bhabha and Gayatri Spivak both insist, at different points, on respect for the irreducible heterogeneity of postcolonial cultural formations, the untranslatable element of identity that, in Bhabha's words, refuses to be "sublated into a similitude." Bhabha, *Location of Culture*, p. 245 Spivak too criticizes attempts to understand and construct postcolonial consciousness as pure or essential forms, calling for a persistent recognition of radical heterogeneity of sub-categories and sub-formations within the postcolonial, such as class and gender. Yet Spivak herself, along with Edward Said and others, also reminds us of the need for what she calls a "strategic politics of essentialism," in which the principle of heterogeneity can be legitimately displaced for pragmatic purposes in the cause of promoting a common alliance between differentially marginalized groups. Rather than accepting as inevitable the fragmentation of the postcolonial or minoritarian terrain into a series of competing or even hostile social and cultural formations, those seeking to resist the hegemony of the Eurocentric center might adopt a strategic—and provisional—commitment to their own kind of master-narrative, in which the essentialism of postcolonial coherence is recognized as a necessary stage prior to cultural decolonization. Ernesto Laclau and Chantal Mouffe suggest, for instance, that the strengthening of specific struggles requires "chains of equivalence" in which struggles of, say, anti-racism, anti-capitalism require a "logic of equivalence" as equivalent symbols of a "unique and indivisible struggle." Ernesto Laclau and Chantal Mouffe, *Hegemony and Socialist Strategy: Towards a Radical Democratic Politics*, W. Moore and P. Cammack, trans. (London Verso, 1985), p. 182.

7. Timothy Kaufman-Osborn, "Political Theory as Profession and as Subfield?" pp. 663–66.

8. Ibid., p. 668.

9. Ibid., p. 662.

10. It is most important, also, to note the material foundations of the hegemony of Eurocentric paradigms and presumptions. As long as certain nations control the material and financial bases of international dialogues, this may ensure that such dialogues continue to be centered on their concerns and presuppositions. It is often expensive to get non-Western participation in such dialogues, and citizens and institutions of non-Western nations often do not have the resources to either host events or to attend events in the West. It is no coincidence that Western ideological hegemony is only now being chipped away at because of China's economic rise. Few people (including liberal and Marxist intellectuals within China) cared about traditional Chinese ideals and values for most of the twentieth century, when China was regarded as the "sick man" of Asia. However, now that China appears economically formidable, it is attracting more attention from both insiders and outsiders about its intellectual heritage, and China now has the resources to fund research, conferences and international dialogues on that heritage. Daniel Bell, personal electronic communication, August 31, 2010. So too with other East Asian economic powers such as Japan, Singapore, Taiwan and Korea, as well as India, whose considerably successful diasporic elite in the West have only recently begun to take on an increasing role in motivating and funding sympathetic discourse about its intellectual traditions. Amy M. Braverman, "The Interpretation of Gods: Do Leading Religious Scholars Err in Their Analysis of Hindu Texts?" *University of Chicago Magazine* (97) 2, December 2004, pp. 32–36.

11. Jenco, "Re-centering Political Theory," p. 32.

12. Ibid., p. 3.

13. Ibid., p. 27.

14. Ibid., pp. 3, 27, 32, 33.

15. Andrew Rehfeld, "Offensive Political Theory," *Perspectives on Politics* 8 (2), June 2010.

16. Jenco, "What Does Heaven Ever Say?" p. 742.

17. Benjamin Barber, "The Politics of Political Science: Value-free Theory and the Wolin-Strauss Dust-Up of 1963," *American Political Science Review*, 100 (4), November 2006, p. 544.

18. Ian Shapiro, "Problems, Methods and Theories in the Study of Politics, or What's Wrong with Political Science and What to Do about It," *Political Theory* 30 (4), August 2002, p. 597.

19. See Donna Haraway, "The Persistence of Vision," in Kate Conboy, Nadia Medina, Sarah Stanbury, eds., *Writing on the Body: Female Embodiment and Feminist Theory* (New York: Columbia University Press, 1997), p. 285; cited in Kaufman-Osborn, "Political Theory as Profession and as Subfield?" p. 672.

20. Kaufman-Osborn, "Political Theory as Profession and as Subfield?" p. 661, 668.

21. Barber, "The Politics of Political Science," p. 544.

22. Rehfeld, "Offensive Political Theory," p. 467.

23. Daniel Bell similarly suggests that we "should be more self-conscious about the interactions between the ideal and the feasible, about how the empirical world sets constraints on workable moral principles." Daniel A. Bell, *Beyond Liberal Democracy: Political Thinking for an East Asian Context* (Princeton, NJ: Princeton University Press, 2006), p. 324.

24. On the lack of "normative" engagement among comparative political theorists, see March, "What Is Comparative Political Theory?"

25. Kaufman-Osborn, "Political Theory as Profession and as Subfield?" pp. 660–61.

26. Bell, *Beyond Liberal Democracy*. See also Daniel A. Bell and Hahm Chaibong, eds., *Confucianism for a Modern World* (Cambridge: Cambridge University Press, 2003); Daniel A. Bell, Kanishka Jayasuriya, and David M. Jones, eds., *Towards Illiberal Democracy in Pacific Asia* (New York: St. Martin's Press, 1995); Daniel A. Bell and Joanne R. Bauer, eds., *The East Asian Challenge for Human Rights* (New York: Cambridge University Press, 1999); Russell Arben Fox, "Confucianism and Communitarianism in a Liberal Democratic World," in Dallmayr, ed., *Border Crossings*.

27. See Bell, *Beyond Liberal Democracy*, pp. 64, 237–43. See also Bell, "Confucian Constraints on Property Rights," in Bauer and Bell, eds., *The East Asian Challenge for Human Rights*.

28. Ruiping Fan, "Self-Determination vs. Family-Determination: Two Incommensurable Principles of Autonomy," *Bioethics* 11 (3–4), 1997, cited in Bell, *Beyond Liberal Democracy*, p. 243.

29. Lusina Ho, "Traditional Confucial Values and Western Legal Frameworks: The Law of Succession," in Bell and Chaibong, eds., *Confucianism for the Modern World*, cited in Bell, *Beyond Liberal Democracy*, p. 248.

30. Bell, *Beyond Liberal Democracy*, p. 247.

31. See Joseph Chan, "Giving Priority to the Worst off: A Confucian Perspective on Social Welfare," in Bell and Chaibong, eds., *Confucianism for the Modern World*. Although Chan's discussion of social-welfare systems is restricted to its theoretical underpinnings in classical Confucian writings, one can see the impact of these ideas in contemporary East Asian legal codes.

32. Nancy J. Hirschmann, "Eastern Veiling, Western Freedom," in Dallmayr, ed., *Border Crossings*, p. 43.

33. Leila Ahmed, *Women and Gender in Islam* (New Haven, CT: Yale University Press, 1992), p. 166.

34. Ibid., p. 151.

35. Nazira Zain al-Din, "Unveiling and Veiling: On the Liberation of the Woman and Social Renewal in the Islamic World" (Beirut, 1928), in M. Badran and M. Cooke, eds., *Opening the Gates: A Century of Feminist Writing* (Bloomington, IN: Indiana University Press, 1990); Timothy Mitchell, *Colonising Egypt* (Berkeley: University of California Press, 1988), p. 169; Qassim amin, *Tahrir al-mar'a*, in Muhammad 'Amara, ed. *Al-a'mal al-kamila li Qassim Amin* (Beirut: Al-mu'assasa al-'arabiyya lil-diraasat wa'l-nashr, 1976), vol. 2, cited in Ahmed, *Women, Gender and Islam*, pp. 155–63.

36. Deniz Kandiyoti, ed., *Women, Islam and the State* (Philadelphia: Temple University Press, 1991), p. 8; Humari Jayawardena, *Feminism and Nationalism in the Third World* (London: Zed Books, 1986), ch. 3.

37. Nancy Hirschmann, *The Subject of Liberty: Towards a Feminist Theory of Freedom* (Princeton, NJ: Princeton University Press, 2003), p. 177. As a result, Ahmed tells us "colonialism's use of feminism to promote the culture of the colonizers and undermine native culture has ever since imparted to feminism"—and perhaps even to discourses about veiling—"the taint of having served as an instrument of colonial domination, rendering it suspect in Arab eyes." *Women, Gender and Islam*, p. 167.

38. Ahmed, *Women, Gender and Islam*, p. 167.

39. We must, of course, be keenly aware that feminist commitments are not to be uncritically elided with liberal ones, nor are either liberalism or feminism to be construed in unproblematically monolithic terms. In using this terminology, I mean only to draw attention to a broad range of criticism that generally takes as foundational the centrality of the values of autonomy and choice to human life and criticizes veiling based on its ostensible denial of these central goods.

40. Randi Warne, "Further Reflections in the 'Unacknowledged Quarantine:' Feminism and Religious Studies," in Sandra Burt and Lorraine Code, eds., *Changing Methods: Feminists Transforming Practice* (Peterborough, Canada: Broadview Press, 1995).

41. Fatima Mernissi, "Virginity and Patriarchy," in Azizah al-Hibri, ed., *Women and Islam* (New York: Pergamon Press, 1982), p. 189. See also Fatima Mernissi, *Beyond the Veil: Male-Female Dynamics in Modern Muslim Society* (Bloomington: Indiana University Press, 1987); Arlene MacLeod, *Accommodating Protest: Working Women, the New Veiling, and Change in Cairo* (New York: Columbia University Press, 1991), p. 83; Anna Elisabetta Galeotti, "Citizenship and Equality: The Place for Toleration," *Political Theory* 21 (4), 1993; Norma Moruzzi, "A Problem with Headscarves: Contemporary Complexities of Political and Social Identity," *Political Theory* 22 (1), 1994; Fatmagul Berktay, "Looking from the 'Other' Side: Is Cultural Relativism a Way Out?" in Joanna de Groot and Mary Maynard, eds., *Women's Studies in the 1990's: Doing Things Differently?* (London: Macmillan, 1993); Haleh Afshar, "Fundamentalism and its Female Apologists," in Renee Prendergast and H.W. Singer, eds., *Development Perspectives for the 1990s* (London: Macmillan, 1991); Marie-Aimee Helie-Lucas, "Women's Struggles and Strategies in the Rise of Fundamentalism in the Muslim World: From Entryins to Internationalism," in Haleh Afshar, ed., *Women in the Middle East: Perceptions, Realities and Struggles for Liberation* (London: Macmillan, 1993), and "The Preferential Symbol of Islamic Identity:Women in Muslim Personal Laws," in Valentine Moghadam, ed., *Identity Politics and Women: Cultural Reassertions and Feminisms in International Perspective* (Boulder, CO: Westview Press, 1994).

42. Azza M. Karam, *Women, Islamisms and the State: Contemporary Feminisms in Egypt* (London: Macmillan, 1998), p. 139. Nancy Hirschmann offers a far more subtle and nuanced account

of this phenomenon, when she argues that even when veiling is voluntary, the "fact of cultural sanction in a closed community also means that this choice is to some significant degree coerced." See her "Eastern Veiling, Western Freedom?" in Dallmayr, ed., *Border Crossings*, p. 49. Here, Hirschmann offers a Foucauldian account of insidious coercion by arguing that such cultural sanction works to frame ideals and values that individuals internalize, thus guaranteeing that they will "desire to do what perpetuates the system." Lila Abu-Lughod, *Veiled Sentiments: Honor and Poetry in a Bedouin Society* (Berkeley: University of California Press, 1986), p. 238. For Foucault, such coercion is violent because it redefines coercion as choice, thereby denying individuals to see the control they are subject to and making them instruments of their own oppression. See also Arlene MacLeod, *Accommodating Protest*, pp. 71, 140.

43. See, for instance, Bhikhu Parekh, *Rethinking Multiculturalism: Cultural Diversity and Political Theory* (Cambridge, MA: Harvard University Press, 2000); and Brian Barry, *Culture and Equality: An Egalitarian Critique of Multiculturalism* (Cambridge, MA: Harvard University Press, 2001).

44. Christian Joppke, "State Neutrality and Islamic Headscarf Laws in France and Germany," *Theory and Society*, 36 (4), 2007; Ellen Wiles, "Headscarves, Human Rights, and Harmonious Multicultural Society: Implications of the French Ban for Interpretations of Equality," *Law & Society Review* 41 (3), 2007; Susan Moller Okin, ed., *Is Multiculturalism Bad for Women?* (Princeton, NJ: Princeton University Press, 1999); Jane Freedman, "Women, Islam and Rights in Europe: Beyond a Universalist/Culturalist Dichotomy," *Review of International Studies* 33 (1), 2007.

45. Chandra Talpade Mohanty, "Under Western Eyes: Feminist Scholarship and Colonial Discourse," *boundary 2*, 12 (3), 1988, p. 334–335.

46. Ibid., p. 336.

47. Ibid., pp. 336–37.

48. Ibid., pp. 337–38.

49. Ibid., pp. 340, 350.

50. Ibid., pp. 347, 352.

51. Lila Abu-Lughod, "Do Muslim Women Really Need Saving? Anthropological Reflections on Cultural Relativism and Its Others," *American Anthropologist* 104 (3), 2003, pp. 783–91; Homa Hoodfar, "The Veil in Their Minds and On Our Heads: The Persistence of Colonial Images of Muslim Women," in David Lloyd and Lisa Lowe, eds., *The Politics of Culture in the Shadow of Capital* (Durham, NC: Duke University Press, 1997), pp. 248–79; Katherine Bullock, *Rethinking Muslim Women and the Veil: Challenging Historical and Modern Stereotypes* (London: The International Institute of Islamic Thought, 2007); Mai Yamani, "Introduction," in Mai Yamani, ed., *Feminism and Islam: Legal and Literary Perspectives* (Reading, Berks, UK: Garnet, 1996); Uni Wikan, *Behind the Veil in Arabia: Women in Oman* (Baltimore, MD: Johns Hopkins University Press, 1982); Lila Abu-Lughod, *Veiled Sentiments*; Elizabeth Fernea, "The Veiled Revolution," in D. Bowen and E. Early, eds., *Everyday Life in the Muslim Middle East* (Bloomington: Indiana University Press, 1993); Nilufer Gole, *The Forbidden Modern: Civilization and Veiling* (Ann Arbor: University of Michigan Press, 1996); Nawar Al-Hassan Golley, "Is Feminism Relevant to Arab Women?" *Third World Quarterly*; Afsaneh Najmabandi, "Gender and Secularism of Modernity: How Can a Muslim Woman Be French?" *Feminist Studies* 32 (2), 2006.

52. It would be absurd to argue, for instance, that the extent of gender-based discrimination practiced in Afghanistan or Iran, where the concealment of the female form is violently enforced,

is not normatively problematic and worthy of criticism. For this reason, examples of veiling I cite draw on contexts in which veiling is largely voluntary rather than coerced.

53. Sherifa Zuhur, *Revealing Reveiling: Islamist Gender Ideology in Contemporary Egypt* (Albany, NY: SUNY Press, 1992); Hessini, "Wearing the Hijab in Contemporary Morocco"; S. Brenner, "Reconstructing Self and Society: Javanese Muslim Women and the Veil," *American Ethnologist* 23 (4), 1996.

54. Zuhur, *Revealing Reveiling*.

55. Tabari, "Islam and the Struggle for Emancipation,"; Azari, "Islam's Appeal to Women"; Nahid Yeganeh, "Women's Struggles in the Islamic Republic of Iran," in Azar Tabari and Nahid Yeganeh, eds., *In the Shadow of Islam: The Women's Movement in Iran* (London: Zed Press, 1982); Yvonne Yazbeck Haddad, "Islam, Women and Revolution in Twentieth Century Arab Thought," *The Muslim World* 74 (34), 1984; Williams, "A Return to the Veil"; Homa Hoodfar, "Return to the Veil."

56. Wikan, *Behind the Veil*; Lila Abu-Lughod, *Veiled Sentiments: Honor and Poetry in a Bedouin Society* (Berkeley: University of California Press, 1986).

57. Fadwa El-Guindi, "Veiling Infitah with Muslim Ethic: Egypt's Contemporary Islamic Movement," *Social Problems* 28 (4), 1981.

58. Hoodfar, "Return to the Veil," p. 119; Arlene Elowe MacLeod, *Accommodating Protest: Working Women, the New Veiling, and Change in Cairo* (New York: Columbia University Press, 1991).

59. Sawsan El-Messiri, "Self-Images of Traditional Urban Women in Cairo," in Nikkie Keddie and L. Beck, eds., *Women in the Muslim World* (Cambridge, MA: Harvard University Press, 1978); Rugh, *Reveal and Conceal*; Safia K. Mohsen, "New Images, Old Reflections: Working Middle-Class Women in Egypt," in Elizabeth Warnock Fernea, ed., *Women and the Family in the Middle East: New Voices of Change* (Austin: University of Texas Press, 1985); Hoodfar, "Return to the Veil"; Macleod, *Accommodating Protest*; Hessini, "Wearing the Hijab in Contemporary Morocco"; and Zuhur, *Revealing Reveiling*.

60. Abu-Lughod, *Veiled Sentiments*, p. 46.

61. Ibid., p. 115.

62. MacLeod, *Accommodating Protest*, p. 105.

63. Ibid., pp. 100–101.

64. See Katherine Bullock, *Rethinking Muslim Women and the Veil*, p. 212. In a private conversation, an American-born Muslim woman described the practices of veiling and gender segregation at her local Washington mosque as providing a sense of personal space and privacy that was not available to her in the rest of her Western life: "Sometimes" she said, "women need their own space to just relax and be by themselves, without worrying about how men view them." Here, the interviewee suggests that the segregation afforded by the veil may fulfill a certain need for privacy that is unavailable to women in modern Western life. Private interview, April 15, 2005, Georgetown University, Washington, D.C.

65. Hirschmann, "Eastern Veiling, Western Freedom?" p. 41.

66. "The Question of Hijab: Suppression or Liberation?" *Institute of Islamic Information and Education* (III&E), http://www.usc.edu/dept/MSA/humanrelations/womeninislam/whatishijab.html.

67. See Bullock, *Rethinking Muslim Women and the Veil*, p. 71: "An aspect of hijab that came through strongly in [my] interviews was how wearing [the hijab] had given these women sources of inner strength and high level of confidence and self-esteem."

68. Ibid., p. 55. For instance, a Saudi Arabian immigrant woman in Canada claims she feels more constrained in Canadian society, where the mixed-sex institutions cramped her ability to learn and made her much less comfortable than the female-only institutions in Saudi Arabia. Ibid., p. 113.

69. Ibid., p. 63.

70. Ibid., p. 199. Indeed, much of Western feminists' reaction to the sexualization of patriarchy sometimes follows a symbol self-marking as modest and desexualized: the refusal to shave one's bodily hair or to wear undergarments or skimpy clothes that emphasize one's feminine shape, the opposition to cosmetic and aesthetic standards that call for painful procedures of self-enhancement, and so on.

71. Ibid., p. 73.

72. Hirschman, "Eastern Veiling, Western Freedom?" p. 45.

73. For Western feminist critiques of gender roles and body images, see, among others, Sandra Bartky, *Femininity and Domination* (New York: Routledge, 1990); Sandra Bem, *The Lenses of Gender* (New Haven, CT: Yale University Press, 1990); Susan Bordo, *Unbearable Weight: Feminism, Western Culture and the Body* (Berkeley: University of California Press, 1993).

74. For instance, Nancy Hirschmann suggests that veiling may introduce new and different ways of understanding the liberal value of freedom. See *The Subject of Liberty*, pp. 192–96. Hirschmann also suggests, however, that veiling cannot be free in any real sense, even when it is chosen, because patriarchy structures this choice, and women do not participate in structuring the contexts in which their choices are formulated. Thus, some might choose to see veiling as a fundamentally illiberal act, devoid of any true autonomy, even when chosen.

75. See Naomi Wolf, *Fire with Fire: The New Female Power and How It Will Change the Twenty-First Century* (New York: Random House, 1993).

76. Martha Nussbaum repeatedly asserts, for instance, the capacity to lead a fulfilling sexual life is central to humanness. See *Women and Human Development: The Capabilities Approach* (Cambridge: Cambridge University Press, 2000), p. 78; "Aristotelian Social Democracy," in R. B. Douglass, G. Mara and H. Richardson, eds., *Liberalism and the Good* (New York: Routledge, 1990); "Nature, Function and Capability," *Oxford Studies in Ancient Philosophy*, suppl. 1, 1988.

77. Isaiah Berlin, "Does Political Theory Still Exist?" in Henry Hardy, ed., *Concepts and Categories* (Princeton, NJ: Princeton University Press; 1988), p. 149.

78. Stephen White, "Introduction: Pluralism, Platitudes, and Paradoxes: Fifty Years of Western Political Thought," *Political Theory* 30,(4), August 2002, p. 474. White notes that Rawls's *Theory of Justice* briefly emerged, but this grand theorizing had a transient quality; Rawls later became skeptical of his own framework and turned to more specific questions in *Political Liberalism*.

79. Charles Taylor, "The Politics of Recognition," in Amy Gutmann, ed., *Multiculturalism: Examining the Politics of Recognition* (Princeton, NJ: Princeton University Press, 1994).

80. Bhikhu Parekh, *Colonialism, Tradition and Reform: An Analysis of Gandhi's Political Discourse* (New Delhi: Sage Publications, 1989), p. 213.

81. For a detailed analysis of Gandhian ontology, see Raghavan Iyer, *The Moral and Political Thought of Mahatma Gandhi* (New York: Concord Grove Press, 1983); Farah Godrej, "Nonviolence and Gandhi's Truth: A Method for Moral and Political Arbitration," *Review of Politics* 68, 2006.

82. Samuel Fleischacker, *The Ethics of Culture* (Ithaca, NY: Cornell University Press), pp. 66–67.

83. John Gray, *The Two Faces of Liberalism* (Cambridge: Polity Press, 2000); Isaiah Berlin, "Two Concepts of Liberty," in *The Proper Study of Mankind: An Anthology of Essays* (London: Chatto

& Windus, 1997); John Kekes, *The Morality of Pluralism*, (Princeton, NJ: Princeton University Press, 1993); Swami Bhaskarananda, *The Journey from Many to One: Essentials of Advaita Vedanta* (Seattle: Viveka Press, 2009); Chandradhar Sharma, *The Advaita Tradition in Indian Philosophy* (New Delhi: Motilal Banarsidass, 2007); Swami Kripananda, *Jnaneshwar's Gita: A Rendering of the Jnaneshwari* (South Fallsburg, NY: Siddha Yoga Publications, 1999); Sarvepalli Radhakrishnan, trans., *The Bhagavadgita* (New Delhi: HarperCollins, 1993); Raimundo Panikkar, ed., *The Vedic Experience: Manramanjari* (Pondicherry: All India Press, 1977); Swami Radhakrishnan, *The Principal Upanishads* (New York: Humanities Press Inc, 1978); Ramavadh Pandey, *Rigveda Bhashya Bhumika* (New Delhi: Motilal Banarsidass, 2007).

84. Fleischacker, *The Ethics of Culture*, p. 173.

85. Ibid., pp. 173–74, 177.

Bibliography

Abu-Lughod, Lila. "Do Muslim Women Really Need Saving?: Anthropological Reflections on Cultural Relativism and Its Others." *American Anthropologist* 104 (3), 2003.

———. *Veiled Sentiments: Honor and Poetry in a Bedouin Society.* Berkeley: University of California Press, 1986.

Ackerly, Brooke A. "Is Liberalism the Only Way Toward Democracy?: Confucianism and Democracy." *Political Theory* 33 (4), 2005.

Afshar, Haleh, ed. *Women in the Middle East: Perceptions, Realities and Struggles for Liberation.* London: Macmillan, 1993.

Ahmed, Leila. *Women and Gender in Islam.* New Haven, CT: Yale University Press, 1992.

Alam, Javeed. "Tradition in India Under Interpretive Stress: Interrogating Its Claims." *Thesis Eleven* 39, 1994.

Alatas, Syed Farid. *Alternative Discourses in Asian Social Science: Responses to Eurocentrism.* New Delhi: Sage Publications, 2006.

Ali, M. C. "The Question of Hijab: Suppression or Liberation?" Institute of Islamic Information and Education (III&E), http://www.usc.edu/dept/MSA/humanrelations/womeninislam/whatishijab.html.

Altekar, A. S. *State and Government in Ancient India.* New Delhi: Motilal Banarsidass, 1958.

Alter, Joseph S. *Gandhi's Body: Sex, Diet and the Politics of Nationalism.* Philadelphia: University of Pennsylvania Press, 2000.

Amara, Muhammad, ed. *Al-a'mal al-kamila li Qassim Amin.* Vol. 2. Beirut: Al-mu'assasa al-'arabiyya lil-diraasat wa'l-nashr, 1976.

Ambedkar, B. R. *Annihilation of Caste.* Jalandhar: Bhim Patrika Publications, 1936.

———. *The Buddha and His Dhamma.* Bombay: Siddharth Publications, 1957.

———. *The Untouchables: Who Were They and Why They Became Untouchables*. New Delhi: Amrit Books, 1948.

Ames, Roger T. *The Art of Rulership: A Study in Ancient Chinese Political Thought*. Honolulu: University of Hawaii Press, 1983.

Ames, Roger T., and Henry Rosemont Jr., trans. *The Analects of Confucius: A Philosophical Translation*. New York: Ballantine, 1998.

Amin, Samir. *Eurocentrism*. Translated by Russell Moore. New York: Monthly Review Press, 1989.

Angle, Stephen. *Human Rights and Chinese Thought: A Cross-Cultural Inquiry*. Cambridge: Cambridge University Press, 2002.

———. *Sagehood: The Contemporary Significance of Neo-Confucian Philosophy*. New York: Oxford University Press, 2009.

Appiah, Kwame Anthony. *Cosmopolitanism: Ethics in a World of Strangers*. New York: Norton, 2007.

Aravamudam, Srinivas. *Guru English: South Asian Religion in a Cosmopolitan Language*. Princeton, NJ: Princeton University Press, 2005.

Aurobindo, Sri. *Essays on the Gita*. Twin Lakes, WI: Lotus Press, 1995.

Azari, F. "Islam's Appeal to Women in Iran: Illusion and Reality." In *Women of Iran: The Conflict with Fundamentalist Islam*, edited by F. Azari. London: Ithaca Press, 1983.

Bajpai, Rochana. "The Conceptual Vocabularies of Secularism and Minority Rights in India." *Journal of Political Ideologies* 7 (2), 2002.

Balagangadhara, S. N., and Jakob De Roover. "The Secular State and Religious Conflict: Liberal Neutrality and the Indian Case of Pluralism." *Journal of Political Philosophy* 15 (1), 2007.

Barber, Benjamin. "The Politics of Political Science: Value-free Theory and the Wolin-Strauss Dust-Up of 1963." *American Political Science Review* 100 (4), 2006.

Barry, Brian. *Culture and Equality: an Egalitarian Critique of Multiculturalism*. Cambridge, MA: Harvard University Press, 2001.

Bartky, Sandra. *Femininity and Domination*. New York: Routledge, 1990.

Basole, Amit. "Whose Knowledge Counts? Reinterpreting Gandhi for the Information Age." *International Journal of Gandhi Studies* 2, 2012.

Beiner, Ronald, ed. *Hannah Arendt: Lectures on Kant's Political Philosophy*. Chicago: University of Chicago Press, 1982.

Beitz, Charles. *Political Theory and International Relations*. Princeton, NJ: Princeton University Press, 1999.

Bell, Daniel A. *Beyond Liberal Democracy: Political Thinking for an East Asian Context*. Princeton, NJ: Princeton University Press, 2006.

———. *East Meets West: Human Rights and Democracy in East Asia*. Princeton, NJ: Princeton University Press, 2000.

Bell, Daniel A., and Joanne R. Bauer, eds. *The East Asian Challenge for Human Rights*. Cambridge: Cambridge University Press, 1999.

Bell, Daniel A., and Chaibong Hahm, eds. *Confucianism for a Modern World*. Cambridge: Cambridge University Press, 2003.

Bell, Daniel A., Kanishka Jayasuriya, and David M. Jones, eds. *Towards Illiberal Democracy in Pacific Asia*. New York: St. Martin's Press, 1995.

Bem, Sandra. *The Lenses of Gender*. New Haven, CT: Yale University Press, 1990.

Benhabib, Seyla. *Another Cosmopolitanism*. New York: Oxford University Press, 2006.

Berlin, Isaiah. *The Proper Study of Mankind: An Anthology of Essays*. London: Chatto & Windus, 1997.

Bernstein, Richard J. *Beyond Objectivism and Relativism*. Philadelphia: University of Pennsylvania Press, 1983.

Beteille, André. "Secularism and Intellectuals." *Economic and Political Weekly* 29 (10), 1994.

Betti, Emilio. *Die Hermeneutik als allgemeine Methodik der Geisteswissenschaften* (HAMG). Tubingen: J.C.B. Mohr (Paul Siebeck), 1962.

Bhabha, Homi. *The Location of Culture*. London: Routledge, 1993.

Bhargava, Rajeev. *Politics and Ethics of the Indian Constitution*. Delhi: Oxford University Press, 2008.

———. *The Promise of India's Secular Democracy*. Delhi: Oxford University Press, 2010.

———, ed. *Secularism and Its Critics*. Delhi: Oxford University Press, 1998.

———. *What Is Political Theory and Why Do We Need It?* Delhi: Oxford University Press, 2010.

Bhaskarananda, Swami. *The Journey from Many to One: Essentials of Advaita Vedanta*. Seattle: Viveka Press, 2009.

Bhattacharya, Harihar, and Ghosh Abhijit, eds. *Indian Political Thought and Movement: New Interpretations and Emerging Issues*. Kolkata: K. P. Bagchi & Co., 2007.

Black, Antony. *The History of Islamic Political Thought: From the Prophet to the Present*. New York: Routledge, 2001.

———. *The West and Islam: Religion and Politics in World History*. Oxford: Oxford University Press, 2008.

Bohman, James, and Matthias Lutz-Bachmann, eds. *Perpetual Peace: Essays on Kant's Cosmopolitan Ideal*. Cambridge, MA: MIT Press, 1997.

Bondurant, Joan. *Conquest of Violence: The Gandhian Philosophy of Conflict*. Princeton, NJ: Princeton University Press, 1988.

Bordo, Susan. *Unbearable Weight: Feminism, Western Culture and the Body*. Berkeley: University of California Press, 1993.

Bowen, D., and E. Early, eds. *Everyday Live in the Muslim Middle East*. Bloomington: Indiana University Press, 1993.

Braverman, Amy M. "The Interpretation of Gods: Do Leading Religious Scholars Err in Their Analysis of Hindu Texts?" *University of Chicago Magazine* 97 (2), 2004.

Breckenridge, Carol, Sheldon Pollock, Homi K. Bhabha, and Dipesh Chakrabarty, eds. *Cosmopolitanism*. Durham, NC: Duke University Press, 2002.

Brenner, S. "Reconstructing Self and Society: Javanese Muslim Women and the Veil." *American Ethnologist* 23 (4), 1996.

Brock, Gillian, and Henry Brighouse. *The Political Philosophy of Cosmopolitanism*. Cambridge: Cambridge University Press, 2004.

Browers, Michaelle. *Democracy and Civil Society in Arab Political Thought: Transcultural Possibilities*. Syracuse, NY: Syracuse University Press, 2006.

———. "Islam and Political *Sinn*: The Hermeneutics of Contemporary Islamic Reformists." In *An Islamic Reformation?* edited by Michaelle Browers and Charles Kurzman. Lanham, MD: Lexington, 2004.

Browers, Michaelle, and Charles Kurzman, eds. *An Islamic Reformation?* Lanham, MD: Lexington, 2004.

Brown, Garrett Wallace. "Kantian Cosmopolitan Law and the Idea of a Cosmopolitan Constitution." *History of Political Thought* 27 (3), 2006.

———. "Theory and Practice: Moving Cosmopolitan Legal Theory to Legal Practice." *Legal Studies* 28 (3), 2008.

Brown, Wendy. "At the Edge." *Political Theory* 30 (4), 2002.

Bruce, F. F., and E. G. Rupp, eds. *Holy Book and Holy Traditions*. Grand Rapids, MI: William B. Eerdmans, 1968.

Buchanan, Allen. *Justice, Legitimacy, and Self-Determination: Moral Foundations for International Law*. Oxford: Oxford University Press, 2004.

Bullock, Katherine. *Rethinking Muslim Women and the Veil: Challenging Historical and Modern Stereotypes*. London: The International Institute of Islamic Thought, 2007.

Burt, Sandra, and Lorraine Code, eds. *Changing Methods: Feminists Transforming Practice*. Peterborough, Canada: Broadview Press, 1995.

Butalia, Urvashi, and Tanika Sarkar, eds. *Women and the Hindu Right*. New Delhi: Kali for Women, 1995.

Butler, Judith. *Bodies that Matter: On the Discursive Limits of Sex*. New York: Routledge, 1995.

———. *Gender Trouble: Feminism and the Subversion of Identity*. New York: Routledge, 1990.

Butler, Judith, and Joan W. Scott, eds. *Feminists Theorize the Political*. New York: Routledge, 1992.

Caney, Simon. *Justice Beyond Borders: A Global Political Theory*. New York: Oxford University Press, 2006.

Chakrabarty, Dipesh. *Provincializing Europe: Postcolonial Thought and Historical Difference*. Princeton, NJ: Princeton University Press, 2000.

Chan, Alan Kam-leung, ed. *Mencius: Contexts and Interpretations*. Honolulu: University of Hawai'i Press, 2002.

Chander, Jag Parvesh, ed. *Gita the Mother*. Lahore: Indian Printing Works, 1947.

Chandhoke, Neera. *Beyond Secularism: The Rights of Religious Minorities*. Delhi: Oxford University Press, 1999.

Chatterjee, Margaret. *Gandhi's Religious Thought*. Notre Dame, IN: University of Notre Dame Press, 1983.

Chatterjee, Partha. *Nationalist Thought and the Colonial World: A Derivative Discourse?* Minneapolis: University of Minnesota Press, 1986.

———. "Religious Minorities and the Secular State: Reflections on an Indian Impasse." *Public Culture* 8 (1), 1995.

———. "Secularism and Toleration." *Economic and Political Weekly* 29 (8), 1994.

———, ed. *Wages of Freedom*. New Delhi: Oxford University Press, 1998.

Chatterjee, Piya. "Taking Blood: Gender, Race and Imagining Public Anthropology in India." *India Review* 5 (3–4), 2006.

Chattopadhyaya, Debiprasad. *Lokayata: A Study of Ancient Indian Materialism*. New Delhi: People's Publishing House, 1959.

Chethimattam, John B. *Patterns of Indian Thought: Indian Religions and Philosophies*. Maryknoll, NY: Orbis Books, 1971.

Childs, Peter, and Patrick Williams. *An Introduction to Postcolonial Theory*. London: Prentice Hall, 1997.

Clifford, James, and George E. Marcus, eds. *Writing Culture: The Poetics and Politics of Ethnography*. Berkeley: University of California Press, 1986.

Cohen, Joshua, ed. *For Love of Country*. Boston: Beacon Press, 2002.

Conboy, Kate, Nadia Medina, and Sarah Stanbury, eds. *Writing on the Body: Female Embodiment and Feminist Theory*. New York: Columbia University Press, 1997.

Cooke, M., and M. Badran, eds. *Opening the Gates: A Century of Feminist Writing*. Bloomington: Indiana University Press, 1990.

Dallmayr, Fred. *Achieving Our World: Toward a Global and Plural Democracy*. Lanham, MD: Rowman and Littlefield, 2001.

———. "Beyond Monologue: For a Comparative Political Theory," *Perspectives on Politics* 2 (2), 2004.

———. *Beyond Orientalism: Essays on Cross-Cultural Encounter*. Albany, NY: SUNY Press, 1996.

———, ed. *Border Crossings: Toward a Comparative Political Theory*. Lanham, MD: Lexington Books, 1999.

———, ed. *Comparative Political Theory: An Introduction*. New York: Palgrave Macmillan, 2010.

———. "Cosmopolitanism: Moral and Political." *Political Theory* 31 (3), 2003.

———. *Dialogue Among Civilizations: Some Exemplary Voices*. New York: Palgrave Macmillan, 2002.

Dallmayr, Fred, and Abbas Manochehri, eds. *Civilizational Dialogue and Political Thought: Tehran Papers*. Lanham, MD: Lexington, 2007.

Dallmayr, Fred, and Thomas A. McCarthy, eds. *Understanding and Social Inquiry*. Notre Dame, IN: University of Notre Dame Press, 1977.

Dalton, Dennis. *Mahatma Gandhi: Nonviolent Power in Action*. New York: Columbia University Press, 1993.

Das, G. N. *Love Songs of Kabir*. New Delhi: Abhinav Publications, 1992.

———. *Mystic Songs of Kabir*. New Delhi: Abhinav Publications, 1996.

Derrida, Jacques. *Of Grammatology*. Translated by Gayatri Spivak. Baltimore, MD: Johns Hopkins University Press, 1976.

———. *Writing and Difference*. Translated by Alan Bass. Chicago: University of Chicago Press, 1978.

Desai, Mahadev, ed. *Anasaktiyoga or the Gospel of Selfless Action: The Gita According to Gandhi*. Ahmedabad: Navajivan Press, 1956.

Deshpande, G. P., ed. *Selected Writings of Jotirao Phule*. New Delhi: Leftword Press, 2002.

Diamond, Irene, and Lee Quinby, eds. *Feminism and Foucault: Reflections on Resistance*. Boston: Northeastern University Press, 1988.

Douglass, R. B., G. Mara, and H. Richardson, eds. *Liberalism and the Good*. New York: Routledge, 1990.

Dunne, Tim, and Nicholas J. Wheeler, eds. *Human Rights in Global Politics*. Cambridge: Cambridge University Press, 1999.

Edwards, Paul, ed. *The Encyclopedia of Philosophy*. Vol. 6. New York: Macmillan, 1967.

Elman, Benjamin A. *From Philosophy to Philology: Intellectual and Social Aspects of Change in Late Imperial China*. Los Angeles: UCLA Asian-Pacific Monograph Series, 2001.

Euben, Roxanne. "Contingent Borders, Syncretic Perspectives: Globalization, Political Theory, and Islamizing Knowledge." *International Studies Review* 4 (1), 2002.

———. *Enemy in the Mirror: Islamic Fundamentalism and the Limits of Modern Rationalism: A Work of Comparative Political Theory*. Princeton, NJ: Princeton University Press, 1999.

———. "Journeys to 'the Other Shore.'" *Political Theory* 28 (3), 2000.

———. *Journeys to the Other Shore: Muslim and Western Travelers in Search of Knowledge*. Princeton, NJ: Princeton University Press, 2006.

Fan, Ruiping. "Self-Determination vs. Family-Determination: Two Incommensurable Principles of Autonomy." *Bioethics* 11 (3–4), 1997.

Fernea, Elizabeth Warnock, ed. *Women and the Family in the Middle East: New Voices of Change.* Austin: University of Texas Press, 1985.

Flavia, Agnes. "Hindu Men, Monogamy and the Uniform Civil Code." *Economic and Political Weekly* 30 (50), 1995.

Fleischacker, Samuel. *The Ethics of Culture.* Ithaca, NY: Cornell University Press, 1994.

Foucault, Michel. *Discipline and Punish: The Birth of the Prison.* Translated by Alan Sheridan. New York: Vintage, 1995.

Fox, Richard G., ed. *Recapturing Anthropology: Working in the Present.* Santa Fe, NM: School of American Research Press, 1991.

Freedman, Jane. "Women, Islam and Rights in Europe: Beyond a Universalist/Culturalist Dichotomy." *Review of International Studies* 33 (1), 2007.

Freeman, Samuel, ed. *John Rawls: Collected Papers.* Cambridge, MA: Harvard University Press, 1999.

Gadamer, Hans-Georg. *Truth and Method.* Translated by Joel Winsheimer and Donald G. Marshall. New York: Continuum, 1989.

Galeotti, Anna Elisabetta. "Citizenship and Equality: The Place for Toleration." *Political Theory* 21 (4), 1993.

Galston, William A. "Defending Liberalism." *American Political Science Review* 76, 1982.

———. "Pluralism and Social Unity." *Ethics* 99, July 1989.

Gandhi, M. K. *Ashram Observances in Action.* Ahmedabad: Navajivan, 1955.

———. *An Autobiography: The Story of My Experiments with Truth.* Boston: Beacon Press, 1993.

———. *The Collected Works of Mahatma Gandhi.* 100 vols. New Delhi: Ministry of Information and Broadcasting, Government of India, 1958–1994.

———. "Discussion with G. Ramachandran." *Young India*, March 1922.

———. *Gita: The Mother.* Free India Publications, 1942.

———. *Key to Health.* Ahmedabad: Navajivan Press, 1948.

———. "On *Ahimsa*: Reply to Lala Lajpat Rai." *Modern Review*, October 1916.

———. *Self-Restraint vs. Self-Indulgence.* Ahmedabad: Navajivan Press, 1927.

———. *Speeches and Writings of Mahatma Gandhi.* 4th ed. Madras: Natesan, 1934.

Gangoli, Geetanjali. *The Law on Trial: The Debate on the Uniform Civil Code.* Bombay: Akshara Women's Resource Center, 1996.

Ganguly, Sumit. "The Crisis of Indian Secularism." *Journal of Democracy* 14 (4), 2003.

Geertz, Clifford. *The Interpretation of Cultures.* New York: Basic Books, 1973.

———. *Local Knowledge: Further Essays in Interpretive Anthropology.* New York: Basic Books, 1983.

Geetha, V., and S. V. Rajadurai. *Towards a Non-Brahmin Millenium: From Iyothee Thass to Periyar.* Calcutta: Samya, 1998.

Gerth, H. H., and C. Wright Mills. *Economy and Society: An Outline of Interpretive Sociology.* Berkeley: University of California Press, 1978.

———, eds. *From Max Weber: Essays in Sociology.* New York: Oxford University Press, 1946.

Ghoshal, U. N. *A History of Indian Political Ideas.* Oxford: Oxford University Press, 1959.

Giddens, Anthony. *The Constitution of Society.* Berkeley: University of California Press, 1984.

Godrej, Farah. "Gandhi's Civic Ahimsa: A Standard for Public Justification in Multicultural Democracies." *International Journal of Gandhi Studies* 1, 2011, pp. 75–106.

———. "Nonviolence and Gandhi's Truth: A Method for Moral and Political Arbitration." *Review of Politics* 68 (2), 2006.

———. "Response to 'What Is Comparative Political Theory?'" *Review of Politics* 71 (4), 2009.

———. "Towards a Cosmopolitan Political Thought: The Hermeneutics of Interpreting the 'Other.'" *Polity* 41, 2009.

Göle, Nilüfer. *The Forbidden Modern: Civilization and Veiling.* Ann Arbor: University of Michigan Press, 1996.

Golley, Nawar Al-Hassan. "Is Feminism Relevant to Arab Women?" *Third World Quarterly* 25 (3), 2004.

Goodin, Robert E., and Philip Pettit, eds. *Contemporary Political Philosophy: An Anthology.* Malden, MA: Blackwell Publishers, 1997.

Gopal, Ram. *The History and Principles of Vedic Interpretation.* New Delhi: Concept Publishing Company, 1983.

Gordon, Neve, ed. *From the Margins of Globalization: Critical Perspectives on Human Rights.* Lanham, MD: Lexington Books, 2004.

Gray, John. *The Two Faces of Liberalism.* Cambridge: Polity Press, 2000.

Gray, Stuart. "A Historical-Comparative Approach to Indian Political Thought: Locating and Examining Domesticated Differences." *History of Political Thought* 31 (3), 2010.

Groot, Joanna de, and Mary Maynard, eds. *Women's Studies in the 1990's: Doing Things Differently?* London: Macmillan, 1993.

Guha, Ranajit, and Gayatri Chakravorty Spivak, eds. *Selected Subaltern Studies.* Delhi: Oxford University Press, 1988.

Guindi, Fadwa -El. "Veiling Infitah with Muslim Ethic: Egypt's Contemporary Islamic Movement." *Social Problems* 28 (4), 1981.

Gunnell, John. G. *The Descent of Political Theory: The Genealogy of an American Vocation.* Chicago: University of Chicago Press, 1993.

———. *Political Theory: Tradition and Interpretation.* Cambridge, MA: Winthrop, 1979.

Gutmann, Amy. *Multiculturalism and the Politics of Recognition.* Princeton, NJ: Princeton University Press, 1992.

———, ed. *Multiculturalism: Examining the Politics of Recognition.* Princeton, NJ: Princeton University Press, 1994.

Habermas, Jürgen. *The Inclusion of the Other: Studies in Political Theory.* Cambridge, MA: MIT Press, 1998.

———. *The Postnational Constellation: Political Essays.* Cambridge: Polity Press, 2001.

Habib, Irfan, ed. *Akbar and His India.* Delhi: Oxford University Press, 1997.

Haddad, Yvonne Yazbeck. "Islam, Women and Revolution in Twentieth Century Arab Thought." *The Muslim World* 74 (34), 1984.

Halbfass, Wilhelm. "India and the Comparative Method." *Philosophy East and West* 35 (1), 1985.

Hammersley, Martyn, and Paul Atkinson. *Ethnography: Principles in Practice.* London: Tavistock, 1983.

Hardy, Henry, ed. *Concepts and Categories.* Princeton, NJ: Princeton University Press; 1988.

Heidegger, Martin. *Being and Time.* Translated by John Macquarrie and Edward Robinson. Oxford: Basil Blackwell, 1973.

Held, David. *Democracy and the Global Order: From the Modern State to Cosmopolitan Governance*. Oxford: Polity Press, 1995.

Henderson, John B. *Scripture, Canon, and Commentary: A Comparison of Confucian and Western Exegesis*. Princeton, NJ: Princeton University Press, 1991.

Herodotus. *The Histories*. Translated by George Rawlinson. New York: Alfred A. Knopf, 1997.

Hessini, Leila. "Wearing the Hijab in Contemporary Morocco: Choice and Identity." In *Reconstructing Gender in the Middle East: Tradition, Identity, and Power*, edited by Fatma Müge Göçek and Shiva Balaghi. New York: Columbia University Press, 1994.

Hibri, Azizah al-, ed. *Women and Islam*. New York: Pergamon Press, 1982.

Hirsch, E. D. *Validity in Interpretation*. New Haven, CT: Yale University Press, 1967.

Hirschmann, Nancy. "Eastern Veiling, Western Freedom?" *Review of Politics* 59 (3), 1997.

———. *The Subject of Liberty: Towards a Feminist Theory of Freedom*. Princeton, NJ: Princeton University Press, 2003.

Honig, Bonnie. *Democracy and the Foreigner*. Princeton, NJ: Princeton University Press, 2001.

Hoodfar, Homa. "Return to the Veil: Personal Strategy and Public Participation in Egypt." In *Working Women: International Perspectives on Labour and Gender Ideology*, edited by Nanneke Redclift and M. Thea Sinclair. London: Routledge, 1991.

Ilaiah, Kanchan. *Why I Am Not a Hindu: A Shudra Critique of Hindutva Philosophy, Culture and Political Economy*. Calcutta: Samya, 1996.

Inden, Ronald. *Imagining India*. Cambridge, MA, and Oxford, UK: Blackwell, 1990.

Ivanhoe, Philip J. *Ethics in the Confucian Tradition: The Thought of Mencius and Wang Yangming*. Indianapolis, IN: Hackett, 2002.

Iyer, Raghavan. *The Moral and Political Thought of Mahatma Gandhi*. New York: Concord Grove Press, 1983.

———. *The Moral and Political Writings of Mahatma Gandhi*. Oxford: Clarendon Press, 1986, 3 vols.

Jayaswal, K. P. *Hindu Polity: A Constitutional History of India in Hindu Times*. Bangalore: Chaukhamba Sanskrit Pratishthan Oriental Publishers, 1967.

Jayawardena, Humari. *Feminism and Nationalism in the Third World*. London: Zed Books, 1986.

Jenco, Leigh. "How Meaning Moves: Tan Sitong on Borrowing Across Cultures." *Philosophy East and West* 62 (2), 2012.

———. *Making the Political: Founding and Action in the Political Theory of Zhang Shizhao*. Cambridge: Cambridge University Press, 2010.

———. "The Past Is Not a Foreign Country: Culture-Centered versus History-Centered Interpretation." Paper presented at the proceedings of the 2008 American Political Science Association.

———. "Re-Centering Political Theory: The Promise of Mobile Locality." *Cultural Critique* 79, Fall 2011.

———. "What Does Heaven Ever Say?: A Methods-Centered Approach to Cross-Cultural Engagement." *American Political Science Review* 101 (4), 2007.

Jha, Shefali. "Secularism in the Constituent Assembly Debates, 1946–1950." *Economic and Political Weekly* 37 (30), 2002.

Jones, K. *Socio-Religious Reform Movements in British India*. Cambridge: Cambridge University Press, 1994.

Joppke, Christian. "State Neutrality and Islamic Headscarf Laws in France and Germany." *Theory and Society*, 36 (4), 2007.

Kandiyoti, Deniz, ed. *Women, Islam and the State*. Philadelphia: Temple University Press, 1991.

Kane, P. V. *History of Dharmasastras*. 2nd ed. Poona: The Bhandarkar Institute, 1977.

Kanth, Rajani Kannepalli. *Against Eurocentrism: A Transcendent Critique of Modernist Science, Society and Morals*. New York: Palgrave Macmillan, 2005.

Karam, Azza M. *Women, Islamisms and the State: Contemporary Feminisms in Egypt*. London: Macmillan, 1998.

Kaufman-Osborn, Timothy V. "Political Theory as Profession and as Subfield?" *Political Research Quarterly* 63 (3), 2010.

Keddie, Nikkie, and L. Beck, eds. *Women in the Muslim World*. Cambridge, MA: Harvard University Press, 1978.

Kekes, John. *The Morality of Pluralism*. Princeton, NJ: Princeton University Press, 1993.

Khan, M. A. Muqtedar, ed. *Islamic Democratic Discourse: Theory, Debates and Philosophical Perspectives*. Lanham, MD: Lexington Books, 2006.

King, Preston, and B. C. Parekh, eds. *Politics and Experience: Essays Presented to Professor Michael Oakeshott on the Occasion of His Retirement*. Cambridge: Cambridge University Press, 1968.

Kögler, Hans Herbert. *The Power of Dialogue: Critical Hermeneutics after Gadamer and Foucault*. Cambridge, MA: MIT Press, 1996.

Kohn, Margaret, and Keally McBride. *Political Theories of Decolonization: Postcolonialism and the Problem of Foundation*. New York: Oxford University Press, 2011.

Krausz, Michael, ed. *Relativism: Interpretation and Confrontation*. Notre Dame, IN: University of Notre Dame Press, 1989.

Kripananda, Swami. *Jnaneshwar's Gita: A Rendering of the Jnaneshwari*. South Fallsburg, NY: Siddha Yoga Publications, 1999.

Kumar, Radha. *The History of Doing*. New Delhi: Kali for Women, 1993.

Kymlicka, Will. *Multicultural Citizenship*. New York: Oxford University Press, 1995.

Laclau, Ernesto, and Chantal Mouffe. *Hegemony and Socialist Strategy: Towards a Radical Democratic Politics*. Translated by W. Moore and P. Cammack. London: Verso, 1985.

Larson, Gerald James, and Elliott Deutsch, eds. *Interpreting Across Boundaries: New Essays in Comparative Philosophy*. Princeton, NJ: Princeton University Press, 1988.

Lau, D. C., trans. *Mencius*. Hong Kong: Chinese University Press, 1994.

Law, N. N. *Aspects of Ancient Indian Polity*. Bombay: Gyan Publishing House, 1960.

Leslie, Margaret. "In Defense of Anachronism." *Political Studies* 18, 1970.

Lewis, Mark Edward. *Writing and Authority in Early China*. Albany, NY: State University of New York Press, 1999.

Lloyd, David, and Lisa Lowe, eds. *The Politics of Culture in the Shadow of Capital*. Durham, NC: Duke University Press, 1997.

Lugones, Maria. "Purity, Impurity and Separation." *Signs* 19 (2), 1994.

Mackenzie, Catriona, and Natalie Stoljar, eds. *Relational Autonomy: Feminist Perspectives on Autonomy, Agency and the Self*. New York: Oxford University Press, 2000.

MacLeod, Arlene Elowe. *Accommodating Protest: Working Women, the New Veiling, and Change in Cairo*. New York: Columbia University Press, 1991.

Madan, T. N. *Modern Myths, Locked Minds: Secularism and Fundamentalism in India*. Delhi: Oxford University Press, 1997.

Mahajan, Gurpreet. "Secularism as Religious Non-Discrimination: The Universal and the Particular in the Indian Context." *India Review* 1 (1), 2002.

Mahmood, Saba. *Politics of Piety: The Islamic Revival and the Feminist Subject*. Princeton, NJ: Princeton University Press, 2005.

March, Andrew. "Are Secularism and Neutrality Attractive to Religious Minorities? Islamic Discussions of Western Secularism in the 'Jurisprudence of Muslim Minorities (*Fiqh Al-Aqalliyyat*) Discourse.'" *Cardozo Law Review* 30 (6), 2009.

———. *Islam and Liberal Citizenship: The Search for an Overlapping Consensus*. New York: Oxford University Press, 2009.

———. "Islamic Legal Theory, Secularism and Religious Pluralism: Is Modern Religious Freedom Sufficient for the *Shari'a* 'Purpose [*Maqsid*]' of 'Preserving Religion [*Hifz Al-Din*]?'" August 14, 2009, Islamic Law and Law of the Muslim World, Paper No. 09–78. Available at SSRN: http://ssrn.com/abstract=1452895.

———. "Theocrats Living Under Secular Law: An External Engagement with Islamic Legal Theory." *Journal of Political Philosophy* 19 (1), 2011.

———. "What Is Comparative Political Theory?" *Review of Politics* 71 (4), 2009.

Martinich, A. P., and Xiao, Yang. "Ideal Interpretation: The Theories of Zhu Xi and Ronald Dworkin." *Philosophy East and West* 60 (1), 2010.

McNay, Lois. "The Foucauldian Body and the Exclusion of Experience." *Hypatia* 6 (3) 1991.

Mehta, Pratap. "Cosmopolitanism and the Circle of Reason." *Political Theory* 8 (25), 2000.

Mehta V. R., and Thomas Pantham, eds. *Political Ideas in Modern India: Thematic Explorations*. New Delhi: Sage Publications, 2006.

Mehta, Ved. *Mahatma Gandhi and His Apostles*. New Haven, CT: Yale University Press, 1993.

Meja, Volker, Dieter Misgeld, and Nico Stehr, eds. *Modern German Sociology*. New York: Columbia University Press, 1987.

Menon, Nivedita, ed. *Gender and Politics in India*. New Delhi: Oxford University Press, 1999.

Mernissi, Fatima. *Beyond the Veil: Male-Female Dynamics in Modern Muslim Society*. Bloomington: Indiana University Press, 1987.

Meyers, Diana Teitjens, ed. *Feminists Rethink the Self*. Boulder, CO: Westview Press, 1997.

Miller, Barbara Stoller, trans. *The Bhagavad-Gita: Krishna's Counsel in Time of War*. New York: Columbia University Press, 1986.

Mitchell, Timothy. *Colonizing Egypt*. Berkeley: University of California Press, 1988.

Moghadam, Valentine, ed. *Identity Politics and Women: Cultural Reassertions and Feminisms in International Perspective*. Boulder, CO: Westview Press, 1994.

Mohanty, Chandra Talpade. "Under Western Eyes: Feminist Scholarship and Colonial Discourse." *boundary* 2, 12 (3), 1988.

Moon, Vasant, ed. *Babasaheb Ambedkar: Writings and Speeches*. Government of Maharashtra, Department of Education, 1979–98.

Moore-Gilbert, Bart. *Postcolonial Theory: Contexts, Practices and Politics*. London and New York: Verso Press, 1997.

Morris, Scott. "Whispering Amid the Canon Roar: The Condition of Comparative Political Theory." Paper presented at Annual Meeting of the American Political Science Association, San Francisco, CA, August 29 to September 2, 2001.

Moruzzi, Norma. "A Problem with Headscarves: Contemporary Complexities of Political and Social Identity." *Political Theory* 22 (1) 1994.

Mowitt, John. "In the Wake of Eurocentrism: An Introduction." *Cultural Critique* 47, 2001.

Mukta, P. *Upholding a Common Life: The Community of Mirabai.* Delhi: Oxford University Press, 1994.

Mundra, Anil. "Mahatma Gandhi's Legacy of Religious Tolerance in India." *Interfaith Voices,* radio broadcast, August 30, 2007, www.interfaithradio.org.

Muraleemadhavan, P. C., ed. *Indian Theories of Hermeneutics.* New Delhi: New Bharatiya Book Corporation, 2002.

Murphy, Tim. "Confucianizing Socrates and Socratizing Confucius: On Comparing *Analects* 13:18 and the *Euthyphro.*" *Philosophy East and West* 60 (2), 2010.

Murty, K. Satchidananda. *Vedic Hermeneutics.* New Delhi: Motilal Banarsidass, 1993.

Najmabandi, Afsaneh. "Gender and Secularism of Modernity: How Can a Muslim Woman Be French?" *Feminist Studies* 32 (2), 2006.

Nakamura, Hajime. *Parallel Developments: A Comparative History of Ideas.* Tokyo: Kodansha Press, 1975.

Nanda, Meera. *Breaking the Spell of Dharma and Other Essays.* New Delhi: Three Essays, 2002.

———. *Prophets Facing Backward: Postmodern Critiques of Science and Hindu Nationalism in India.* New Brunswick, NJ: Rutgers University Press, 2003.

Nandy, Ashis. "An Anti-Secularist Manifesto." *Seminar* 314, 1985.

———. "The Politics of Secularism and the Recovery of Religious Tolerance." *Alternatives* 13 (2), 1988.

———. "The Twilight of Certitude: Secularism, Hindu Nationalism and Other Masks of Deculturation." *Alternatives* 22 (2), 1997.

Nasr, Seyyed Hossein. *Islam: Religion, History and Civilization.* San Francisco: Harper, 2003.

Needham, Anuradha Dingwaney, and Rajeswari Sunder Rajan, eds. *The Crisis of Secularism in India.* Durham, NC: Duke University Press, 2007.

Nelson, Cary, and Lawrence Grossberg, eds. *Marxism and the Interpretation of Culture.* Chicago: University of Illinois Press, 1988.

Nigam, Aditya. *The Insurrection of Little Selves: The Crisis of Secular-Nationalism in India.* New Delhi: Oxford University Press, 2006.

Nussbaum, Martha. *For Love of Country.* Boston: Beacon Press, 2002.

———. "Kant and Stoic Cosmopolitanism." *Journal of Political Philosophy* 5 (1), 1997.

———. "Nature, Function and Capability: Aristotle on Political Distribution." *Oxford Studies in Ancient Philosophy.* Supplementary Volume 1, 1988.

———. *Women and Human Development: The Capabilities Approach.* Cambridge: Cambridge University Press, 2000.

Oakley, Francis. *Kingship: The Politics of Enchantment.* Oxford: Blackwell, 2006.

Okin, Susan Moller, ed. *Is Multiculturalism Bad for Women?* Princeton, NJ: Princeton University Press, 1999.

Ormiston, Gayle L., and Alan D. Schrift. *The Hermeneutic Tradition: From Ast to Ricoeur.* Albany, NY: SUNY Press, 1990).

Oz-Salzberger, Fania. "The Enlightenment in Translation: Regional and European Aspects." *European Review of History* 13, 2006.

———. "'Lost in Translation' Meets Political Thought: Some Modern Tales of Misreception." Working Paper Series, April 7, 2010, pp. 22–23. http://papers.ssrn.com/sol3/papers.cfm?abstract_id=1585891.

———. *Translating the Enlightenment: Scottish Civic Discourse in Eighteenth Century Germany.* Oxford: Clarendon Press, 1995.

Palmer, Richard. *Hermeneutics: Interpretation Theory in Shleiermacher, Dilthey, Heidegger and Gadamer.* Evanston, IL: Northwestern University Press, 1969.

Pandey, Ramavadh. *Rigveda Bhashya Bhumika.* New Delhi: Motilal Banarsidass, 2007.

Panikkar, Raimundo, ed. *The Vedic Experience: Manramanjari.* Pondicherry: All India Press, 1977.

Pantham, Thomas. "Indian Secularism and Its Critics: Some Reflections." *Review of Politics* 59 (3), 1997.

Pantham, Thomas, and Kenneth Deutsch, eds. *Political Thought in Modern India.* New Delhi: Sage Publications, 1986.

Parasher, Archana. *Women and Family Law Reform in India.* New Delhi: Sage Press, 1992.

Parekh, Bhikhu. *Colonialism, Tradition and Reform: An Analysis of Gandhi's Political Discourse.* New Delhi: Sage Publications, 1989.

———. *Gandhi's Political Philosophy: A Critical Examination.* Notre Dame, IN: University of Notre Dame Press, 1989.

———. "The Poverty of Indian Political Theory." *History of Political Thought* 8 (3), Autumn 1992.

———. *Rethinking Multiculturalism: Cultural Diversity and Political Theory.* Cambridge, MA: Harvard University Press, 2000.

Parel, Anthony. "Gandhi and the Emergence of the Modern Indian Political Canon." *Review of Politics* 70 (1), 2008.

———, ed. *Gandhi: Hind Swaraj and Other Writings.* Cambridge: Cambridge University Press, 1997.

———. *Gandhi's Philosophy and the Quest for Harmony.* Cambridge: Cambridge University Press, 2006.

Parel, Anthony, and Ronald C. Keith, eds. *Comparative Political Philosophy: Studies under the Upas Tree.* Lanham, MD: Lexington Books, 1992.

Patton, Laurie L., ed. *Authority, Anxiety and Canon: Essays in Vedic Interpretation.* Albany, NY: SUNY Press, 1994.

Periyar, E. V. Ramaswami Naicker. "Matakkirukku" *Pakuttarivu,* January 1, 1939.

———. Ramaswami Naicker. "Matam Een Ozhiyaveendum?" *Pakuttarivu,* September 9, 1934.

Phule, J. *Collected Works of Mahatma Phule.* Bombay: Government of Maharashtra, 1873.

Pogge, Thomas. *World Poverty and Human Rights: Cosmopolitan Responsibilities and Reforms.* Cambridge: Polity Press, 2002.

Pollock, Sheldon. "Cosmopolitan and Vernacular in History." *Public Culture* 12 (3), 2000.

Prakash, Gyan. "Subaltern Studies as Postcolonial Criticism." *American Historical Review* 99 (5), 1999.

Prasad, Beni. *Theory of Government in Ancient India.* Allahabad: The Indian Press, 1958.

Prendergast, Renee, and H. W. Singer, eds. *Development Perspectives for the 1990s.* London: Macmillan, 1991.

Rabinow, Paul, and William Sullivan, eds. *Interpretive Social Science: A Reader.* Berkeley: University of California Press, 1979.

Radhakrishnan, S., ed. *The Principal Upanishads.* New York: Humanities Press, 1978.

Radhakrishnan, Sarvepalli, trans. *The Bhagavadgita.* New Delhi: HarperCollins Publishers India, 1993.

Radhakrishnan, Sarvepalli, and Charles Moore, eds. *A Sourcebook in Indian Philosophy.* Princeton, NJ: Princeton University Press, 1957.

Ramaswamy, V. *Divinity and Deviance: Women in Virasaivism*. New Delhi: Oxford University Press, 1996.

Rao, Badrinath. "The Variant Meanings of Secularism in India: Notes Toward Conceptual Clarifications." *Journal of Church and State* 48 (1), 2006.

Rawls, John. *Political Liberalism*. New York: Columbia University Press, 1993.

Rehfeld, Andrew. "Offensive Political Theory." *Perspectives on Politics* 8 (2), 2010.

Reiss, Hans, ed. *Kant: Political Writings*. Cambridge: Cambridge University Press, 1991.

Robbins, Bruce. "The Weird Heights: Cosmopolitanism, Feeling, and Power." *Differences* 7 (1), 1995.

Robbins, Bruce, and Pheng Cheah, eds. *Cosmopolitics: Thinking and Feeling Beyond the Nation*. Minneapolis: University of Minnesota Press, 1998.

Roy, Ramashray, ed. *Gandhi and the Present Global Crisis*. Shimla: Indian Institute of Advanced Study, 1996.

Rudolph, Lloyd I., and Susanne Hoeber Rudolph. *The Modernity of Tradition: Political Development in India*. Chicago: University of Chicago Press, 1967.

———. *Occidentalism and Orientalism: Perspectives on Legal Pluralism*. Ann Arbor: University of Michigan Press, 1997.

Rugh, Andrea B. *Reveal and Conceal: Dress in Contemporary Egypt*. Syracuse, NY: Syracuse University Press, 2000.

Said, Edward. *Culture and Imperialism*. New York: Random House, 1994.

———. *Orientalism*. New York: Vintage Books, 1979.

———. *The World, the Text and the Critic*. London: Faber and Faber, 1984.

Salkever, Stephen G., and Michael Nylan. "Comparative Political Philosophy and Liberal Education: 'Looking for Friends in History.'" *PS: Political Science and Politics* 27 (2), 1994.

Sandel, Michael. *Democracy's Discontent: America in Search of a Public Philosophy*. Cambridge, MA: Harvard University Press, 1996.

———. "Political Liberalism." *Harvard Law Review* 107, 1994.

———. "The Procedural Republic and the Unencumbered Self." *Political Theory* 12 (1), 1984.

Sandoz, Ellis, ed. *The Collected Works of Eric Voegelin*. Vol. 12. Baton Rouge: Louisiana State University Press, 1989.

Sangari, K. "Mirabai and the Spiritual Economy of *Bhakti*." *Economic and Political Weekly* 25 (28), 1990.

Sankhdher, M. M., ed. *Secularism in India: Dilemmas and Challenges*. New Delhi: Deep and Deep, 1995.

Satchidananda, Sri Swami. *The Yogasutras of Patanjali*. Buckingham, VA: Integral Yoga Publications, 1990.

Scheffler, Samuel. *Boundaries and Allegiances: Problems of Justice and Responsibility in Liberal Thought*. Oxford: Oxford University Press, 2001.

Schneck, Steve F., ed. *Letting Be: Fred Dallmayr's Cosmopolitical Vision*. Notre Dame, IN: University of Notre Dame Press, 2006.

Scott, Joan W. "The Evidence of Experience." *Critical Inquiry* 17 (4), 1991.

Senthamizko, Vellore. *Periyar in History*. Vellore: Periyar-Gora-Kovoor Atheist Centre, 1987.

Shapiro, Ian. "Problems, Methods and Theories in the Study of Politics, or What's Wrong with Political Science and What to Do about It." *Political Theory* 30 (4), 2002.

Sharma, Arvind. *Modern Hindu Thought: An Introduction*. New Delhi: Oxford University Press, 2005.

Sharma, Chandradhar. *The Advaita Tradition in Indian Philosophy*. New Delhi: Motilal Banarsidass, 2007.

Sharma, R. S. *Aspects of Political Ideas and Institutions in Ancient India*. Delhi: Motilal Banarsidass, 1968.

Sharpe, Eric. *Comparative Religion: A History*. London: Duckworth, 1975.

Shatz, Edward, ed. *Political Ethnography: What Immersion Brings to the Study of Power*. Chicago: University of Chicago Press, 2009.

Shogimen, Takashi, and Cary Nederman, eds. *Western Political Thought in Dialogue with Asia*. Lanham, MD: Lexington Press, 2009.

Singerman, Diane. *Avenues of Participation*. Princeton, NJ: Princeton University Press, 1995.

Skinner, Quentin. "Meaning and Understanding in the History of Ideas." *History and Theory* 8, 1969.

Smith, Jane I. *Islam in America*. New York: Columbia University Press, 1999.

Smith, Vincent A. *Asoka: The Buddhist Emperor of India*. Oxford: Clarendon Press, 1909.

Spellman, J. *Political Theory in Ancient India: A Study of Kingship from the Earliest Times to Circa A.D. 300*. Oxford: Oxford University Press, 1964.

Spivak, Gayatri Chakravorty. *In Other Worlds: Essays in Cultural Politics*. New York: Routledge, 2006.

———. *Outside in the Teaching Machine*. New York: Routledge, 1993.

Steger, Manfred. *Gandhi's Dilemma: Nonviolent Principles and Nationalist Power*. New York: St. Martin's Press, 2000.

Strauss, Leo. *City of Man*. Chicago: University of Chicago Press, 1977.

———. *Natural Right and History*. Chicago: University of Chicago Press, 1953.

———. *What Is Political Philosophy?* Glencoe, IL: The Free Press, 1959.

Sykes, Marjorie, trans. *Moved by Love: The Memoirs of Vinoba Bhave*. Wardha, India: Paramdhan Prakashan, 1994.

Tabari, Azar, and Nahid Yeganeh, eds. *In the Shadow of Islam: The Women's Movement in Iran*. London: Zed Press, 1982.

Tan, Kok-Chor. *Justice Without Borders: Cosmopolitanism, Nationalism and Patriotism*. Cambridge: Cambridge University Press, 2004.

———. *Toleration, Diversity and Global Justice*. Philadelphia: Pennsylvania State University Press, 2000.

Thomas, Megan. "Orientalism and Comparative Political Theory." *Review of Politics* 72 (4), 2010.

Tilak, Bal Gangadhar. *Srimad Bhagavadgita Rahasya or Karma-Yoga-Sastra*. Poona: Tilak Bros., 1935.

Timm, Jeffrey R., ed. *Texts in Context: Traditional Hermeneutics in South Asia*. Albany, NY: SUNY Press, 1992.

Tully, James. *Meaning and Context: Quentin Skinner and His Critics*. Cambridge: Polity Press, 1988.

Vanita, Ruth. "The Special Marriage Act: Not Special Enough." *Manushi* (58), 1990.

Varma, V. P. *Philosophical Humanism and Contemporary India*. New Delhi: Motilal Banarsidass, 1986.

Vincent, Andrew. *The Nature of Political Theory*. Oxford: Oxford University Press, 2004.

Viramma, Josiane, and Jean Luc Racine. *Viramma: Life of an Untouchable*. London: Verso, 1997.

Voegelin, Eric. *The Ecumenic Age*. Vol. 4 in *Order and History*. Baton Rouge: Louisiana State University Press, 1974.

Waldron, Jeremy. "What Is Cosmopolitan?" *Journal of Political Philosophy* 8 (2), 2000.

Wallerstein, Immanuel. "Eurocentrism and Its Avatars: The Dilemmas of Social Science." *New Left Review* 1 (226), 1997.

Walzer, Michael. *On Toleration*. New Haven, CT: Yale University Press, 1997.

White, Stephen. "Introduction: Pluralism, Platitudes, and Paradoxes: Fifty Years of Western Political Thought." *Political Theory* 30 (4), 2002.

Whorf, Benjamin L. *Language, Thought and Reality*. Edited by John B. Carroll. Cambridge, MA: MIT Press, 1956.

Wikan, Uni. *Behind the Veil in Arabia: Women in Oman*. Baltimore, MD: Johns Hopkins University Press, 1982.

Wiles, Ellen. "Headscarves, Human Rights, and Harmonious Multicultural Society: Implications of the French Ban for Interpretations of Equality." *Law & Society Review* 41 (3), 2007.

Williams, J. A. "A Return to the Veil in Egypt." *Middle East Review* 11, 1979.

Winch, Peter. "Understanding a Primitive Society." *American Philosophical Quarterly* 1 (4), 1964.

Wolf, Naomi. *Fire with Fire: The New Female Power and How It Will Change the Twenty-First Century*. New York: Random House, 1993.

Yamani, Mai, ed. *Feminism and Islam: Legal and Literary Perspectives*. Reading, Berks, UK: Garnet, 1996.

Yanow, Dvora, and Peregrine Schwartz-Shea, eds. *Interpretation and Method: Empirical Research Methods and the Interpretive Turn*. Armonk, NY: M.E. Sharpe, 2006.

Zaehner, R. C., ed. *The Bhagavad-Gita*. London: Oxford University Press, 1969.

Zuhur, Sherifa. *Revealing Reveiling: Islamist Gender Ideology in Contemporary Egypt*. Albany, NY: SUNY Press, 1992.

Index